CREOLE TROMBONE

CREOLE TROMBONE

Kid Ory and the Early Years of Jazz

John McCusker

UNIVERSITY PRESS OF MISSISSIPPI

Jackson

www.upress.state.ms.us

The University Press of Mississippi is a member of the
Association of American University Presses.

Material from *Slide Man*, Kid Ory's Autobiography versions,
copyright by Elan/Daniel Kegan; used by his permission.

Ory musical compositions copyright by Elan/Saniel Kegan;
used by his permission.

First printing 2012

∞

Library of Congress Cataloging-in-Publication Data

McCusker, John (John P.), 1963–
Creole trombone : Kid Ory and the early years of jazz / John
McCusker.
p. cm. — (American made music series)
Includes bibliographical references and index.
ISBN 978-1-61703-626-2 (cloth : alk. paper)
— ISBN 978-1-61703-627-9 (ebook)
1. Ory, Kid, 1886–1973. 2. Jazz musicians—Biography.
3. Trombonists—Biography. I. Title.
ML419.O77M33 2012
781.65092—dc23
[B]   2012005303

British Library Cataloging-in-Publication Data available

To Johanna M. Schindler (1956–2010)

CONTENTS

ACKNOWLEDGMENTS

This book is the result of inspiration and support from a variety of sources over a fifteen-year period.

Foremost is the support of my family. Ian, Katie, and Ellen Mc-Cusker, 22, 17, 15, have endured seemingly endless treks through graveyards, archives, and libraries while I dogged the Ory story. Their mother and my wife and soulmate of twenty-five years, Johanna M. Schindler, looked after them while I jetted off to Los Angeles, San Francisco, and Honolulu seeking to unearth new pieces to the Ory puzzle. She shared in my enthusiasm and cheered on my latest discoveries. She knew I had doubts about my abilities as a writer. It was her tireless encouragement that saw me through my phobias. I could not have written this book without her bottomless well of love, friendship, and understanding. We lost Johanna unexpectedly in 2010 and our lives are forever diminished. This book is dedicated to her life and memory.

The original inspiration for the project came from Dr. Bruce Boyd Raeburn of the Hogan Jazz Archive at Tulane University. In 1995 Dr. Raeburn told me that a comprehensive book on Kid Ory was in order and that I might be the person to do it. He has been a reliable sounding board for my research and has provided me with reams of information to support my efforts. Another inspirational figure has been Lynn Abbott, also of the Hogan Jazz Archive, who suggested parallel research to use in buttressing my arguments and who took me to task on ready conclusions. I think the world of both these men and am honored to consider them my mentors.

The late Tad Jones was, at the time of his death, researching an in-depth biography of Louis Armstrong's life in New Orleans. It was Tad who discovered Louis's real birthday. Since we both researched some of the same material, he from Louis's point of view, I from Ory's, he was a valuable sounding board for my research and theories. He was a good friend too and I miss him very much.

Others who offered support and inspiration along the way include Joseph H. McCusker III, Ruth McCusker, Alma Freeman Williams, Sybil Morial, Marc Morial, Jacques Morial, Lorraine Dedeaux and the descendants of Annie Ory, Harold Ory, Rudolph Dinvaut, Joy Lodrigues, Randy DeSoto, Sybil Ory Levet, Danny Barker, Dr. Jack Stewart, Steven A. Werkow, Hal Smith, Sue Fischer, Lolis Eric Elie, Christer Fellows, Sid Bailey, Daniel C. Meyer, Trevor Herbert, Gene Anderson, Dr. Larry Gushee, Alexandra Johnson, Natalie Pompilio, Albert "Pud" Brown, Floyd Levin, Donald M. Marquis, Peter Gerler, Louise G. Bill, Percy Humphrey, Dr. Richard B. Allen, Renee Lapeyrolerie, Bill Carter, George Probert, Paul Harris, T. Brian Wood, Bill and Chris Stotesbury, George Avakian, Stephan Sargent, Robert Parker, Will Allen, Tom Saunders, Sue Hall, Nina Buck, Julie Ahrend, Barry Martyn, Wendi Schneider, Bridget O'Brian, Susan Feeney, Nan Powers Varoga, Craig Gill, the Ken Colyer Trust, the Swedish Bunk Johnson Society, the Kid Ory Society, the DART Society, and the staff of the New Orleans *Times-Picayune.*

This book almost became a victim of Hurricane Katrina. When the Federal levees failed on August 29, 2005, our home filled with eight feet of water, destroying everything we owned. Emotionally wrecked by losing my home and possessions, and haunted by the pictures I made for the *Times-Picayune* during the first horrible week after the storm, the farthest thing from my mind was writing a biography of Kid Ory.

Thankfully for this project, I had boxed a decade's worth of research notes and most of my Ory collection, including his trumpet and clarinet, and squirreled them away in the photo studio at the

Times-Picayune before the storm made landfall. When we abandoned the building on the day after Katrina, I was not sure if this book would ever be written. Thankfully, in October 2005 when the building reopened, the boxes were found safely where I had left them.

Eventually, writing became a sort of therapy for me, a way to assert my fragile sanity against the weight of living in post-Katrina New Orleans. I turned to it again after Johanna died as a way of maintaining some continuity in the face of an uncertain future.

So hopefully you hold not only a biography of a great jazzman, but also a testament to my recovery.

CREOLE TROMBONE

WHO WAS KID ORY?

In 1994 I led a history tour of jazz sites in New Orleans. Trombonist and educator Dave Ruffner, a member of the tour group from California, thought I gave Kid Ory the short shrift. He said Ory was more than just a sideman on the records of Louis Armstrong, King Oliver, and Jelly Roll Morton. He believed Ory to be bridge between the earliest jazz pioneers, like Buddy Bolden, whom Ory knew, and the ultimate jazzman Louis Armstrong, who got his start in Ory's New Orleans band. Further, said Ruffner, recent scholarship on Ory suggested his reported December 25, 1886, birthday was suspect. Peeved, I went to Dr. Bruce Boyd Raeburn at the Hogan Jazz Archive at Tulane University. To my surprise he sided with Ruffner and said that Ory was indeed a major, if overlooked, figure in jazz history. And there was indeed a controversy of sorts about his birthday. In his 1989 article "Johnny Dodds in New Orleans," Gene Anderson of the University of Richmond makes a convincing argument that Ory was actually born in 1889. Anderson's article was the first real scholarship on the Ory band even though the essay was not specifically about him. Raeburn said the ground was ripe for an Ory biography.

Taking this as a challenge, I sought out Ory's baptismal certificate in his hometown of LaPlace, Louisiana. Having worked there as a photojournalist for the New Orleans *Times-Picayune*, I was well acquainted with the area and knew which church Ory would have attended. I found the baptismal certificate confirming his Christmas 1886 birthday and was hooked.

Since 1995 I have researched Ory's life and those of the people around him. In 1999 I presented some of my findings to Ory's daughter, Babette, who in turn entrusted me with Ory's unpublished autobiography.

The autobiography is far from a cohesive document. It is composed mostly of loose pages recalling a memorable story or event. The documents indicate the autobiography was dictated beginning in 1950 by Ory to Barbara GaNung, who was then his mistress. Ga-Nung would later become Ory's second wife and Babette's mother. This dictated material produced what I call Version I of the autobiography. Unfortunately, the document is in Gregg shorthand and I have been unable to find anyone to transcribe it. Version I was translated by GaNung to prose on the typewriter, resulting in what I call Version II. GaNung eventually rewrote some of these stories along with other material to produce Version III, which is an attempt at a cohesive narrative.

The problem with Version III is that its events could not have happened in the order GaNung presents. In the end the stories are real, but the narrative timeline is artificial. Once I realized this, I was freed from the confusion the document had created for other Ory enthusiasts lucky enough to read it, including the late Floyd Levin. Working in New Orleans and St. John the Baptist Parish, I was able to find vital statistical, sacramental, and public records to place Ory's stories in a reliable timeline. For example, I was able to date a story about Ory building a house for his sister once I found a notation in the 1903 St. John the Baptist Parish property tax records.

Babette has been a source of unbridled enthusiasm for the project. Despite many trying times, she has kept her father's collection together. Once I met Babette I had materials at my disposal that included everything from a picture of Ory's father to the saxophone on which he composed "Muskrat Ramble." Holding Ory's instruments and going through his music library, most of which was written out by Arthur "Bud" Scott, was climactic. It also encouraged me to dig deeper. Researching Ory's early life, particularly his genealogy, was uncharted territory.

A disclosure: I am neither a musicologist nor a trained historian. I have worked as a journalist in New Orleans for twenty-five years, and I went after the Kid Ory story the way I would any other. I looked at what he said and what others said about him. What I found was the story of a pioneering New Orleans musician bearing witness to the dawn of jazz.

The record finds Ory to be an oracle of those days. Yet, his story is one that has not been explored in a cohesive way like those of Louis Armstrong and Buddy Bolden. So much has been written about Armstrong that his tale has become the stuff of celebrity. Bolden's story is near mythic. Ory is neither celebrity nor myth. He was a flesh-and-blood jazzman who, fortune would have it, was widely interviewed. Further, his autobiography contains many stories not found in interviews. These serve as Ory's primary voice in this telling of his story. Whenever possible, I try to get out of the way and let him speak.

The purpose of this book is to tell the story of a jazz musician arriving on the scene at the same time as the music itself. The man and the music came up together, reached maturity together and, ultimately, faded from the scene together. The tale covers the years between 1900 and 1933 and that is what the majority of this book is about. Ory's remembrances carry the story only to this point, and it would have been difficult to fill the remaining years without his voice. Further, while the tale of his career revival in the forties is interesting and covered to some degree, it is far less so than the earlier period and frankly less relevant to the historical question: "Who was Kid Ory?"

CHAPTER 1

1886–1896
LE MONDE CREOLE EN CAMPAGNE

⬤⬤⬤⬤⬤⬤⬤⬤⬤⬤⬤⬤⬤⬤⬤⬤⬤⬤⬤⬤⬤⬤⬤⬤⬤⬤⬤⬤⬤⬤⬤⬤⬤⬤⬤

The Woodland Plantation was a sprawling 1,882-acre sugar cane farm twenty-five miles upriver from New Orleans in a tiny St. John the Baptist Parish hamlet called LaPlace. Its main house—a raised, elongated cottage with a modest tin roof, cistern, and two stained-glass dormer windows—was built in 1839. About two dozen build-ings, many of which had been slave quarters, ran along a dirt road behind the main house.[1] It was there on a cold Christmas morning in 1886 that Edward "Kid" Ory was born. Ory's family lived about a half mile behind the main house across the cane fields, next to the massive multi-story sugar mill where his father worked.

At least two sets of railroad tracks ran through the plantation between the main house and the mill. One ran to other places like New Orleans and Baton Rouge. The other, a spur line, curved through the fields back to the sugar mill. The overland route was the River Road, an often-murky thoroughfare that followed the Mississippi downriver southeast to New Orleans and upriver northwest to Baton Rouge. Most folks called it simply "the road."

In the nineteenth century most of the population of St. John Parish lived close to the river on the plantations and farms daisy-chained along its banks. An earthen levee hemmed the waters in, providing some small protection from the spring floods that were responsible for the rich soil that made farming possible. The fields fanned out like thinly cut pie slices originating at the water's edge: large wedge to the river, thin to the swamp.

The Woodland was part of the village of LaPlace, which was little more than a few homesteads, some rental property, and a store. Further upriver was Reserve, which had more of a town feel, including stores, social clubs, and the only Catholic church for miles, St. Peter's. The church was about five miles from the Woodland sugar house, so the Ory family would have needed transportation to get there. They would have traveled down the red dirt road that crossed the railroad tracks until they arrived at the River Road. From there they would have headed upriver, winding and turning with the river until reaching the simple wooden church. Built in 1867, it sat some distance off the road, allowing parking space for dozens of buggies. Out back, surrounded by a wrought-iron fence, was the cemetery that took over as the burial location for east bank Catholics who previously would have been buried across the river in Edgard at the St. John the Baptist Church.

Father Etienne Badoil was the Ory family's priest from the founding of St. Peter's until his death in 1905. He baptized most of the Ory kids. He was out in the community and could often be found playing euchre, a card game, at the Planters and Merchants Social Club hall down the road from St. Peter's.[2] Other than the Latin he spoke during mass, he always conversed in French, as did most of his parishioners.

Across the river from Reserve is Edgard, comprised largely of the parish courthouse, St. John the Baptist Church, the Caire Store, and a few other businesses. Apart from a couple of villages up and downriver, the rest of the parish was sugarcane fields and swamp.

The majority of the population of St. John the Baptist Parish was of African ancestry, though one would never get this impression from the names on the 1860 census. A puny document compared to its postwar counterparts, the census lists white planters and a few free blacks. The 1870 count, the first after the Civil War and Emancipation, would present a very different view. The nameless masses that had been noted merely as numbers on the 1860 slave census had become a political majority.[3] With the support of occupying federal forces, which arrived in 1862 with the fall of New Orleans, and the disenfranchisement of white voters, St. John voters elected black officials. Even after the troops withdrew in 1877, black politicians like Sheriff John Webre held on to power. For the better part of a generation former slaves enjoyed, if not a radically changed life, the promise of one and the assurance that the American democracy might at last embrace them as full citizens.

But, for the most part, the everyday lives of people of color were largely unchanged from the days of slavery. White men still held the property of the parish and black laborers did most of the back-breaking work. Many still lived on plantations in much the same manner as before. On the 1880 census, long lists of black families—who are generally noted as tenant farmers and laborers—often follow the names of major landowners.

The agricultural economy based on slavery was gone, and some wondered if crops could be produced at a profit in the South without a free labor source. Many large landowners whose money was tied up in slaves prior to the war lost a big chunk of their capital with Emancipation. They had land, little money, and loans outstanding. As late as 1869, few fields in the parish had crops in the ground apart from what was needed to eat.[4] Through foreclosures and auctions many small farmers, who owned few or no slaves before the war, took over former plantation lands. Other owners tried to hang on to their land by letting it out to sharecropping.

Sugarcane had been the number one cash crop in antebellum St. John, and planting slowly increased after the war. By the time Ory arrived, production levels were outstripping those of the pre-war period, though the method of growing and harvesting had changed very little.

Late summer and early fall marked the busiest time in the parish. It was called "grinding season," a reference to the process that yielded molasses, cane syrup, and sugar from the freshly cut stalks. The process began out in the fields, where laborers grasped the cane by the stalk with the left hand while swinging a machete, sharply and precisely, with the right. The field hands expended just enough effort to cut the cane cleanly, no more. Inexperienced hands learned quickly how to conserve their energy for those long summer days under the searing Louisiana sun. The cane was then loaded onto trailers that traveled along the cane rows and hauled to the sugar mill. There the sticky sweet juice was ground from the cane stalks and cooked until it crystallized. The process gives off a sweet (to some, sickly) aroma that can be smelled a mile away. The leftover stalks, reduced to a stinky pulp called *baggasse*, were piled up in mounds around the sugarhouse.

People living nearby would have smelled little else. For the Orys, who lived in the middle of a cane field across the dirt road from this industrial operation, the odors were accompanied by a cacophony. The roar of boiling caldrons of crystallizing cane juice, the hammering shut of barrels, and the clang and boom of uncoupling railroad cars would have filled Ory's ears with a din not usually associated with such a rural setting.

His father, Ozeme Ory (1850–1901), was known to his friends as John. He was white, a child of the plantation and once slave-owning Ory family of St. John the Baptist Parish. In 1850, Ozeme and his extended family lived in a tiny village called Terre Haute on the east bank of the Mississippi River near Reserve. The family had been there for several generations.[5]

The patriarch of the family was Nikolas Ory (1705–ca. 1775) who came to America from the Alsace-Lorraine region of France in 1736. Nikolas settled in Berwick Township, York County, Pennsylvania, until around 1750, when he moved to Frederick County, Maryland, with his wife Anna Strasbach and their children. Anna died there in the 1750s, and Nikolas later married Christine Michel, a native of German-held Lorraine born in 1728. Nikolas and Christine had several more children.[6]

The Orys' decision to move to Louisiana was rooted in the migration of the Acadians from British-controlled Canadian territories in the aftermath of 1763 Treaty of Paris, which ended the

French and Indian War. After France ceded Canada and Nova Scotia to Britain, the French Catholic Acadians were forced out, and many came to French-speaking, Spanish-controlled Louisiana. There they were welcomed by Spanish authorities, such as Governor Antonio de Ulloa, who liked the idea of having colonists with anti-English sentiments. Other Acadian communities in exile, including the one in Frederick County, Maryland, heard favorable reports from their countrymen in Louisiana and soon joined their people there. The Orys and other German Catholics threw in their lot with the Acadians and relocated to Louisiana as well.[7] They set sail in January 1769 aboard the schooner Britannia with 100 passengers, including 56 Germans, 32 Acadians, and 12 British sailors. Sailing in a heavy fog, the ship missed the mouth of the Mississippi River and went on to Galveston, arriving in February 1769. There, a perplexed Spanish Authority, apparently unaware of Governor Ulloa's feeling on the matter, held them in detention. They had trouble understanding why a group of Germans would relocate to Louisiana. That they were traveling on a British ship whose passenger roster included a group of soldiers contributed to Spanish suspicions that they were spies. Their property was seized and they were detained until September, when they at last received permission to head to Louisiana, where they eventually settled in an established German Catholic colony. St. John and part of St. Charles Parish became known as the "German Coast."

As early as 1724, there were 330 Germans farming upriver from New Orleans. In the generations between Nikolas Ory and Edward "Kid" Ory, the German language gave way to French. German surnames such as Heidel, Zehringer, and Traeger became Haydel, Zeringue, and Tregre. French-speaking census takers and bureaucrats who wrote down subjective spellings of German names on population rolls helped eradicate the German language, and over time the settlers married into French families, becoming Creoles like the French around them. In many cases, the German language disappeared in a generation.[8]

By the early fall of 1850, when Ozeme was born, the Orys were a prominent and successful family. Ozeme's parents, Edmond Ory (1811–1853) and Marie Irene Tregre (c. 1816–1853), were first cousins who had grown up as neighbors in Terre Haute. They married around 1834 and had the first of their seven children in 1835. Edmond was a planter in partnership with his older brother, Omer. The pair bought property together, grew sugarcane, and thrived. Edmond and his family lived with his wife's grandmother, Margarethe Vicknair Ory, and mother Marie Ory Tregre. Ozeme, the youngest of seven children, would never get to know his parents. They died when he was three.[9] Their deaths coincided with a devastating yellow fever epidemic that killed about seven thousand people in New Orleans. The fever eventually spread to the outlying areas and proved just as deadly there, wiping out entire families.

The Orys' movable property, including a steam engine and a sugar mill, was liquidated and the children were divided among Edmond's siblings and friends. Each was to receive several thousand dollars in inheritance, a sum that grew when Ozeme's great-grandmother Margarethe Vicknair Ory died in 1856. Responding to a petition from Omer Ory, the court made Evariste Triche, a neighbor, the guardian of three-year-old Ozeme. Triche owned a plantation, which included nearly two hundred acres and twenty slaves and had children about Ozeme's age. The Triches lived in Terre Haute no later than 1870, when they appear on the parish property tax records downriver near LaPlace.[10]

Apart from a few items in the 1860s, little is certain about Ozeme's childhood. All of his siblings owned property at one time or another; he did not. He is not on the 1860 census (though the Triches are), and he did not fight in the Civil War (though his brother Edmond did). In summer 1867 Ozeme stood as godfather for the baptism of brother Edmond Ory's daughter Marie. A year and a half later, Edmond became Ozeme's new guardian though Ozeme continued living with the Triches.[11]

According to the 1870 census, twenty-year-old Ozeme was a journeyman. Benjamin Triche was also listed as a journeyman. The man listed on the census after Ozeme was a cooper, as were several other men enumerated after him. The young men were probably learning from the established coopers to make barrels to transport sugar, molasses, and other products produced on the Triche plantation. One of these coopers was named Jacques Thomas. He was the son of a free man of color and lived with his mother and sisters in the LaPlace area. In the summer of 1869 Jacques had a son, Charles Octave Thomas, with a woman named Octavie Devezin. They never married and apparently did not live together. A year later Octavie bore the first child of Ozeme Ory.[12]

Marie Octavie Devezin had light brown, reddish skin with straight black hair that "shined like polished ebony in the sunlight." Ory remembered that she sang to him in French as she rocked him to sleep. Listed as mulatto on the 1880 census, she was born sometime between 1848 and 1852. She worked as a washerwoman and spent most of her life having children.[13] Joy Lodrigues, a granddaughter of John L. Ory (one of the partners who owned the Woodland Plantation), remembered hearing tales about Octavie as a child. She was well-regarded on the plantation, where she watched the owner's kids during the day. The Ory children, Lodrigues suggested, would have played with John L. Ory's youngsters in the plantation yard. She said that was the way it was when she grew up and, from what she could tell, that was the way it always had been.

Octavie's genealogy has proven elusive. On the baptismal certificates of her children she is listed variously as "Marie Octavie," "Octavie Devezin," "Octavie Devesin," and "Octavie Ory." On her son John's death certificate her last name is given as "Madere." There is no Octavie Devezin on the 1870 Louisiana census and the Octavie Madere listed is another woman. There were free blacks in St. John Parish named both Devezin and Madere prior to the Civil War but there is no definitive record of Octavie prior to 1869.

Since Octavie is listed as native to Louisiana, she may have been a slave, which would explain her absence from the 1860 census. At the time she was born, around 1850, there were slaves named Devezin on the Berthelot, Sorapuru, and Balvet plantations in St. John Parish.[14]

Ory always referred to himself as a Creole, a distinction that is a tinderbox of controversy. There is agreement that the term was widely employed after the Louisiana Purchase in 1803 as a way of distinguishing the native "Creole" population from the Americans who were flooding the city. In this context Creole is a cultural term that includes both whites and blacks.[15] Beyond this, consensus is difficult to come by.

By some traditions, only the descendants of eighteenth-century French and Spanish settlers are Creole. Still, in *The Settlement of the German Coast of Louisiana and Creoles of German Descent* (1909), J. Hanno Deiler sought to apply the term to Germans, like Ory's ancestors, who settled St. John Parish at the behest of the French. In another context, Creole applies to the pre–Civil War *Gens de Coleur Libres* or "free people of color." This French-speaking, generally Catholic, mixed-race caste was, in part, the result of exploitive sexual relationships, termed *plaçage,* between white men and black women.[16] More generally, Creole is sometimes applied clumsily to denote a mixed racial heritage within the African American populace, thus ignoring the cultural, linguistic, and religious components entirely.

Ory is a Creole by any of these definitions. His genealogy embraces French and German ancestry on his father's side and African ethnicity on his mother's. Further, he was a Catholic whose first language was French. Still, Creole is only a label, one that in Louisiana is applied to different peoples in different regions. Some French-speaking blacks living in proximity to the Acadian, or Cajun, people in south central and southwestern Louisiana call themselves Creoles. Theirs is a rural existence, not unlike that of the Cajuns around them, of hunting, trapping, farming, and fishing. Another rural Creole community, dating back to the late eighteenth century, can be found around Cane River south of Natchitoches, where descendants of a Creole named Nicholas Augustine Metoyer still gather annually at a church he paid to have built in 1803. He was the son of a freed African slave and a prominent Frenchman. Some Creoles operated stores there, while most worked on the farm.[17] Conversely, in New Orleans, a century ago there was a Creole of color urban community composed largely of descendants of the *Gens de Coleur*. New Orleans Creoles often were educated and worked not as laborers, as most blacks did, but as skilled craftsmen and artisans. The New Orleans Creoles had their own neighborhoods, social clubs, and gathering places and were usually Catholic.

Ory's Creole experience in LaPlace is closer to that of the rural blacks living in Acadiana. After all, his education was minimal and he grew up on a farm. Still, he lived among Creoles in St. John Parish who were themselves descendants of white plantation owners and free blacks. Like the Creoles of New Orleans, Ory's family tended to be insular when it came to marriage and socializing.[18]

Certainly the Orys were not pleased with Ozeme's choice for a common-law wife. They were a prominent family with political connections and Confederate sympathies. *Plaçage* relationships and sex across the color line were uncomfortable relics in the Reconstruction era. French customs and language, already under assault before the war, were on the wane. French communities that had once tolerated and even legally validated relationships like the Orys were caving in to American sensibilities. Cross-ethnic families are less common on the 1900 census returns than those from 1880, though a ban on interracial marriage was not codified into law until 1894.

Despite the disapproval of their relatives and the community, Ozeme and Octavie had a relationship that spanned thirty years and produced a large family. Octavie and Ozeme had their first child, Simon Leonce, or Leonee, in November 1870. According to the census, Ozeme lived with the Triches in LaPlace the summer before his son's birth and not with Octavie.[19]

The 1880 census found Ozeme and Octavie living together with their four children back upriver near Ozeme's ancestral home in Terre Haute, later called Lions. The Thomas family, including Ory's half-brother Charles Octave, had also moved upriver. It appears that Ozeme did not stay on track with his apprenticeship, as he is listed as a farm laborer, not a cooper. By 1886 when Edward Ory was born, the family was back downriver in LaPlace, living at the Woodland Plantation. Edward joined a family that included his 13-, 12-, and 7-year old sisters Nellie, Louisa, and Lena, respectively, and his big brother John, 3 (the oldest sibling, Simon Leonce, or Leonee, died after the 1880 census but before Edward's birth). Within the family Edward was known as "Dutt," which he said was Creole for "Dude." Eventually it caught on and his friends called him this throughout his life. The Orys had two more children. Maria Lesida, or Lizzie, came in 1889 and Annie followed in 1893. Dutt said that his family was very poor.[20]

In 1895 Dutt's sister Louisa married Victor Bontemps, a native of Avoyelles Parish in central Louisiana. His parents had been free people of color and owned property. He and his brother Louis had set up residence in St. John in the 1890s. After the marriage, the couple lived next door to the Orys at the Woodland.[21]

Later that year, Nellie married a man of similar station. Clay Haydel was the fifth of nine children from a family that owned land on the west bank of St. John near the town of Edgard. Like the Orys, the Haydels had family on both sides of the color line. The Caucasian branch of the Haydel family owned Whitney Plantation, one of the biggest in the parish. Clay Haydel's family grew rice and cane and later operated a store.[22]

Up to between the ages of seven and eight, I led the normal life of any plantation child. During the fall, winter and spring seasons, I attended classes after I reached school age. In the

summers, I was around the fields and woods of the plantation
and the surrounding countryside, fishing in the Mississippi
River from the banks of the levee and doing all of the hundred
and one things that any child of that time could and would
do.[23]

The Fourth Ward Colored School in LaPlace was the only public
school available to the Ory kids. Ory attended school until about
the fifth grade, and other times an after-hours tutor was paid to
educate him. Unlike the white schools, which ran for nine months,
the black schools were only in session for five consecutive months.
He placed little value on his education and said he never thought
he needed more than he got. Copies of his writings, devoid of the
editing of his well-educated second wife, reveal a man whose lit-
eracy level was that of an elementary school student.[24]

Of life on the plantation, Ory said there was always work to
be done and that everyone was "pressed into service when not in
school." The kids worked alongside the adults in the fields and the
mill, and Ory freely admitted that he "hated it."[25]

The poor Orys found themselves working for and living on the
land of the rich Orys. In 1898 a partnership, made up in part of
the sons of Lezin Ory Sr. (Ozeme's cousin), bought the Woodland
plantation. The Ory brothers—Lezin Jr., Emydge, Felicien, and
John L. Ory—and other partners (including Louis Keller and Augustine Lasseigne) pooled their money and bought up a succession
of plantations after the war. The Woodland went for $45,000—
lock, stock, and sugar mill. John L. Ory (1846–1920), then a member of the parish police jury (city council), took over the Woodland
as on-site manager.[26]

In the 1870s John L. Ory farmed under the tenant or sharecropping system and worked odd jobs until the brothers' partnership bought Ingleside Plantation on Bayou Lafourche in 1878.
The Golden Gate in Iberville Parish was added a few years later
and then sold to buy the Woodland. In 1904 the San Francisco

and Union plantations, both in St. John Parish, joined the family holdings. The two Ory families were similar in their makeup. John L. and his wife Victoria Chauff settled down about the same time Ozeme and Octavie did. Most of their children, including the oldest, were girls. Their only son, named John Daniel, was two years younger than Dutt. The mothers of both had probably been attended to by the same *traiteurs* (midwives)—usually black women experienced in birthing children. "People didn't go to the hospital (to have children)," Harold Ory, son of Johnny Ory, remembered. "If you went to the hospital you're gonna die. Babies were born at home."[27]

Dutt and Daniel played together as kids around the Woodland big house, under the eye of Octavie who was one of seven servants in the house. "He was Octavie's son, they were good to him," Joy Lodrigues said. "He would have worked in the wash house at an inside job. We (the white kids) played with the servants' children. There was no babysitting, children were brought (to work) and accepted. We made mud pies together."[28]

Working on a Louisiana plantation compound in the nineteenth century was a rough existence filled with harsh labor, long hours, and punishing heat. Drinking water at the big house was stored in a cistern that collected water from the gutters. For families without a cistern, or in times of drought, water had to be hauled from the river and boiled.[29]

Of course, sometimes the river would come to the people. During the spring, the snow up north melted and caused the Mississippi to rise. There was a levee system but it sometimes failed, as major crevasses revealed themselves every few years. In Dutt's youth, the largest of these cracks contributed to a levee breach near Reserve in 1893.[30] The flooding destroyed homes and crops, leaving a foot deep layer of silt behind. Eventually, the water would drain away from the river to the swamp and on to Lake Pontchartrain and Maurepas, but not before agitating the alligators, snakes, and muskrats, which often came wandering into populated areas.

It did not take much effort from Mother Nature to reduce the parish to a near primordial state.

Hurricanes brought similar strife during the summer and early fall. Late-season storms could wreak havoc on the sugarcane harvest, and ultimately on the larger economy of the parish and region. Many farmers, particularly tenants, took crop loans against the anticipated revenue of the harvest. Storms could reduce the size and quality of the harvest or, in some instances, destroy it altogether. A farmer, weeks from harvest, could find himself broke and deeply in debt. Every year was a roll of the dice.

Many plantation houses were surrounded by rough-hewn picket fences made of driftwood and scrap lumber. The goal was to keep the chickens in the yard and deer and other pests out. Pears, figs, and plums were grown in orchards, and sliced cane was chewed as a snack during the harvest. Breakfast consisted of grits, bacon, eggs, boudin (sausage), and *pain perdu* (literally, "lost bread," or French toast) with cane syrup. Mattresses were stuffed with Spanish moss, which was first boiled to rid it of parasites.

The places where the farm laborers lived were described in writing at the time: "Down the dusty country lanes were the Negroes' quarters with rows of identical cabins. The yards out front with constant pounding of barefooted playing children looked like cement. It was living at the poverty level. Many worked on the plantations. The children would go crawfishing and pick blackberries to sell to village people."[31] Ory recalled collecting berries and catching crawfish and fish and selling some of the take.[32] In addition to cane, rice and corn were grown for commercial and feed purposes as well as for consumption by families in the home.

At harvest time, Dutt was picked to be the water boy, which meant he was responsible for hauling water barrels by mule cart out to the fields for the workers. He described a typical day:

> *I stopped for the mule I would be driving all day and led him over to the cart. It took some coaxing and pushing to convince*

that old mule that he should go between the shafts of the cart. That didn't bother me, I just kept whistling and working and finally, there he was . . . all ready to have the hitching finished. Then came filling the buckets and loading them in the wagon and I was ready to sit on the seat and take up the reins. They paid me .60 a day. You had a wagon with a barrel on it and a mule to pull it around and every morning about 7 you'd pick up the laborer's breakfast and take it to them in the field getting there about 8 or 8:30. The water had to be hauled from the well to the field and the farthest stop was about 45 minutes from the well, as the mules didn't go very fast. We made two trips a day in the summer time, with a break for midday dinner, and three in the winter when we gathered up the sugar cane at grinding time and we had no midday return to the farm then.[33]

Ory earned points with the overseer by keeping a separate dipper for his use, so that he did not have to use the same one as the workers.

By the age of eleven, Dutt was big enough to go with his brother Johnny to the west bank to help Nellie and brother-in-law Clay Haydel on their rice farm. He said he went there three times to help harvest and process the rice. He paints a difficult life of endless work.

To begin with, I'll tell you it was hot as hell. The sun was shining very bright and the heat was intense as it always is in August when the rice harvesting begins. It lasts for four to six weeks and the heat right along with it. At times, there would be a big rain shower and the workers would have to hide under the trees or get a little shelter if they had anyone living near enough to be able to get under roof. Usually the rain would pound down very hard for about five or six minutes then the sun would come out again and we'd all just steam.

The fields of (rice) just looked like level ground, some of it green, some of it off green and some of it yellow. When they cut it, in a few days all of it would turn yellow. They cut it with a rice maul by hand. The cutter would stoop, gauging the distance very nicely and when he finished cutting, the shock would be just as level as the field of growing rice had been, and the rice would pike up on top of the stubble. Then the next worker would come along and bundle it, taking just about an armful each time, and tying it. Then he would set it up right there for the gatherers to come along. They would take the bundles and put them in enough bags, like a kiln, you might call it. They would let it dry there for a few weeks until the wagons and carts came to take it up to the riverbanks where they always did the threshing. When it went through the thresher the rice would go in a bag and there was a big crane that would take the straw out and throw the straw right in the water. The straw would float down the Mississippi River for miles and miles from there, all you would see was straw, just floating down. It would finally rot and disappear.

I went over there in the rice fields and gathered up the broken stalks while the wagons were being loaded with the shocks. The Creole name for these was gropp *and at the end of the season my brother-in-law, Clay Haydel, would see that it was loaded on the steamboat and dropped off at Woodland Plantation across the river for me and I've always felt grateful to him for that. But, this was only the beginning of the work because after the sacks were home, then we had to cut big logs and hull them out to make mortars. We'd make beaters to pound the rice to get the husks off but by adding some corn shuck it would break off the husks quicker and easier. After pounding awhile we'd empty the mortar and hold it up and the wind would blow the chaff away and the rice would drop into the container below, that's why it was always best to work this on a windy day.*[34]

Free time at the plantation was sometimes spent hanging around the Woodland Store, which sat a short distance from the main Woodland house by the river. According to Ory, the store had the only liquor license for miles. A rural superstore, it featured a blacksmith, wheelwright, groceries, tobacco, medicines, lumber, coffins, carts, and carriages. Everyone, regardless of race, went there for supplies. As early as 1895, when the area's only telephone was installed, the store became the place to catch up on news from outside of the parish. The store's operators, Augustine Lasseigne and Louis Keller, were also investors in the Woodland Plantation.[35]

"Every plantation had its own store. The company store. I remember it at San Francisco [plantation]. Every month they [workers] settled their bill," remembered John L. Ory's grandniece, Maria Ory Levet.[36] Among the black workers it was known that the best way to guarantee continued employment on the plantation was to maintain a debt at the store. Such a debt would insure that the bosses at the Woodland would hire you back if for no other reason than to make sure the debt was paid. Institutions like this were links in the chains that kept blacks confined to the plantation in the post-slavery era. There were few retail options in a rural setting like this, and it would be a few more years until non-plantation stores came to the fore.

Through the 1890s and beyond, laws were passed, and case law decided, restricting the rights of people of color to a level not seen since before the Civil War. Despite the passage of the 13th Amendment to the U.S. Constitution, which prohibited slavery, and the 14th Amendment, which promised equal protection under the law, southern states passed laws limiting the rights of black citizens. Freedom, it turned out, did not necessarily translate into African Americans being allowed to avail themselves of public institutions and accommodations.

Like jazz, the racial doctrine of "separate but equal" had origins in New Orleans, but this contribution came from a courthouse, not a dance hall. In 1890 the Louisiana legislature passed a law requiring that railroads provide separate accommodations for the races. A light-skinned, New Orleans Creole shoemaker named Homer Plessy ran afoul of the law when he sat in a whites-only car. His case resulted in the U.S. Supreme Court ruling *Plessy v. Ferguson* on May 18, 1896, in which the court found that, while the races were equal before the law, that did not mean that there were not "distinctions" between them. Thus segregation was legal, provided the respective facilities in question were "equal." *Plessy* set the double standard for race relations that endured through most of Ory's life.[37]

Ory called himself a Creole when the question of race was brought before him. It was a distinction he identified with much more than being called black or negro. And though the term applied as much to his culture as to his color, it was as accurate a racial identifier as any. With a white father and a mother of mixed ancestry Ory was as white as he was black, and this was certainly at the heart of his Creole identity in a racial context. Still, self-identity is one matter; the law is another. Though he had straight hair, Anglo features, and red skin, Ory legally may as well have been black as coal.

Back in St. John, Jim Crow oppression manifested itself in specific ways. Since the war, blacks had controlled many parish offices including the sheriff's. They held on to those positions until a wave of white backlash succeeded in reclaiming political power by fiat. Emboldened by an out-of-parish militia sent by Governor Murphy Foster, the whites seized the ballot boxes from the 1896 election.[38] When they were located and the votes counted, the white, Democratic ticket had won. The defeat of Republican Sheriff John Webre in the 1896 election meant that whatever checks and balances blacks enjoyed were gone. Blacks were disarmed, voter rolls were purged, and poll taxes and intimidation did the rest. Blacks would not return to elected office in St. John Parish until the 1960s.

Beyond race, there were cultural shifts under way as well. In the 1890s French was still the common conversational language in St.

John Parish, though English had been the legal tongue since before the Civil War. By 1900 St. John's steadfast French-language newspaper, *La Meschacébé*, was publishing some articles in English. Many of the early bilingual items were parish legal ads that, by law, had to be printed in English. Traditions held on more stubbornly in some arenas. At St. Peter Church, Fr. Badoil's sacramental register was written in French. He consistently used Francophone spellings of given names such as "Edouard" rather than "Edward." Conversely, census enumerators after the Civil War leaned toward Anglicized versions of names.[39] The eventual domination of English was a foregone conclusion.

Like the insular, rural Creole world from which he came, Ory's first tongue would soon be an anachronism; but English would not be his only new language.

ca. 1897–1900

MUSIC

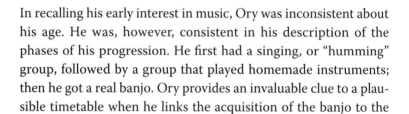

In recalling his early interest in music, Ory was inconsistent about his age. He was, however, consistent in his description of the phases of his progression. He first had a singing, or "humming" group, followed by a group that played homemade instruments; then he got a real banjo. Ory provides an invaluable clue to a plausible timetable when he links the acquisition of the banjo to the death of a relative in the summer of 1901, when he was 14.[1]

In those years before 1901, Dutt befriended several like-minded youngsters, some of whom would eventually accompany him when he brought his band to New Orleans in 1910. Lewis "Chif" and Joseph "Stonewall" Matthews, originally spelled Mathieu, grew up with Ory at the Woodland. Both brothers were dark and little. Lewis, born 1887, was the same age as Dutt and showed real aptitude at music, mastering several instruments, including bass and guitar, before settling on trumpet. He was good looking, with a steely, determined gaze. His older brother Joseph was called Stonewall, probably in reference to his square face. He was not the musician Chif was. Irresponsible and slovenly, his rumpled appearance was a stark contrast to the sharp-dressed Chif. Over the years Stonewall was forced on more than one bandleader who really just wanted to hire Chif. Stonewall would get fired and Chif would quit in protest.[2] Stonewall and Chif were cornerstones of Ory's bands through 1914, in that time rising from childhood pretenders to professional musicians. Together, the boys traveled the parish seeking out music and ultimately found a way to make it themselves. Dutt recalled many experiences in those early years in which he and the Matthews brothers literally begged, borrowed, and stole to feed their voracious musical appetites.

Joining the trio along the way was Edward "Rabbit" Robertson, sometimes spelled Robinson, born ca. 1887, who eventually took to the drums. Like the Matthews brothers, Rabbit would follow Ory to New Orleans and play with his band for several years. There was Jake "Bull" White who would later become the group's violinist. Ory said he was the "world's worst" but he managed to find a place in the group. Finally, there was Lawrence Duhe (1887–1959), easily the most talented of all of Ory's early bandmates. Duhe was born in LaPlace, where his father Evariste worked at the sugar mill with Ozeme Ory. Evariste played violin in various bands around St. John, while his sons performed as the Duhe Brothers Band. Both of Duhe's sisters played piano and organ in church.[3]

To appreciate the awakening of Ory's musical muse, it is helpful to remember that he was first a listener, then a player. To this end, a survey of the music played in St. John the Baptist Parish in this period is helpful. Ory suggested nothing remarkably musical about his surroundings or upbringing, but his contemporaries, including former bandmates and neighbors, paint a more colorful canvas. Mathilda August Clementin said that locals sang in French in St. John Parish when she was growing up: "In the community . . . people used to sit on the porch in the evening and sing old French tunes in the dark. They went out about eight when it was cool."[4]

It is apparent from Ory's post–World War II French-language recordings that he was familiar with Creole folk songs. In 1939 musicologist Irene Whitfield documented numerous nineteenth-century Creole songs sung in St. John Parish. One song Whitfield encountered, "Vous Conne 'Tite La Maison," or "Our Little Home," offered this verse:

Mo Cher Cousin
Mo chere cousine
Mo l'aime la cuisine
Mo bois du vin
Mo Mange bien
Ca pas coute moi a rein[5]
[My dear cousin (male), my dear cousin (female),
I love the kitchen! (or food)
I drink wine
I eat good
it costs me nothing.]

Ory recorded a song called "Eh La Bas" in 1946 that included a version of this verse, though others, including New Orleans trumpeter Dede Pierce, also claimed authorship. Since Whitfield's documentation beats Ory's recording by seven years, it is safe to assume Ory appropriated "Eh La Bas" from "Vous Conne 'Tite La Maison." Regardless of authorship, the tune was popular in Louisiana through the 1940s when there are accounts of men wearing dresses, playing guitars, and performing "Eh La Bas" on Mardi Gras.[6]

Another Creole tune Ory later recorded, and claimed authorship of, was "Blanche Touquotoux," which tells the antebellum story of a light-skinned woman passing for white who is called out by others as being "negre." The unnamed woman sued her accuser and the case ended up in court where the woman, known only by her nickname "Touquotou," lost. As the trial went on, barber and musician Joseph Beaumont, a Creole of color, wrote a musical critique of her actions. "Toucoutou" "mocked the woman's aspirations to whiteness, ensuring that the annoyingly repetitive and catchy tune would follow her around the city and would live after her death." "Toucoutou" was sung in New Orleans as late as the 1920s.[7]

Dutt's first regular exposure to organized band music of any kind may have come from a combo comprised of extended members of the John L. Ory family. They played at local theatres and at functions throughout the community with regularity and are mentioned in newspaper accounts of the time. Among them was John L. Ory's son John Daniel Ory (1889–1918), who showed promise as a wind musician. John Daniel was two years younger than Dutt, and Ory alludes to him in a 1957 interview, though in a context apart from music.[8] Having an organized band on the scene, regardless of type, surely provided some sort of model for the future jazzmen.

A string band in name, featuring guitars, bass, and violin, the group included horns despite the terminology. In interviews, musicians from St. John commonly called sit-down configurations of brass bands "string bands." In other words, string bands were considered synonymous with dance bands. "The brass bands were used for brass band music, and the string bands played for dancing; quadrilles, mazurkas, waltzes, etc. In the string bands you had bass violin, violin, clarinet, guitar, trumpet and trombone. Drums were not used," St. John parish bandleader Peter Valentine, who was active in the 1890s, remembered. String bass replaced brass bass; alto horns were replaced by guitar or banjo—thus a "string band."[9]

But it was the brass bands of St. John, including the Pickwick of Reserve and the Onward of LaPlace, that initially piqued Ory's curiosity. "In LaPlace I used to hear brass bands all the time," he said. Brass bands marched in parades and funerals and played for church affairs. In Reserve the bands played while riding around in horse carts and later trucks. The Pickwick and the Onward regularly squared off on Sundays at bucking contests where the winner would be determined by audience acclaim.[10]

Itinerant music teachers were common in the hinterlands of New Orleans from at least the 1880s onward. Frank Clermont, born 1869, taught bands from the west bank of St. Charles Parish southwest to Houma, and was billed as the "Creole Cornetist." He instructed students in numerous communities including Boutte,

Luling, Raceland, Gibson, and Houma. One citation in the *Indianapolis Freeman* states that he trained the Ory band in St. Charles, Louisiana.[11] St. Charles is one parish downriver from St. John. Intriguing as this is, musicians in St. John Parish cite the influence of primarily one "professor."

James Brown Humphrey (1859–1935) led the Onward Brass Band in LaPlace and taught most of its members to play music in the early 1880s. Later he instructed members of another St. John band, the Pickwick. These were only two of many Humphrey tutored in Southeast Louisiana over a forty-year career. He was the father of six children: Willie, Eli, Lilly, Eva, Bernice, and Jamesetta; all were musicians. His grandsons included jazzmen Willie, Percy, and Earl Humphrey. Humphrey was born in Sellars, Louisiana, in 1859, the son of plantation owner James B. Humphrey of Reserve and Eva Kelson, a Creole woman of color. Humphrey grew up with his mother in New Orleans' Third Ward, living on Green Street where he later settled with his wife Ella in 1878. By 1879 they had son and future clarinetist William. The family later moved to South Liberty Street, though they maintained a home in Reserve.[12] The professor was a big man, over six feet tall, who traveled a circuit throughout southeast Louisiana, teaching children and young adults on plantations and other remote communities.

Humphrey led the Crescent City Band in the 1880s and temporarily took over the professorship of music at Straight and Southern Universities in 1887, when Professor William Nickerson went on tour. He was a leader and solo cornetist in the Pelican band after 1889, while continuing to lead the Crescent City band. A report in the *Weekly Pelican* confirms Humphrey leading the Onward Band of St. John Parish in 1889. St. John native "One Eyed" Babe Phillips (1879–1960) remembered having heard the band before the Spanish-American War (1898). He said some members read music though others did not. Edmond Hall (1901–1967), renowned clarinetist with Louis Armstrong's All-stars and a St. John native, recalled his father being in the Onward when it traveled to New

York to participate in a competition.[13] The trip was in support of the Louisiana delegation to the gathering of the Knights of Pythias, a black fraternal organization.

Closer to home, Humphrey was known for bringing his country bands to New Orleans during Mardi Gras and other holidays when there was extra work for musicians.

Before taking up an instrument Humphrey's students learned music, working from exercises he wrote out himself. Trombonist Charles "Sunny" Henry (1885–1960) studied with the professor at the Magnolia Plantation downriver from New Orleans in Plaquemines Parish. Henry described the rehearsals. Humphrey started with what he called "the batterie"; the bass, trombone, and drums. When they played to his satisfaction he added the cornets, followed by the rest of the band. Only then would Professor Humphrey take out his cornet and join the band. The rehearsals lasted about two hours and centered on march pieces and popular tunes like "Suwannee River (Old Folks at Home)" and "Whistling Rufus," which Humphrey arranged.[14]

Some of Humphrey's students, like Manny Gabriel of Reserve, born in 1898, were intimidated by "the old man." Humphrey expected results from his students and had little tolerance for slackers. So sought-after was Humphrey that he was known for charging spectators admission to band rehearsals. These practices attracted both "white and colored," according to grandson and jazz trombonist Earl Humphrey. Rehearsals, he said, were held every Friday night no matter who was there.[15]

Henry remembered the professor's visits the Magnolia Plantation to teach the band there: "Jim Humphrey used to come there and teach the boys. I was a little kid. I'd get in the window. Jim Humphrey used to show them fellows everything. They did have sixteen men in that band. When Jim Humphrey was gone, I could go there and show them everything what Jim Humphrey showed them. When I growned a little more older they wanted me to get in the band."[16]

The other band Humphrey started, the Pickwick Brass Band, played from sheet music but also featured some fakers. There was also a string band version of this group that played for dances. They were popular with the clubs and benevolent societies in the area and were led by Peter Ferdinand Valentine. Born in the 1870s, Valentine led the Pickwick band from its inception in the 1890s. The Pickwick played for funerals for deceased bandmates and, like the Onward, marched in New Orleans' carnival parades. Valentine lived in Reserve, as did most of the members. The band varied their repertoire to gauge audience taste, according musician Marshall Lawrence, whose uncle Joseph played drums in the band.[17]

Professor Humphrey drilled the ensemble at its inception, though Valentine, and later cornetist Dejan Alexandre, were the leaders. Valentine recalled the band: "I joined the Pickwick brass band of Reserve, after Jim Humphrey had taught the members. They were all from around Reserve. Edward Hall was our clarinet player. Dejan Alexandre taught the band most of what they knew, after the professor had organized it."[18]

Ory did not like to dwell on stories where he was not a bandleader, but he did say that he played with the Pickwick Brass Band in Reserve. He recalled watching brass bands rehearsals when he was a youngster: "I remember sometimes they had a rehearsal in a big house. They wouldn't let kids in. Sometimes they would have it at my friend's house and I'd get there early and get underneath the bed and hear them play."[19]

Ferdinand Peter Valentine's son, "Kid" Thomas Valentine (1896–1987), had similar memories. He and Robert Hall, brother of future Louis Armstrong All-Stars clarinetist Edmond, messed around with instruments stored at Valentine's house when the Pickwick band was not playing.[20] They would try to blow the horns and pretend they were playing a dance. Ory had similar memories of trying his hand while attending functions in St. John: "Sometimes when a brass band would be playing for a big banquet the guys would put the horns down and be drinking beer. I'd slip in and get one of the horns and try and blow it. I noticed how they were putting it into their mouth and I'd just kept on till I got a tone. We were all self taught."²¹

The annual musical high point in St. John came at grinding season when the raw cane was refined into sugar, syrup, and molasses. Activity centered around the sugar mill every payday, where refreshments and music brought a celebratory atmosphere to the harvest ritual. Bands played for the workers as they partied, wages in hand, into the evening. The grinding continued for weeks, as did the music every Friday after work. Living across the dirt road from the mill, Dutt was in a position to take it all in. Groups from New Orleans, including Henry Peyton and his band, were regulars at the harvest. Peyton played a button accordion and featured guitars, mandolin, violin, and other strings. By comparison, Ory said, Charlie Galloway and Edward Clem featured horns in a combination that was closer to the construction of a jazz band:²² "(Clem) had four or five pieces; he played something like Bolden, played trumpet good. Our town was too small for Bolden."²³

John Joseph (1877–1965) equated Clem to New Orleans cornetist Buddy Bolden in that theirs were the first two groups he heard play the blues for dancing.²⁴ Joseph, a bass player, noted that Clem's brother Jesse was the first man he ever saw slap a bass. At the time he saw him Joseph said everyone he knew was still bowing and would only pick, not slap, if a bow broke. Slap bass later became a regular feature among New Orleans jazz bands.

Sometimes John Robichaux would come into town to play for grinding season, a parish fair, or train excursion. Robichaux (1866–1939) was from Thibodaux originally but relocated to New Orleans in 1891, where he led bands till his death in 1939. "They played for the elite and had the town sewed up," Robichaux bandsmen Bud Scott remembered. It was a traditional dance band that played the popular music of the day from a library of scores to which new arrangement were constantly added. Robichaux is said to have boasted that he had a score for any request. They played parlor music and sentimental ballads sprinkled with raggy melodies, cakewalks, and novelty pieces.[25] It is not remembered as an improvising group in this time period, though future jazz stars did play with him, including Scott and guitarist Johnny St. Cyr. Songs played by Robichaux included "Belle Marie," "Naval Cadet March," "Nigger in the Hen Coop," and "Whistling Rufus."

Another regular at grinding season was cornetist Claiborne Williams. Williams, born 1869, was based in Donaldsonville, where he led a dance band for about as long as Robichaux. At one time he played about every parish festival and gathering up and down the river. Noted for their musicality and professionalism, Williams's orchestra is not remembered as a hot band. The brass band version of the Williams group was called the St. Joseph Brass Band. John Joseph said the violin played the lead in Williams's band and that at one time it featured members of Joseph's family, including John's brothers Henry, Kaiser, and Nelson.[26]

Professor Anthony Holmes's band from Lutcher, a few miles up-river from LaPlace, was also active in the region during this period. They are remembered as a talented unit that bested many bands— including Ory's, according to some people. They played from sheet music, according to Kid Thomas, who heard them at his home in Reserve. Joseph Harris, a musician born in 1909, said his father studied clarinet with Holmes and taught musicians throughout the area. The band traveled to Baton Rouge and was a regular at carnival parades in New Orleans. Musician Manuel Paul studied with Holmes as well, and said the professor knew enough about reading music to tell the others what to play and how to read their parts. John Joseph remembered the band from an earlier period. Joseph said all the musicians in the band were good and that he later played with the group.[27]

Visiting musicians came by water as well as by land. Steaming down the river every fall was the French and Price showboat, complete with dancers, an orchestra, and moving pictures. "The

French and Price showboats in the winter, had good bands who sold sheet music," Marshall Lawrence recalled. Mathilda August Clementin, who lived in Lucy on the west bank of St. John, saw the boats, too.[28] The showboat would spend about a week in a parish going from community to community, mooring up against the riverbanks where it would sit securely in the mud for the duration of its stay. The shows were open to white and black and are remembered as being a highlight of the year, particularly to youngsters.

There were benevolent society halls, where musical events were held, throughout the river parishes, many near Ory's home. Mutual aid and benevolent societies, based on old world fraternal and service organizations, were popular in southeast Louisiana throughout the nineteenth and much of the twentieth centuries. They arose from the need for a social safety net for people to deal with catastrophic events like illness and death. For a few pennies a week, the members earned a sickness and death benefit whereby their healthcare was paid for, or at least subsidized, and upon death the funeral was covered. Their membership books often were illustrated with a pair of hands joined in friendship with the motto printed below: "To care for the sick and bury the dead."

Societies located in the river parishes that served members of Ory's community included the Good Hope, Israelite, and Bon Savance organizations, located in respective halls on the River Road between LaPlace and Reserve. On the west bank there were the Mayflower and the Bonsecour Benevolent Associations, among others. The groups sponsored parades for funerals and the organization's anniversary. The parades were a pro-bono party for the community, as well as a means to market the group to potential members. This was essential: like insurance companies, societies needed a broad membership to insure their financial well-being. The society halls where these groups held their functions also served as community centers where fish fries, banquets, and dances were held featuring local and visiting bands.

There was a hall called the Bonsavance [sic] and several halls
around Reserve that held fish fries and dances. This was when
I was nothing, but a kid. Usually, I would have a few of "my
boys" with me. We all loved music and wanted to hear it
whenever we could. We couldn't play it ourselves or at least
please ourselves with our playing; we felt we were only pre-
tending. So, we always wanted to go to the hall whenever any-
thing was going on that included music.[29]

During a society dance, when a march song was played, it was
customary for the boys to buy the girls with whom they danced
refreshment. Sometimes the roles were reversed.

I didn't want to be embarrassed by being the only one without
treating. It wasn't the rule that the girl asked the boy to dance
but, occasionally, the girls would do just that if there were a
special boy they liked. Then, the mother of the girl, sitting on
the sidelines, and well equipped with a bag filled with fruits of
the season, would give the girls something from the bag, if she
approved of her dancing with the boy the girl had asked. In
those days, no girl could attend a dance without her mother
or some other suitable chaperon. Then. If the boy felt equal to
accepting being treated by the girl and her mother, he would
dance with her to the tune of the special march.[30]

Eventually Dutt developed a reputation as a successful fruit gath-
erer at the dances, and over the years he faced his share of angry
boyfriends and brothers.[31]

The halls were some distance from the plantation, but Ory, always looking for an angle, had a plan. He noticed that the Orys and
Lasseignes let their horses graze and water on the Mississippi River
levee batture, the land between the levee and the waters edge, at
night. Ory fished at that spot in the evening. He noticed, whenever

he lifted his line and exposed his bait, the horses would come over looking to be fed. That was all the fishing he needed to do.

It was easy enough to do, I'd get a few ears of corn and the horses would just come to you, they were always hungry. All I had to do was slip that (bridle) on a horse and get on his back. The boys said that we couldn't all ride on one horse, so I had another bridle made. It was very cheap. Thereafter, on the night of any big dance . . . with the country folk going wild, for miles and miles around, all wanting to get to the hall and hear them, we'd help ourselves to a horse or two and slip the bridles on them.[32]

It sounded easy enough, but the plan needed refinement.

We had no saddles, not even a blanket to throw over them, so we just rode them bareback into Reserve. By the time we arrived at the dance hall in Reserve, we were so dirty sweaty. (From) all the dust and the perspiration—from the horse (that it) made us look as though we had combination trousers on. The backs of them were all black and the rest of the pants were their original colors. We were sort of ashamed to go into the hall and we stayed out on the lawn where they served the food and drinks and listened to the music from there. After all, we had gone there mostly to get ideas from the bands for our own playing.[33]

Ory and the Matthews brothers kept the practice up for a while until they got the nerve up to ask John L. Ory, whose horses they had been stealing, if they could borrow a buggy to ride to the hall. John L. gave his approval and the Ory gang showed up at the dance clean and pressed. Among the bands Ory heard in the society halls around the parish were those led by Charlie Galloway, Edward

Clem, Henry Peyton, John Robichaux, Claiborne Williams, and eventually Freddie Keppard.

There were several white clubs with music and dancing. The Woodmen of the World hall in LaPlace was a favorite venue of extended members of the white Ory clan, who played there for concerts and dramatic presentations. Vaudeville shows from New Orleans traveled to play the W.O.W. hall, too. The New Sugar Belt Club in Reserve featured bands, both black and white, for dancing and concerts. One popular local band was the Donaldson-Edrington Orchestra, led by H. A. Donaldson. Even the St. John Progressive Euchre Club held dances after card tournaments "until a late hour." The club was for whites, but black folks would stand outside to take in the music.[34]

Brass bands, music teachers, professional bands from New Orleans, and musicians on the scene at the Woodland created a diverse canvass for Ory to take in. Ory acted on his musical impulses early and deeply. In the beginning, without instruments and a merely rudimentary understanding of music, Ory and his friends gathered after hours to join voices and harmonize. Recreational singing and harmonizing, particularly among African Americans, was ubiquitous in America during Ory's youth. By the 1890s, what came to be known as barbershop harmonizing "was thoroughly woven into America's cultural fabric, across all race and class barriers." Indeed, membership in vocal quartets was a common experience among future jazzmen in New Orleans. Though born in different decades, Louis Armstrong (1901–1971) and Jelly Roll Morton (1889–1941) both refer to being in harmonizing groups early in their careers.[35] Lee Collins (1901–1960), another New Orleans jazzman, remembered singing groups from his youth:

Speaking about singing, There used to be lots of guys around New Orleans that could sing real good. They got up quartets. My Aunt Esther's husband was the leader of many a one and would go around to some of the funeral homes to sing eat and

drink beer or maybe it would be a cowein [turtle] with plenty
of wine to go with it. That was some of the most beautiful sing-
ing you could ever hope to hear. After everyone was drunk, the
last song would always be their old favorite "Sweet Adeline."³⁶

Ory recalled his early harmonizing experiences: "We would stand
on a bridge at night and hum different tunes with different harmo-
nies. It was dark and no one could see us, but people could hear
us singing and they'd bring us a few ginger cakes and some water.
We hummed and when we knowed the tune itself, the melody, the
others would put a three or four part harmony to it. It was good
ear training."³⁷ Finding variations of chords is basic music theory
so singing served as a medium for the Woodland boys' education.

Popular songs in the river parishes included "Hiawatha," known
in St. John as "Lizard on a Rail." The song apparently became so
popular that it replaced "Dixie" as a top request.³⁸ "Silver Threads
Among the Gold," "Home Sweet Home," and "Here Comes Your
Daddy Now" were all tunes regularly played in St. John, according
to violinist Marshall Lawrence. These songs were in common cur-
rency throughout the country, and all were commercially recorded
at the turn of the century. Still, Ory makes it clear that they composed their own material as well.

We were all so interested in our own music by this time that
on our way home from Milesville, a village about a mile from
LaPlace, one of us would get an idea for a new number. Of-
ten, we would stop wherever we were, in the road, by the rail-
road track and rehearse on the spot. We could see the lights
in the houses of LaPlace where the people would be making
their preparations for breakfast, and those people would tell
us later how they had enjoyed our impromptu sessions.³⁹

I suggested to the boys that we make ourselves a banjo, a gui-
tar and bass. I first used a cigar box to make my banjo, with

different sizes of thread and fishing line for the strings on it and the other two instruments. Later, I used a regulation din- ner pail (for the body) which would resonate better. To do this I cut a hole in the bucket and pushed the neck of the banjo through the hole and tacked it with braids. For the bucket banjo I changed from thread to wire for the strings, then later I got regular musical strings from New Orleans for it. I used wire for my frets and after getting used to it, I liked the tone of it (not like a real banjo, but more like a ukulele as to loud- ness of tone), but the five strings made it different. We played mostly in rooms, just hustlin' around, so the lack of carrying power didn't make too much difference. For the bass, we used a regular wooden soapbox and added a neck to it and worked it down just like a regular bass. (For the guitar) we couldn't make a machine head, but copying the banjo we worked it out of a large, deep cigar box and the usual six strings and fol- lowed the same general pattern of the banjo and other than the box, practically the same materials. After finishing the three instruments, we started practicing in the daytime but evenings would find us drifting to our favorite spot . . . the bridge . . . and the people, especially the youngsters found us there and would hang around listening to us play and they would start dancing there in the dusty road. It made us feel wonderful that they would want to spend time listening to us beginners and like it enough to start dancing.[40]

How Ory knew how to string an instrument and at what pitch to tune it is unclear, but it is not something one would just know how to do. John Daniel Ory, John L.'s son, would have known how, though he may have been away at school in 1898. Lawrence Duhe's father Evariste, who worked at the sugar mill with Ozeme, could have been another source of information. A violinist, Duhe could have shown the boys what strings were needed and to what pitch they should be tuned. He then could have shown Dutt and the boys how to form chords.

The instruments eventually consisted of a five-string dinner-pail banjo, cigar-box guitar, cigar-box violin, and soapbox bass. If drums were needed, Rabbit tapped out the rhythm on a chair top. As each instrument was completed, Ory took time to refine both the instrument and his playing. As Dutt moved from one instrument to the next, the other boys took up his castoffs and he tutored them. "I played five string banjo and taught the other boys to play the violin, bass, drum and guitar," Ory said.[41] He said they bowed the bass but had to use lots of rosin to avoid sawing through the G string. Realistically, the instruments had irregular strings and intonations, and were certainly difficult if not impossible to get in tune with one another. He said the sound did not carry very far and the instruments were suited only to playing indoors, and there is no doubt that they were difficult to play. Still the Woodland boys plowed on, cutting their musical teeth along with many fingertips.

Ory said that when they started out they were pretending, like being a musician was an extension of child's play. However, his determination to make the instruments playable, and his desire to promote the resulting product, makes it clear that at some point music became a serious endeavor. What the resulting sound was from this bizarre amalgamation of instruments is anyone's guess. That they stuck with it and became professional musicians is testament to the sincerity of their efforts. They were genuinely committed to make their way, cigar-box instruments notwithstanding. Ory had created his first band. He said they played songs that they made up and other tunes. They may have started with songs from their singing repertoire. The group at first was probably as much about singing as playing.

Kid Thomas Valentine recalled similar musical adventures with his pals at his house in Reserve. "Me and my friends started on

home-made instruments made out of cane reeds. We used fishing
line to make the bass."[42]

Florence Dymond, who lived on the Bel Air Plantation, remembered the kids there having a similar group:

> *Some of the small colored boys on Bel Air varying from 10 to*
> *14 years, decided they would have their own band. They used*
> *an old lard can for a drum and an old, discarded sugar house*
> *pipes, varying in length and diameter, some straight and some*
> *bent, formed the other instruments. The boys sang and blew*
> *through the pipes with the drummer keeping time on the lard*
> *can and it was really remarkable the harmony they could get*
> *out of all that junk.*[43]

In New Orleans, Emile "Stalebread" Lacoume (1885–1946) led
just such an irregular outfit in the streets around this time. Made
up of kids with such nicknames such as Warm Gravy and Family
Haircut, the ragtag outfit was well known in the city and a picture
of the group was displayed in the window of the Werlein's for Music store. Like Ory, Lacoume would go on to become a professional
jazzman.[44]

The band practiced and learned what tunes they could as they
continued working on making their instruments more playable.
Bringing his entrepreneurial proclivities to the fore, Ory organized
a fish fry at an abandoned house at the Woodland. John L. Ory
thought Dutt was wasting his energies, but he signed off on the
party. Dutt strung fishing lines in the river and spread the word
among the kids along the road behind the plantation that there
would be food and cold drinks. Featuring both catfish from the
river and perch from the bayous behind the plantation, Ory fried
the fish and arranged for the drinks on credit at the Woodland
store and collected money at the door. "I was the leader, the promoter, the bookkeeper, treasurer and fish fryer," Ory said of his
first venture.

We kept every dollar we made with me acting as treasurer and put it aside to buy real instruments. As we started the fish fries, we had to add two more instruments and decided on a lead violin, made out of a small cigar box and patterned on the same scale as the other instruments. We also wanted drums, but we used a chair for this and beat on the rounds and the seat. Afterward, changing over to a big tub and making the chair to be used as the snare drum. We kept saving like mad for real instruments.[45]

Ory and the boys performed when Ory was not busy frying fish. At the next fish fry, he hired a couple of girls to fry the fish. "I was a big shot then," Ory said.

Ory planned more events and his mind was occupied more and more by music. Eventually, he said, he could see nothing else. But in a pattern that would be repeated throughout his life, Ory would discover his highs were often tempered by life-changing lows. Hard times were around the corner.

CHAPTER 3

1900–1904

ORPHAN

⬥⬥

During the third week of a stay at the Haydels' rice farm in Edgard, news reached Dutt that his mother had passed away. He recalled her in his autobiography:

I kept remembering she had said she felt bad and several times she stayed in bed for a day or so, and that just wasn't like my mother. To this day, I have never learned what caused her illness or her death. I don't think it could have been from some old age ills because she wasn't that old. My mother's death really broke my heart. To me, it was the end. That was when my hard times really did start.[1]

Burials took place immediately after death, as there was limited embalming available in St. John and the Ory family surely could not have afforded it anyway. Octavie's jaw would have been tied shut and coins placed on her eyes to hold them closed. She was laid out in the home on a board between sawhorses or on the bed with the mattress removed. Since it was summer, she was most likely placed over buckets of ice. The vigil over the body would have lasted for hours, with several meals being consumed before the funeral mass. On September 5, 1900, the family gathered at St. Peter's in Reserve on the upriver side of the cemetery behind the church. This is where people of color were buried. Typically graves there were marked with a flat iron cross about two feet high. Sometimes the name of the deceased was etched into the crossbar but within a few years rust would obscure the writing. This was the custom, and even today a few deteriorating metal crosses may be found along the fence at St. Peter's. Father Badeaux, who had watched the Ory children grow up, said prayers at graveside.[2]

She was a very happy person until she became ill. She was an excellent cook. I remember that on all holidays, but especially on my birthday, Christmas, she would prepare wonderful dinners and we would all get together and enjoy ourselves until our stomachs were filled to bursting. On Christmas, we would always have a tree. In those days, we never had to buy one, we would go about two blocks from the house and cut one down and drag it home. Then, my mother and my older sisters would get together and help us decorate the tree. But, the best memory of all that I have of my mother is her picking me up and sitting me on her lap. Then she would rock me while she sang to me in French.[3]

As Octavie lay ill, Dutt had promised her that he would take care of Ozeme and his younger sisters Annie and Lizzie. As the oldest child at home, responsibilities were on Dutt. It was a hardscrabble existence. By this time Ozeme was also in declining health. "I never was sure that my mother's death was the actual cause of it, but after she passed, my father's health grew steadily worse and more and more of the burden of supplying the household with food, money and any and all necessities fell on me. I was happy to do anything at all to help my Daddy because I loved him so."[4]

By this time the family had moved from the Woodland Plantation and were living in a house near the LaPlace train station, known as the "Battery Village."

After my dad got so ill, I rented a house for $3 a month and I continued working as a water boy (at the Woodland) but after I found out that .60 cents a day couldn't support my dad, my

sisters and myself, I decided that in my spare time, I would
supply my water wagon with fishing equipment . . . crawfish
nets, fishing pole lines and an extra bucket and when the peo-
ple weren't in need of water, I'd take time out and fish because
there were lots of fishing ponds, mushrooms, blackberries,
dewberries and anything I could pick up quickly and easily
that could be used for food. During the crawfish season, I'd
get up very early and catch them and sell the catch right af-
terward for 25 cents for a pail and I'd usually get three or four
pails a day during the season.[5]

Somehow, between all these hand-to-mouth activities Ory still
found time for music. By 1901 he had outgrown his homemade
instruments and was interested in moving on to the real thing.
Ozeme was proud of Dutt's progress on his homespun banjo and
decided he deserved a real one. He placed an order through the
Woodland store and their buyer took the train to New Orleans
where he fetched specialty items and catalogue orders. The day the
grocery man, as Ory called him, was due to come back with his
banjo he sat on the tracks and waited.

He jumped at the sound of the train and ran to meet the grocery
man. The banjo was wrapped in brown paper, which Dutt quickly
tore away. At last he had a real instrument, which meant he could
be a real musician. His joy was tempered when he went to show
his father the prize.

When I got back to the house, just a few steps from the tracks,
my sister told me that daddy was very sick but, I went on
in and showed him my banjo. He just nodded his head and
said it was fine, but he was too ill to listen to me play it. Back
to the railroad tracks I went and sat there and played and
played with only myself the air and the birds to hear me. Ev-
ery day after that daddy grew steadily worse. Approximately
two weeks after my "banjo day," he passed away without ever

having heard me play. I loved him so. He had always been so
kind and patient with me and even encouraged me on with
my music. He spoke almost no English. Our conversations
were in French, but to this day I can remember them almost
word for word. He was a wonderful man.[6]

Ozeme "John" Ory died on July 29, 1901, at age 50. His obituary
ran on page one of the Frencholanguage newspaper *La Meschacébé*,
but with no mention of his late wife and family. A bastard, mixed-
race family would not be recognized in such a public way, so for
readers that day they did not exist. Still, the family gathered at St.
Peter's cemetery to lay him to rest. Fr. Badeaux recited prayers in
Latin, as he had done a few months earlier for Octavie. His simple
notation in the sacramental register reads, "I buried John Ory today." The period after his father's death in the summer of 1901 was
difficult for Dutt, and he described it as the "doldrums." Dutt, now
14, and his eight-year-old sister Annie moved in with their sister
Louisa and her husband, Victor Bontemps, back at the Woodland
Plantation.[7] "Again, I was tied down to plantation life and working
at whatever jobs the superintendent felt like handing to me. I felt a
deep, yearning emptiness inside me. It was a pit that needed to be
filled but, by what, I wasn't sure. In fact, I wasn't sure of anything
for those first six months or so of being an orphan."[8]

With the death of Ozeme, the most influential men in Dutt's
life became his sister's respective husbands. These men set a high
bar of success for Dutt, which probably had him longing for his
father's easygoing ways. Men of color did not get ahead at the turn
of the century very easily, and their work ethic must have been
one that they tried to imprint on the adolescent. Surely, pressure
was brought on the boy approaching manhood to find his way and
"learn a trade."

So it was right after Ory completed his work at the sugar mill
in the wake of the 1901 harvest that he sought employment beyond the plantation. Ory was not interested in working at the

Woodland, where he said he was "pushed around" for a very small salary. That first summer, though, he kept close to home and participated in the familiar routines of the harvest, driving the water cart, and working in the mill. He heard the bands as they came from New Orleans to play for the workers when they got their payout., but probably without the lighthearted joy with which he had listened to them before. He had a new seriousness about him and a determination to get away from the plantation to leave its hard life and sad memories behind. Perhaps anxious to impress his brother-in-law Victor Bontemps, Ory proposed turning over his salary from the harvest to make a down payment on a lot in La-Place's Cherokee Town on which they could build a home.[9] "I told him that I felt grateful to my sister for being a sort of mother to me after my Dad passed, and if he would just let me pay for my room and board while I worked at the sugar mill, I would pay so much per week on a lot and have it all paid for her by the end of the sugar season. By the time I left the sugar mill, the lot was bought and paid for by me."[10]

Childhood friend Joe Millet had bought the lot next to Ory's and was anxious for him to finish his house. He told Ory about a lumber mill being built three miles downriver in Montz, and together they went to seek work there.[11]

The entire river parishes region was in the throes of a timber rush, as centuries-old cypress trees were felled and milled from Jefferson Parish to Baton Rouge. By 1902, lumber camps could be found up and down both sides of the river. For plantation workers brought up in the cycle of the harvest and obliged to the weather for success, the lumber camps were a godsend. In 1902 most plantation workers got well under a dollar a day. The lumber mills sometimes doubled that. "Joe (Millet) and I decided that if we got there early enough we would get the best jobs. We didn't have any experience and what with our ages, we were offered jobs on the cut-off saw, at $1.75 a day . . . the toughest job in the mill. Shortly after that, I started thinking about a way to get my house built."[12]

Ory cut a deal with the manager of the mill to buy $150 worth of lumber to build the house. Dutt's weekly wage was garnished while he paid off the lumber bill.[13] In classic Louisiana fashion, the house raising became a party: a boucherie. A pig was roasted and family friends came over to frame the house out. In the weeks that followed Dutt and Victor Bontemps finished out the siding and trim and papered the walls. The pride Dutt felt about the three-room cottage was apparent in his retellings of the story. This was his first real foray into manhood, and perhaps Dutt sensed his father smiling down on him. He had helped his sister Louisa by providing a home for her family and had ensured that sister Annie, whom his parents had asked him to look out for, would have a roof over her head. This was his first big money transaction and it surely filled him with confidence.

Ory said he spent about eighteen months at the lumber mill before getting a lead on another job, this time from Joe Millet's brother James, who had been away working with a bricklayer. When James returned to LaPlace he came upon Dutt laboring to repair a brick fireplace. Ory did not really know what he was doing and this must have been obvious to Millet. "James was watching me and he said, 'Why don't you come with me and learn that trade?'"[14] Ory decided to take Millet up on it.

Apparently Millet had engaged in some bait and switch, as Dutt thought they were going to Donaldsonville, about thirty miles upriver. One of the reasons Dutt had taken the job was because he thought he might get a chance to hear Claiborne Williams's band, which was based there. Donaldsonville was an important city then, a railroad hub at the convergence of Bayou Lafourche and the Mississippi River. Dutt had never been to a city. To his dismay, he discovered the bricklaying crew was laboring miles downriver from Donaldsonville, repairing the old Choppin Plantation.

Choppin had been a large plantation before the war but by 1903 had been reduced to a relic. Whatever optimism Dutt had for the rest of the trip evaporated after a few days in the sun working for overseer John Tureau, whom he compared to Simon Legree. Toureau was a ruthless taskmaster, and a drunk. He paid the workers $1 a day, but he required that .50 be paid back for room and board. He cursed at the crew, made them work overly long shifts, and confined them to the plantation after hours. After working all day, the only thing the crew looked forward to was eating. Tureau fouled this up, too, by making a pass at the "old shanty woman," as Ory described her, who had been hired to cook for the men. She quit and the men were left in a fix. With only one pan, they washed, cooked, and ate out of it every day. "We'd fall to work and make a fire and mix the hotcakes in an old pitcher and cook them in that same darned pan (that we washed in). We had a couple gallons of sorghum, which was plentiful in the country. We'd eat the cakes soaked with the sorghum and that's all we had for a few days. Before I got away from him, I went through other forms of torture."[15]

After hours, when Dutt retreated to his bedroll to play his guitar, a drunken Tureau would burst in and demand to hear the blues.[16] Many times Tureau promised Dutt that if he played the blues for him he would not have to work in the morning, only to renege in the light of day. "Most nights I would play for old man Tureau until twelve or one o'clock. If I had managed to fall asleep and he felt like hearing me play, he would come around my room and wake me and say, 'Come on and play me some blues.' I'd tell him, 'I'm sleepy, man. Let me rest. I've got to carry all those bricks tomorrow.' That would mean nothing to him."[17]

The confines of the plantation were getting to Dutt; he longed for a decent meal and some fun. Tureau's requirement that the crew remain at the plantation flew in the face of Dutt's reason for making the trip in the first place. He soon heard about a sawmill town between Donaldsonville and Choppin. Tureau was usually passed out drunk early on Saturdays, so Dutt figured he would make a run for it. He threw his guitar on his shoulder and headed for the bright lights off in the distance.[18] When he arrived at the boomtown, a row of saloons and businesses lay before him. He went to the first saloon, where someone spotted his guitar and announced his presence.

> *Someone started to pass a hat around saying, "If we give him something, he'll play us something." I started in playing some blues and I saw that by that time about $4 had poured into the hat and I said to myself, "Oh man, this is more money than I earned in two months, working for Tureau, carrying bricks on my head and mixing mortar." Just then, along came a nice brown-skinned gal. She walked right up to me and said, "You must be a stranger in town." I said, "Yes, I am. I'm just scuffling, trying to make a living." "You're going to make one right here," she told me.[19]*

Dutt discovered she was a madam connected with the boss of the saloon. He said she slipped him a few dollars and made arrangements for him to play every Saturday night. Ory arranged to have a bottle of wine on hand Saturday afternoons, to get Tureau out of the way. The strategy worked a few times, but ultimately the old man began to get suspicious. He discovered Dutt missing and traced him to the honky-tonk, where he broke up the gig. Ory had had enough of the sadistic overseer and plotted an exit.

The next morning, as Tureau yelled for the crew to work faster, the 5' 7", slightly built Ory struggled up a shaky ladder carrying bricks and mortar to the crew above. Tureau let fly another curse at Ory who had had enough. He dropped his entire load of bricks on Tureau's head. The taskmaster hit the ground hard, unconscious. Ory grabbed his guitar and knapsack and lit out of Choppin as fast as he could, rambling down the River Road in a stolen wagon. A stunned Tureau rose to his feet. Still wobbly from the blows to his head, he gave chase determined to teach Ory something once and for all. He found him at the train station.

When he got to the station, I was already on the train and we were ready to pull out. Tureau spotted me and started for the train. Just then, the cars started to slide out of the station, and I leaned out the window and waved to Tureau and called, "goodbye." The last I saw of him he was standing there with his face almost purple in color, waving his buggy whip at me and yelling something that I couldn't hear and to this day, I've never been curious what it was.[20]

The train clacked away southeast, toward Edgard, where Dutt retreated to the safety of his family at the Haydel rice farm, where he shared the whole story with Nellie, Clay, and Johnny. When the laughter subsided, and Dutt had been fed, Johnny walked his brother to the ferry and wished him good luck. Dutt crossed the river and fell in with his old crowd again.[21]

The most telling item in the bricklaying story may be that it sheds light on Ory's musical leanings early on. The essential thrust of the story hinges on him playing the blues, be it under duress from Tureau, or delight at the sawmill saloon. It is interesting that both a white overseer and Ory's peers at the sawmill saloon, wanted, and apparently expected, the blues.

If Ory returned to LaPlace with his tail between his knees from the bricklaying fiasco, it was soon forgotten in a new eagerness to get something going musically. His forays into playing music and following the bands back home were now childhood memories. The adolescent Ory probably looked back with some embarrassment at his childhood noisemaking. Realistically, Ory's seriousness about music, and his ownership of a real banjo, separated him from his childhood accomplices who were still fooling around with their homespun instruments.

The situation would change rapidly upon his return to the Woodland. About this time, Dutt heard about a used trombone for sale a few miles upriver. "The boys told me that Jules Duhe had an old beat-up valve trombone that he wanted to sell for $7.50 so I walked six miles that very day to go buy it and I came back with it and we started in rehearsing again."[22] The horn was so full of holes that Ory had to plug them with soap. After playing a few minutes he found himself blowing bubbles. Still, it was a trombone. Undeterred, Ory hatched a plan to buy instruments for the rest of his gang.

> I had a hunch that I might be able to do business with the clerk at the grocery store there who made a practice of lending money at 6 percent interest, when he thought he would be sure to get it back. I propositioned him for $100 to pay for the instruments for the other three boys so that we would all be playing on real ones. He let me have it and I went to New Orleans and picked up a bass violin, a guitar and a lead violin. Then we had some real rehearsing with the honest-to-God instruments and decided we were good enough to play at the ball games when the teams would come to LaPlace from New Orleans and get the crowd interested enough during game time to come to the picnics later in the evening that I promoted. For my first picnic, I went around and told all the business people why it was I wanted to put on the affair and it was to help me get two more instruments and to enlarge my band (trumpet and drums). All the business men and women who were both interested and able to do so, gave me chicken, potatoes, ham and beer, lemons, sugar, soda pop and most anything that I could sell to help me out on my first venture and it turned out to be a huge success.[23]

Ory sold sandwiches and fruit, and his band played after the ball game. He said he made enough money to pay part of his $100 note to the Woodland clerk and buy a trumpet and drums for the group. "Then we really went to town for my second picnic and it was so successful that I paid off the rest of the $100 and the interest and still had plenty left for the boys and myself," Ory said.[24]

Now they were a real band.

CHAPTER 4

1905–1907
WALKING WITH THE KING

By 1905 Ory was spending much of his time with his brother Johnny across the river in Edgard. Johnny had become a partner in the
Haydel and Ory store with his brother-in-law Clay Haydel. "It was
a regular store on the [river] road," remembered Haydel's granddaughter Sybil Haydel Morial. She said they had pickles and pig
feet in jars and just about anything else people might want. According to Harold Ory, Johnny's son, there was usually a card game
going on in a back room, complete with a signal bell in case the
sheriff came around. Johnny had a dog trained to carry messages
between his home and the store.[1]

A store full of groceries and Johnny's easygoing ways were probably a relief to Dutt, who no doubt was tired of Louisa and Victor
Bontemps's attempts at parenting him. He took advantage of this
freedom and in 1905 made his first trip to New Orleans to buy a
new trombone.[2]

Dutt really had no concept of what a city would look like. In
St. John Parish the biggest thing around was the Woodland sugar
mill, which was several stories high. Imagining dozens of buildings
that big must have filled him with anticipation. Approaching the
city from its rural northwest, the train traveled southeast with the
swamp at the left and the river at the right. The cypress marsh of
St. Charles Parish gave way to the cow pastures of Jefferson Parish.
The train passed Carrollton Avenue and crossed the New Basin
Canal. Shotgun houses and Creole cottages spanned block after
block. Dutt disembarked at the Y&MV station at Poydras and

Villere Streets and headed to Werlein's for Music on Canal Street. As the streetcar turned right onto the giant thoroughfare, Ory took in the expanse of it all. The buildings reached five to ten stories in the air and electrical lines ran everywhere overhead. Streetcars converged from far-flung points around the city, bells dinging against the gentle *errrrr* sound created by the giant steel wheels against the smooth track. Dozens of wagons and carts plowed the streets, some carrying produce that, like Ory, was fresh from the country. He got off the car at Royal and Canal Streets and crossed to Werlein's. Generations of New Orleanians bought instruments, sheet music, and other items from this one-stop store that opened in 1834. Entering the store, he likely marveled at the shining silver and gold cornets, alto horns, saxophones, clarinets, and bass drums. In the string department he spied a double bass, violin, and guitar. Looking back in the wind band department, he found his prize, a York valve trombone. After parting with $67, Dutt grabbed the streetcar to his sister's house uptown.

Ory's sister Lena had taken up with a widowed carpenter named Warren Cotton and gone to live in Baton Rouge. Around 1905, Warren's brother Henry moved to New Orleans with his wife Emma, renting a house at 2123 South Robertson Street near the corner of Jackson Avenue; by late 1905, Lena and Warren had moved in.[3] It was there that Ory went with his new horn.

Few days in Ory's life made an impression on him like the one on which he met Buddy Bolden. He often included the story in interviews and he recounted the details in his autobiography. Charles "Buddy" Bolden (1877–1931) is the man many people point to as being the first jazz band leader in New Orleans.[4] Clarinetist George Baquet (1883–1949), a contemporary, described the effect Bolden had on an audience and his own musical philosophy: "They played 'Make me a pallet (on the floor).' Everybody rose and yelled out 'Oh, Mr. Bolden, play it for us, Buddy, play it!' I'd never heard anything like that before. I played legitimate stuff. But this, it was something that pulled me in. They got me up on the stand and I played with them. After that I didn't play legitimate so much."[5]

Musical contemporaries say emphatically that Bolden's major innovation was playing blues for dancing. "Buddy Bolden is the first man who played blues for dancing," said bassist and St. James Parish native John Joseph. Bolden was a good player, he said, though not a good reader. Robichaux had a good unit, Joseph said, but Bolden bested him by playing the blues.[6] This was an innovation that apparently had not happened previously in New Orleans. Ory bandmate Lawrence Duhe added: "Buddy Bolden would put them out, then everybody'd go listen. That's how jazz came about. That's where all New Orleans musicians got that idea, from Buddy Bolden. We used to go listen. There is no question Buddy Bolden started jazz."[7] Future Ory trumpeter Thomas "Mutt" Carey concurred: "When you come right down to it the man who started the big noise in jazz was Buddy Bolden. Yes he was a powerful trumpet player and a good one too. I guess he deserves credit for starting it all."[8]

He stood about six feet tall, according to most people. He had a reddish tint to his brown skin and hair and wore a medium moustache, which arched around his wide mouth. He favored tight pants and a box back coat, which accentuated his rugged frame. When the night was young he sported a bow tie atop a detachable starched collar. As the evening wore on and his audience got rougher, the King would sometimes remove the cumbersome tie and collar. He then unbuttoned the neck of his sweat drenched white shirt to reveal his red firemen's underwear. This was hot stuff in 1901 and Bolden never missed an opportunity to "stir the pot," musically or otherwise.

When his rival, John Robichaux, was playing the pavilion at Lincoln Park in uptown New Orleans, Bolden would stick his horn over the fence from nearby Johnson Park and play a tune. The clarion call was meant to deride Robichaux and steal his audience. Bolden referred to the practice as "callin' my children home." Some say he had a signature series of notes he would blow to call his children home while others recall him actually launching into a song like "Funky Butt." There are many versions of the lyrics to "Funky Butt," some obscene. A typical passage went: "I thought I heard Buddy Bolden say, funky butt, funky butt, take it away. Funky butt, funky butt, take it away. I thought I heard him say." "The rendition of this number became an over-night sensation and the reputation of the Bolden Band became a household word with patrons of the Oddfellows Hall, Lincoln and Johnson Parks and several other popular dance halls around the city."[9]

Bolden also drew attention to himself with volume. His horn playing is often remembered as being powerful or simply loud. Ory recalled: "Bolden was very rough. You have to give him credit for starting the ball rolling, you know? But he really wasn't a musician. He didn't study. I mean he was a gifted player with effect but no tone, you know? He played loud, not high, but loud. And people loved it. They went for it."[10] Bolden may not have been playing jazz as it was recorded a decade later, but he played music that made people move their feet and clap their hands. Bolden was what Dutt Ory wanted to be.

Bolden was known in LaPlace and even played there on occasion, though only during short whistle stops at the train stations between New Orleans and Baton Rouge. Ory knew of these visits but says he first saw Bolden in New Orleans on the day he bought his trombone at Werlein's. The meeting happened at a transitional time for both men. For Ory, things were falling into place musically. Bolden was in twilight. His last complete year as an active musician would soon be behind him. Evidence suggests that Bolden's behavior was erratic. He failed to show up for gigs and spent advances, leaving nothing for the band. There are many references to his drinking. Musically, the great innovator of 1900 may have been on his way to becoming old hat by 1905. The original Bolden band had broken up and Buddy landed in trombonist Frankie Duson's band. On the day Bolden met Ory, he was between trombonists, and perhaps, between bands. At this point in Bolden's life, it is possible he was just between barrooms.

> *I had just bought my horn from the Werlein's music store. I had my sister living in New Orleans and I stopped with her. This was my first time (in New Orleans). And I was running over the horn, running over, blowing to see how it—you know, it would sound, to see how I liked it—I had already tired it in the music store—Bolden happened to pass by, and he heard the trombone, and he knocked on the door. At Jackson and Robertson Street. I was on Jackson. He heard the horn and he stopped and rapped on the door. "Young man," he said, "Are you blowing the trombone?" I said, "Yeah." He said, "Well you know who I am?" I said "I don't really." He said, "I'm the king." I said, "King who?" He said, "Bolden." "Glad to know you, Mr. Bolden." He said, "You live here?" I said, "No not exactly. My sister lives here. I live out in the country." He said, "Well I'd like to have you to work with me. You sound very good." He must have stayed out there and heard me play a little. And so I said, "Wait a minute," I was so tickled, you know? I thought, "Oh, man I'm going to play with King Bolden." Went back to my sister, and I said, "Come here" (to Bolden), "explain to my sister what you want." She said, "Oh, no, he has to go back home. He can't leave home now till he's twenty-one years old."[1]*

Denied the opportunity to play with Bolden, Dutt was nevertheless energized by the meeting. He told his friends back at the Woodland about the encounter, and they accompanied him on trips back to New Orleans. On the first trips there, they probably confined themselves to Lena and Warren Cotton's neighborhood and nearby Lincoln and Johnson parks off Carrollton Avenue.

Opened on April 14, 1902, Johnson Park was used primarily as a baseball venue. Owned by Pierre Larroux, it was leased by George W. Johnson, a Storyville waiter. With another waiter, James

Flowers, Johnson opened the Johnson Saloon across the street at 7935 Oleander.[12] Baseball may have had a role in drawing the LaPlace boys to Johnson Park. The baseball team Ory followed, at whose games he had held picnics in LaPlace, probably played against the New Orleans teams at Johnson Park.

Lincoln Park, which was across the street, was a combination amusement park, vaudeville theatre, and skating rink that also opened in 1902. It was a favorite destination of visitors from the country who rode in by train to spend their Sundays in the city. Parks became a crossroads of various popular bands in the city. "At that time, Lincoln Park was one of the most popular amusement places in New Orleans operated by colored people. Mention is made of Lincoln Park because it probably made a large contribution to New Orleans jazz music. It was here that several popular bands of the city rendered music for balls, picnics, banquets and other like affairs."[13] The park had been built by the Standard Brewery to sell their beer, and featured vaudeville entertainment including pianist Clarence Bush's Ragtime Opera Company and Allen's Troubadours.[14] Another piano professor, Albert Carroll, was the musical director for two seasons, including 1907 and 1909.

Lincoln Park was also the scene of many battles-of-the bands that Ory witnessed between the John Robichaux Orchestra and Buddy Bolden's Band. The rivalry originated when Bolden played across the street at Johnson Park. Mathilda August Clementin remembered that the Johnson Park bunch was a rougher crowd and that "Mr. Bolden and them shined" there. She said Lincoln Park was larger and drew a bigger crowd.[15] Later, according to Ory, Lincoln Park hired Bolden to play Sunday evening dances at the skating rink. From then on, Robichaux and Bolden competed for customers at respective stages at the same venue.

I used to run out to Lincoln Park on Sunday afternoon where John Robichaux's band was playing for the afternoon sessions of the balloon ascensions. They had a big pavilion for dancing, also a big skating rink on the same grounds for roller skating but no music at the rink until 8 p.m. when Bolden played. At this time, Bolden played in the afternoons out at Milneburg at picnics on the water and would come into Lincoln Park at 8 p.m. to play at the rink when the skating was over. The people would really crowd both the pavilion where Robichaux played and the grounds to watch the balloon ascension but, when Bolden would enter the skating rink, he would just stick his horn out a window and say, "Let's call my children home" and then start blowing "Pallet on the Floor."

You could see the people stop, listen and then frantically start pushing toward the skating rink to get to their idol, Bolden. I used to try to get there fast myself. Poor John Robichaux would be left flat without an audience whenever the King started to play. Robichaux would respond to Bolden's trumpet call with a rendition of Bolden's own number, "I Thought I Heard Bolden Say" but he would parody it to "I thought I heard Robichaux say, Buddy Bolden take it away," but he didn't mean it in a nice way.[16]

This was likely the summer of 1906, Bolden's last at Lincoln Park. Ory recalled once seeing Bolden sitting on the stoop of his house practicing. "And he never practiced in the house; he practiced on the box step, out in the street, on the sidewalk. He blew so loud he'd blow everyone out of the house when he practiced. Then he'd get out on the sidewalk, on the step, he'd practice a tune, and the kids would all gang around, 'King Bolden, King Bolden,' oh man."[17]

The Woodland boys went on to develop one-on-one friendships with members of the Bolden band. Ory sought out trombonist Willie Cornish (1875–1942) and went to hear music with him at Funky Butt Hall. Duhe befriended Frank Lewis (ca. 1870–1924), one of Bolden's clarinetists, and learned what he could. Ory recalled a night out with Willie Cornish, the original trombonist in the Bolden Band.

When I first started visiting New Orleans. I went down to the Masonic Hall. It was a church . . . the Baptist Church. When I moved to New Orleans, I found that the Baptist minister had changed his church into a dance hall. He called it Funky Butt Hall. I went there one night with a good guy named Willie Cornish. The Galloway band was playing there then. I kept wondering why a Baptist church would have been changed into a dance hall. I found out the reason that night. It seemed that the pastor decided he could make more money out of dancehall since that district had changed and was becoming faster and faster in the sporting life. His collections had fallen off so much that he felt that changing over the church to a dancehall was the sensible thing to do and that he did.

The place was always packed. The dances would be held on Saturday sand Monday nights. This amazed me as there were no decorations, the building was just a shell and a honky-tonk if I ever saw one but of fairly good size. It would accommodate about 700 people, the way they jammed themselves into those places in those days. All they wanted to do was move around just a little, rubbing against each other, and they called it dancing.[18]

Ory eventually discovered what he believed to be Bolden's inspiration and the wellspring of hot music. Ory said Bolden "got most of" his tunes from "the Holy Roller church," and then "he'd put his own feeling to it." He remembered the congregation at a church that he identified as Bolden's exiting services doing "the closest thing" to dancing. The term Holy Roller refers to churches where congregants get caught up in the spirit and collapse to the floor, rolling in a Pentecostal ecstasy. Often called sanctified or holiness churches, the Sunday goings-on there stood in stark contrast to the services Ory had grown up attending at St. Peter's Catholic Church back in St. John Parish. He said he went there for ideas, just as he had seen Bolden do, adding that sometimes drums and horns would augment the piano and the place would swing. Ory said the music he played goes back to that:[19] "Oh, yeah, they had drums and piano while they sang, clapping their hands. Even the Baptists, some of the Baptist Churches had it. They'd have guests; invite a trumpet player, trombone player to come play with them. What we're doing now we're about sixty years behind what happened. Yeah, they'd get to swinging, you know?"[20] Mutt Carey said: "Hell, that music was swinging all the way back in Bolden's time and before him in the Holy Roller churches he got it from. You know, all those churches, like the Baptist and Methodist, got hot now and then—but the Holy Rollers were hot all the time."[21] Future Ory bandmate Bud Scott also cited the influence of the sanctified and holiness churches he called "holy rollers": "Each Sunday, Bolden went to church and that's where he got his idea of jazz music. They would keep perfect rhythm there clapping their hands. I think I am the first to start 4 beat (as opposed to 2 beat) on guitar. And that's where I heard it."[22]

The minor hitch in this telling of church music as a precursor to jazz is that St. John the Fourth, which Bolden attended, was not a sanctified church but a Baptist one. It may be that Ory, a Catholic, painted Protestant groups with a broad brush and simply applied a vernacular term to St. John the Fourth's Baptist congregants. Since Ory and Carey mention some Baptists churches going the Holy Roller route musically, the distinction may be moot. If St. John the Fourth was not the church from which Bolden drew his inspiration, there were many others within walking distance in the neighborhood, including six Baptist and two Methodist congregations.[23]

Among the old-fashioned Orthodox Baptists, shouting, waving the arms, springing up in the air, walking over the tops of benches and performing other feats of acrobatic strengths, are common forms of religious demonstration seen in the churches when song has reached the rhapsodic stage, or when the congregation has succumbed to the spell of eloquent preaching.

With the sect calling itself the Sanctified Servants of God, the condition of mind during religious services reaches a state bordering on frenzy. Dancing before the altar is an important feature of their ritual, in which men, women and children participate, each one doing an original expressive of his religion, to all appearance totally oblivious to one another.[24]

By 1906 Ory had formed an opinion of the New Orleans bands. His favorite one, at least at first, was Bolden's; they played the blues, and that set them apart. Still, Ory ultimately came to appreciate the musicality of the John Robichaux group: "Well it [Bolden's band] was a great band in those days. It was the onliest [*sic*] band that was playing that stuff and people was crazy about it. I liked it too. Until I began to understand more about it, music you know? Then I could see John Robichaux's band. They played chords and (had) good tone. But Bolden's . . . they just blew."[25]

Much is often made in jazz histories between the respective styles of the Bolden band and the Robichaux orchestra. The Bolden group is termed "rough," while the Robichaux group is remembered as a more refined unit.[26] It is noteworthy that Ory said John Robichaux's band was his second favorite in New Orleans. If Ory, the jazz pioneer, liked both bands fairly equally, then both groups were offering something to the mix of what became Ory's style and genre. How different would the bands have sounded from each other?

There were other bands that played roughly in the same style as Bolden. Both Charles Galloway and Edward Clem were regulars with Bolden and headliners in the river parishes, where Ory first heard them. He got the idea for his band from watching them, more so than his exposure to the brass bands that had ignited his earliest musical interest. Ory's primary career was as a dance-band leader. His experience hearing Bolden and his contemporaries playing for dances clearly influenced his band model. Along the way, Bolden and Robichaux, and other bands, provided the LaPlace boys with a musical standard to aim for. Ultimately, the combination of Robichaux's musicality with Bolden's blues for dancing became the Woodland boys' template for success: play the rough stuff, but play it sweeter and softer. Ory saw he could have an edge. Before he went to New Orleans, he had a bunch of boys with instruments and ambition. After a few trips there, he had an idea of what he wanted to play and how he was going to play it.

He learned how to build a set of songs so the dancers could dance all their steps. Building a set is a special gift, one that Ory was credited with having by those who heard his bands over extended periods.[27] He likely noted Bolden's shifts between blues, waltzes, rags, and marches. The King knew how to pulse his audience, and Ory studied him.

Dutt landed a gig for the band close to home. Since the death of Ozeme, Woodland Plantation co-owner and manager John L. Ory had taken a paternalistic attitude toward young Dutt. John L. seemed set on making Dutt into a straw boss or overseer. "He thought I was lazy and would turn out no good because I would rather make music than work on a plantation," Ory remembered. John L., however, had children who were musicians, and it was they who came to Dutt's rescue. The upcoming June 27, 1906, wedding of John L. Ory's daughter Maria to Sidney Levet was sure to be a musical affair. Knowing their father's feelings about Dutt's musical exploits, two of John L. Ory's daughters, Ida and Noelie, hired Ory's band to play at the reception at the Woodland house.[28] John L. surely expected the Ory family band featuring his son John Daniel to play, but he was caught by surprise when Dutt's group took to the porch. No one remembers what they played, but whatever it was, it was good enough to begin to change the old man's attitude about his distant cousin. After hearing the band play at a dance around this time, John L. Ory finally warmed to Dutt's musical exploits. "The night of the dance, the big party, he came up to me, and he said, 'You know, I'm sorry.' He told me in French, that he accused me of being a lazy boy. He said, 'You know, everyone is good for something in this world. If there's anything I can help you with, let me know."[29]

As Ory's dance band took its first steps in the summer of 1906, the man they had followed lost his way. In New Orleans one night, Ory observed Bolden as he wrapped up his Monday night gig at the Oddfellows Hall at Perdido at South Rampart Streets.

> *The last time I saw Bolden, King Bolden, I saw him at the Masonic Hall. He had a little trouble with—I stayed there until the dance was over on Monday night. He was short. He had spent all the deposit he received on the engagement. When they paid him the rest he didn't have enough money to finish paying the boys. So he started issuing it out. He said "Here's your (street) car ride, boys." He looked in his hand. He had .60 cents left. He said this is for Chookie. Ain't anyone going to get this but Chookie and he walked away. Chookie was his wife.[30]*

Ory never saw Bolden again.

While playing a 1906 Labor Day parade in Algiers, Bolden collapsed halfway through the route. In 1907 he was committed to the mental hospital in Jackson, Louisiana, where he spent the rest of his life.[31]

CHAPTER 5

1908–1910

KID

⟨⟨⟨⟨⟨⟨⟨⟨⟨⟨⟨⟨⟨⟨⟨⟨⟨⟨⟨⟨⟨⟨⟨⟨⟨⟨⟨⟨⟨⟨⟨⟨⟨⟨⟨⟨⟩

Shortly before they died, Dutt made a promise to his parents that he would remain in St. John Parish until he turned 21. He was supposed to look out for his younger sisters Annie and Lizzie. This, he said, was why in 1905 he did not take Bolden up on his offer to play with him. "I had to go back home," he said. Ory should have been released from his bond on Christmas Day, 1907, when he turned 21. Somehow, however, Ory had come to believe that he was born in 1889. By 1957, when he realized that he was older, he claimed he went to New Orleans in 1907 instead of 1910, changing the date of the event instead of his age in the story.[1]

Christmas 1907 marks not his move to New Orleans but the continuation of increased musical activity and, significantly, exposure to and participation in the music of that city. In the coming years he would play his first job in the city, study with a trombone master, and buy his first slide trombone. He also played marching jobs in New Orleans and Reserve with the Pickwick Brass Band. He took to ducking into New Orleans whenever he could. Sometimes the whole band would go into town, listen to the city bands, and take what they could back with them to the country. "We used to go down to New Orleans to hear different bands that played in the parks. They play a tune once, that's all I want to hear so we could play it too. Take two and make one out of it, if we couldn't get all of it."[2]

This could best be termed the Ory band's apprenticeship among the hot musicians of New Orleans. They heard the best bands the city had to offer. Notable areas of exploration for Ory included episodes in Storyville, the Rampart and Perdido area, Bolden's neighborhood, and Lincoln Park. The boys heard different bands playing in different contexts for very different audiences. There were polite society dances at benevolent society halls and raucous brass band parades, where the street dancing shut down traffic. Then there were the bands at the Storyville clubs that played for the sporting crowd. A musician had to know how to handle playing in all these places to make a go of it in New Orleans. Ory was observing not only the music itself, but how each leader handled his band. How did he count off tunes? How did he build a set of music? What type of songs should a band open with? Did the audience seem to enjoy the louder bands or the softer ones? Should a band play hot all the time? How did the leader guide the players during the performance? Ory needed to learn all of these things.

In the summer of 1908, as they had the two previous summers, Ory and the boys spent much of their free time at Lincoln Park. It was a brief train ride from St. John, where Dutt was spending most nights in the room above Johnny Ory's store in Edgard. While Bolden, who had made the biggest impression, was gone, there was always plenty of music at Lincoln and Johnson Parks to keep the gang interested.

Ory ingratiated himself to the manager at Lincoln Park, Buddy Bartley, and ultimately the band was hired to play on advertising wagons and for dances there. Bartley, whose real name was Joseph Haywood, was the manager of the park and worked for a Mr. Snow. He also worked as a waiter and lived uptown on Dryades Street. Ory described Bartley (he called him Bottley) as a promoter, though he had other titles. Variously described by the police as a pimp and a small-time criminal, he was arrested for fighting, loitering, discharging firearms, disturbing the peace, and catching on streetcars. Bartley was the emcee of Lincoln Park as well as its aerial attraction: he rode a smoke-filled balloon up to the sky and then, on cue from a shotgun blast fired from the ground, parachuted out. Sometimes he landed in the park, but stories are legend of him coming down on unintended targets. Bartley once was cast adrift in the balloon by high winds, and came down in Lake Pontchartrain.[3] "He would climb into the basket, and they would cut him loose and he would start casting off ballast. One Sunday, he drifted too far because of the high winds and when it was time for his parachute jump back to earth from the balloon, instead of landing in the park as usual, he wound up in the chimney of one of the houses fairly close to Lincoln Park and what a mess he was."[4]

A Professor L. B. Hadlock had originally performed the stunt at Lincoln Park, before training Bartley, who took it over and made it famous.[5] "But it did not stop there. My new boss was quite a dancer; in fact, he started one that became the rage of New Orleans. At first it was called 'Ping Pong,' but later it was generally known as 'Buddy Bottley's [sic] dance.' It was rather a combination of the fox trot with a breakaway in it almost similar to one done by today's [1957] jitterbugs."[6]

It was Bartley, in his role as promoter, who dubbed Ory "Kid" in 1908. Arriving for a gig on a promotional wagon for Lincoln Park, Dutt noticed the sign said "Kid Ory."

I asked him why the name "Kid" and he answered, "That's what all the girls call you and the name seems very right for you, so from now on you're the Kid" and it has stuck to me ever since. This was about the time that I started working there regularly for him on the basis of three sessions a week. To make money, Bartley believed in letting the people know what he had to offer in the way of entertainment. There was no newspaper advertising then, but he used the mediums available at that time, such as huge cloth streamers across streets, placards any place he could put them, wagon advertising with the band riding in the wagon on the day before the

performance. This was my first real publicity campaign and
Bartley was the one responsible for my nickname.[7]

His friends still called him Dutt or Ory, but the public called him
Kid from that summer onward. It fit his personality, his attitude,
and his diminutive size. Further, since he thought he was only 17
that summer (he was actually 20), he really was a kid. The preco-
cious upstart from LaPlace was developing a reputation.

Who exactly was in the band at this point, and on what instrument, is difficult to tell, though the lineup would soon solidify:

When I first got the band together I played bass. Lawrence
Duhe, the trombone player, wanted to play clarinet. He came
with a long story after I got the trombone. He wanted to play
trumpet, then he wanted to play violin. Finally when every-
body switched around so they were satisfied (the) only one left
was trombone, so I played that. Lawrence Duhe was on clari-
net, Louis Matthews on trumpet, Joseph Matthews on guitar,
Alfred [Foster] Lewis on bass, Eddie [Robertson] on drums,
Bull White on violin.[8]

There is an undated photo of Ory's early band that is, for the
most part, the band he brought to New Orleans, minus Lawrence
Duhe. The photo was probably not taken after Lawrence Duhe
left the group in 1911–12, as Ed Garland, who is not the bassist
in the picture, was a member by then. It is more likely that Duhe
simply was not there the day the picture was made. The identi-
fications vary according to source. Beyond dispute is Ed "Rabbit" Robertson, on drums, Ory on trombone, and the Matthews
brothers, Lewis "Chif" and Joe "Stonewall," on trumpet and guitar
respectively. Some captions credit Foster Lewis as the bass player,
while Ory himself misidentified him in several interviews as Alfred Lewis. There was a Foster Lewis who later played trombone,

and Ory claims in an interview that his old bass player now plays trombone.[9]

Foster Lewis, and his new wife Odina, appear in the 1910 St. John census for LaPlace. Ory said Louis did not come to New Orleans because he had just gotten married. Notably, the other Ory bandsmen show up in New Orleans on the census. If it is Foster Lewis in the photo, it was probably taken no later than 1910, when the band moved to New Orleans.[10] But this is not a certainty. Ory said that Lewis still played with them on country jobs after the band's move to New Orleans, so perhaps his tenure overlapped with that of Ed Garland.

Historian Bill Russell identifies the violin player as Raymond Brown. Ory never mentions Brown in his stories of the plantation band, saying on numerous occasions that Jake "Bull" White was their violinist. "Papa" John Joseph, in an interview in 1962, said Ory's violin player as seen in the band photograph, was alive and living in New Orleans. He said the musician had a son who played trumpet who was blind and another son who played piano, but could not remember the man's name. Further, Harrison Verrett said that Ory's band in New Orleans featured a musician named Johnny Brown who played clarinet. Others remember him playing violin. The kicker to Verrett's story was that he said Johnny Brown was the father of a blind trumpet player whose name was Raymond and another son who played piano. Since there is no mention of a violinist named Raymond Brown in all of the oral histories at Tulane, and William Russell's source remains elusive, it might be concluded that it is in fact Johnny Brown in the photo. Many mention him playing with Ory, including Clarence "Little Dad" Vincent.[11] If it is Johnny Brown, then the photo was probably taken after the band's move to New Orleans in 1910.

A further question is the name of the band. Prior to 1950, Ory identified his group as Ory's Brown Skin Band or Ory's Brown Skinned Babies. In interviews after 1950, when his relationship with future wife Barbara GaNung was well underway, Ory began referring to the group as the Woodland Band. No musicians refer to this name except Ory. The probable culprit is GaNung, who was instrumental in getting Ory to deny any black ancestry in his autobiography and in interviews post-1950.[12]

The name is significant, as Pops Fosters points out: "Up until Ory's band, most of the bands had names like Crescent Band, Silver Leaf Band, Eagle Band and so on. He made such a big hit that all the other bands started changing the names of their band to the leader's name to copy Ory."[13]

The early steps were tenuous, and that first summer Ory and the band suffered several unfortunate encounters with established bands that likely convinced them that they still had some practicing to do. According to Ory, a particular weakness was Lewis Matthew's trumpet playing, though everyone in the band was probably below the New Orleans standard at this point. Still, the band must have had something going on musically, or Bartley would not have hired them to promote the park.

In late 1909 Ory and the band played at Frank Moseman's Saloon in the sawmill boomtown of Garyville in St. John Parish. Moseman showed Ory a slide trombone that a patron had hocked but never returned for.[14]

Mr. Moseman, the saloon owner, in telling me how much he had liked our performance, mentioned to me that he had a slide trombone in the place, on which he had loaned $10 bucks to a guy and the man had never shown up to redeem his horn. He asked me if I had ever played one and I told him no, but, that I would like to have one to try. He offered to sell me this one for the $10 and what he had loaned on it. I answered that I didn't have the money then, but I would come back the following Saturday with the $10. I had to borrow the money from my brother-in-law, one Louis Bontemps, at six percent interest. I went to Garyville the next Saturday and picked up the new horn.[15]

The purchase of a slide, rather than a valve, trombone is significant. The trombone style Ory came to play is called "tailgate." The term comes from the practice of bands playing out of the back of advertising wagons. The trombonist often found himself sitting in the back of the wagon working his slide over the tailgate. Tailgate style is marked by its use of the glissando, or sliding, effect. The New Orleans men referred to glissando as slides, smears, and slurs. This can only be done with a slide trombone so it follows that the style developed as trombonists shed their valve instruments for slide trombones.[16] For Ory, that process began in 1909 with the used horn he bought from Frank Moseman.

The standardization of the voicing of the trombone in a wind band ensemble derives largely from written, military band music of the late 1800s. "The trombone, due to its range and technical tendencies was pretty much designated a rhythmic part, providing strong punctuations beneath the melody and an occasional countermelody." So too, the pre-glissando origins of the tailgate style can be found in "the patterns that trombonists played in marching bands, which included melodic conjunctions and countermelodies to the treble instruments, and the punctuations that marked and emphasized harmonic progressions." While turn-of-the-century marching pieces contributed to the development of the tailgate style, so did the players themselves.[17] Ory did not invent tailgate playing, but he perfected it and, due in large part to the many recordings he made in his lifetime, became the practitioner most identified with it. Ory's understanding of the role of the trombone in the jazz ensemble was to play a supporting role, injecting rhythmic upper bass parts and countermelody to the lead instrument, usually the trumpet.

One place Ory learned was playing with the established Pickwick Brass Band of LaPlace, led by Dejan Alexandre. Ory mentions playing with the LaPlace-based brass band in an interview but not in any detail. Mathilda August Clementin confirmed Ory's membership in the band.[18]

Ory was not a music reader at this point and he would have had to learn parts by rote to play them correctly within the ensemble. With an excellent reading musician like Alexander leading the band, Ory certainly got some instruction in playing his horn. Working with other wind players, most of whom were superior to him at this point, afforded Ory the advice of experienced musicians who knew their instruments and could help a fledgling player along. August Piton played valve trombone and baritone horn in the Pickwick, as did Alexandre's nephew Paul Ben. Ory likely sat down with one of them and went over the parts to tunes in the Pickwick repertoire. The Pickwick's regular gigs included funerals, parades, and Sunday bucking contests with other bands. The group also played regularly at St. Katherine's Hall in New Orleans.

Another influence on Ory in this period was trombonist Alvin "Zue" Robertson (1891–1943).[19] Ory befriended Robertson, an established member of the Excelsior and Onward brass bands as well as the Olympia orchestra, and began taking lessons.

I liked Zue Robertson's trombone a lot too. He played with the Olympia band and in Storyville. Smooth trombone—he was good. We played duets. We practiced together and he used to say "Let's blow a little bit." We played in a brass band together sometimes. He was radical to play with. If you had a wrong note on the paper he'd say "I'm playing what you got. I ain't gonna move it." He was a good piano player and a good bass too, studied piano, read music.[20]

People who heard Zue said he was a reader who could play hot. Bill Matthews said Zue Robertson would cross his legs and make more stuff on a trombone than a man can with a saxophone. Much of Robertson's career was spent traveling in tent shows around the country. In fact some said his nickname was actually "Zoo," in reference to his years playing in the circus. He started out on piano as a youngster but turned to trombone around the age of 13.

He was a cousin of Baptist Delisle (1868–1920), a well-respected trombonist in the John Robichaux Orchestra. Ory said Delisle was the first slide trombonist he ever heard. Robertson made records in 1923 with Jelly Roll Morton, playing on "Someday Sweetheart" and "London Blues." While Ory would ultimately progress beyond the "popping" (playing short notes in a sometimes percussive way) style of trombone practiced by Robertson on these recordings, some elements similar to Ory's phrasing, rhythmic sense, and voicing are readily discernable, though with less glissando.[21]

The other trombonists that Ory cites as influences are Vic Gaspard, Buddy Johnson, and Frankie Duson.[22] By the time Ory arrived on the scene, these older horn men were already well established. Duson (1881–1936) led the Eagle band and would become one of Ory's fiercest rivals in the city. Johnson (1870–1927) was the trombonist with Manuel Perez's Imperial Orchestra. Gaspard (1875–1957) was a regular in both John Robichaux Orchestra and Bab Frank's Peerless Orchestra. Gaspard and Johnson played in bands that read music, while Duson's Eagle band was a gut-bucket band. Unfortunately, none of these men recorded, so it is difficult to say what influence they had on Ory.

Ory mentions a number of gigs and experiences that occurred around 1909, the year before his move to the city. Some are more illuminating than others, but they all give a inkling of what sort of work he was doing as he prepared the band for the move to New Orleans.

The next summer found me back at Lincoln Park for the season, but halfway through, Buddy Bottley became ill and the park closed down, so I went out to Lake Pontchartrain. I got lots of jobs out at the lake for the afternoons, but that still left the evenings to be filled and I moved into National Park, playing evening picnics there after the ballgames were over. We were becoming better known all the time and had developed a wonderful following.[23]

It was an established practice for musicians to play at the lakefront on Sunday afternoons and then play a dance that night. That was the context for Bolden's shows at Lincoln Park; he played the late dance there after spending the afternoon at the lakefront. The lakefront featured three major resorts: West End, Spanish Fort, and Milneburg.

The West End was at the end of the New Basin Canal, where it met the lake. Oyster luggers, fishing boats, produce haulers, and shell barges all plied the canal from the lake to its point of origin in the city's interior near Rampart Street. The West End, which featured a roller coaster, had a bandstand and picnic areas where various bands performed. Formal concerts were a regular attraction and were advertised in the *Times-Picayune*. West End was accessible by streetcar, a shell road, or by boat.

Spanish Fort, a short eastern trip along the Lake Pontchartrain shoreline, was a full-blown amusement park and casino with rides, tent shows, caged alligators, restaurants, and a salvaged Confederate submarine. Perched at the mouth of Bayou St. John at the lake, it had a bandstand, but there were also picnic areas where various bands could dig up work. Spanish Fort also featured dancing contests and concerts. It could be reached by railroad, shell road, or boat via the twists and turns of Bayou St. John.

Conversely, Milneburg, a mile to the east, was a hodgepodge collection of camps, clustered around the Port Pontchartrain lighthouse, which stood in Lake Pontchartrain at the end of Elysian Fields Avenue. There were a series of boardwalks that connected the camps to a main boardwalk, which ran out into the lake. The easiest way to get to Milneburg was to take the "Smokey Mary" train from the French Market out Elysian Fields Avenue. The train went forward on the way to the resort and backed up on the way back. Cornetist Ernest "Punch" Miller (1894–1971) recalled the scene: "At Milneburg, four or five bands would play every Sunday from 9am–4pm then come into town and play until 4 in the morning. Out at Milneburg people would buy lunches and drink beer and whiskey and love and court. Sometimes there would be fights."²⁴

In between the three major resorts were clusters of camps dotting the shoreline. Much of the work jazz bands got came from going door to door and playing a song or two. "We played most every camp out at Milneburg. The camps were about twenty feet apart and different bands would play for them. We played from nine o'clock in the morning to six in the evening."²⁵

As daylight faded, Ory and the band caught the West End streetcar back into town. They disembarked at Claiborne Avenue and made their way uptown to the corner of Third and Willow streets to National Ball Park. Though a baseball park, prizefights and dances were also presented there. The main musical attraction was the Peerless Orchestra, led by a piccolo player named Gilbert "Bab" Frank, (1872–1933). Bass player Wellman Braud said that Frank had "good control, fine tone and could improvise." Frank was an "old time piccolo player who played with jazz bands," Braud said. John Joseph said, "He was one of the best I ever heard.²⁶ He always carried his piccolo in his pocket, in the side pocket, you know, wrapped in a piece of paper. When them guys out there, their clarinet player didn't show up, you know, Bob say 'Maybe I can help you.' Pulled out the piccolo and they hired him. He could play some piccolo, man he could play."²⁷

He was also in Kid Ory's path. Ory moved into the evening slot playing dances at National Park on Sundays.²⁸ Bab Frank's band played the late afternoon session for picnickers. Ory knew that a cutting contest was coming and that his band had to be ready. One band would play and then the other; the people would vote with their feet, leaving the losing band without an audience.

If he was nervous, Ory had cause to be. He was a virtual newcomer in a city filled with top musicians. Still, he had some strengths in his column. He had grown up watching the Sunday bucking contests in St. John between the Onward and Pickwick brass bands. He probably participated in a few. He had studied the devices Bolden employed to lure Robichaux's audience away. Finally, his men were young and good-looking and certainly more appealing to the youthful audience. Frank's men were middle aged. More importantly, these were different types of bands. Ory's was strictly a faking band, while Frank's men read music. Some of the men Frank used included trombonist Baptist Delisle, drummer Louis Cottrell, trumpeter Adolph Alexander, and violinist Alcide Alexander.

Ironically, the showdown happened not at National Park but at Dixie Park on Bienville Street. What was played and what it sounded like are details lost to history, but the outcome is not: Ory's band cut Frank's. Ory solidified his gig at National Park, and he played there often on Sunday nights throughout his New Orleans residency.[29]

It was at a society hall around this time that Ory first encountered Freddie Keppard. At this point Keppard (1889–1933) was a violinist, but in a few years he would become the city's most exciting horn player. In 1914 he would tour the country with the Original Creole Orchestra, placing New Orleans jazz on the national stage. Keppard's and Ory's bands were booked in St. James Parish, the next one upriver from St. John, to play respective benevolent society halls. At Beehive Hall, where Ory was playing, the club sponsoring the dance ran out of refreshments and shut down early. Rather than go home, the band, along with Ory's brother Johnny and a few drunken hangers-on, traveled by wagon to the hall where Keppard was playing.

There was no such thing as a two o'clock curfew then and we rolled along, jamming and jiving until we reached the Friends of Charity Hall and stopped to hear the Keppard band. We drove into the yard, right next to the ballroom. I said to the boys, "Take it easy, they're playing, but as soon as they stop playing, we'll do a number." As soon as they stopped, we hit a number and Freddie's whole band came out and Freddie

said, "This is it." He started sawing on his violin with us and
his valve trombone player, Will Cornish, said to me, "Man, let
me try that horn. It looks so good and sounds better, I want
to blow it." I let him try it, but he was just as bad on it as on
his own. Then we went into the hall and Freddie said to me,
"Come on and blow one with me."[30]

On Christmas Eve 1909, Ory and the boys played Good Will
Hall, a benevolent society headquarters on the road from La-
Place to Reserve. Though the band had played all over by this
time, there must have been something special about playing the
hall that sat right in the middle of Ory's community. The Good
Will Hall was the place where the bands Ory came up listening to
played. The boys had emulated these groups, and on Christmas
Eve they played the place where they had listened to so many others. People were looking at the boys in a different way, and Ory
could see this. The kid who had hustled around LaPlace ten years
earlier with a toy banjo had evolved into a professional. The Good
Will gig went over well, and the band began to plan its move to
the city.

In early 1910, Ory got a job playing trombone in New Orleans
with singing bass player George Jones, born 1880. Jones lived in the
rough neighborhood around the Girod Street cemetery, sometimes
referred to as the battlefield. All who heard him, including Ory's
future bass player Ed Garland, said he was a terrible musician. Still,
Jones had a knack for improvising lyrics and rhymes, which made
him popular in the sporting circles at the clubs bordering the red
light district on Iberville Street. He became a favorite at Pete Lala's new club at Villere and Iberville streets, where he would spot a
well-known sport at the door and sing an introduction about him
as he walked in. He was also popular for his version of the New
Orleans standard "Little Liza Jane" and for singing smutty songs.
Johnny St. Cyr said Jones was referred to as "George the Rhym-
er" and that he had extra pockets sewn into his pants to steal tips

intended for the whole band. He sawed through his bass' G-string every night and re-haired his bow with sewing thread.[31] Jones got a lot of convention work because of his entertaining rhymes and he enjoyed extended residencies at Thom's Roadhouse and the Bungalow, both at the West End.

Ory's pal Zue Robertson was an acquaintance of Lala and may have helped get Ory the gig. Music teachers were sometime conduits for plugging students into work. Through early 1910 Ory stayed on playing with George Jones in Storyville at Lala's and other places. The gig was growing tedious, but not nearly so much as the problems developing for the band. Bass player Foster Lewis did not want to move to the city as he had just gotten married, though he did not want to leave the band. White, on the other hand, was in Ory's words the "world's worst" musician.[32] With the move to New Orleans on the horizon, Ory was left searching for a bass and violin player. Part of the answer arrived driving a horse-drawn liquor wagon.

The driver was a five-foot five, strongly built man a year older than Ory. Edward Garland (1885–1980) was born in New Orleans, near the old prison at Basin Street between Tulane and Gravier streets. Around the age of 10, Garland began studying with Henry Kimball, a well-respected bassist, who played with many top bands in New Orleans including Robichaux's Orchestra. Finally, he settled as a regular sub in Manuel Perez's Imperial Band. George Filhe, the Imperial Band's trombonist, tipped Garland off about Ory needing a bass player.[33]

Garland drove a liquor wagon as a day job but was one of the city's hottest young bass players by night. He had married Jenny White a year earlier and they lived at 743 Felicity Street, in the Lower Garden District near the Mississippi River. Ory says they met at his sister's house, meaning either 3201 Freret or 2823 Second Street. Here Garland differs again, saying they meet at Conti and Claiborne, which was the location of Pete Lala's other club. Ory sometimes slept there while visiting New Orleans.

We sat in that wagon and talked of this and that. He told me
he had just been jobbing around New Orleans with his bass,
but that he wanted a chance to play it all the time. I told him
that this would be just a job for gigs right then, but I was plan-
ning to move to the city permanently not too long in the fu-
ture and that I thought he could be a steady man then if he
worked out all right. After that, he asked me if I would care
to have a drink at the corner saloon. I said to him, "Man, I'm
drunk already from the past hour's inhaling the fumes from
your wagon. In fact, I feel as though I'd had a 'mickey.'" Gar-
land really laughed at that and thought I had a good sense of
humor. What with his laughing, I laughed too and we did go
to the corner for a beer. From then on, I used Tudi whenever
we played New Orleans. After we moved there, Garland was
my regular bass player.[34]

Ory liked that Garland was his age and approved of his musical taste. Garland had played with both of Ory's favorite bands,
Bolden's and Robichaux's. At the rehearsal, Garland knew none of
the tunes: "They was nothing but some made up tunes from out in
the country. Like '1919 March,' you know. I played with them and
they said 'Oh Can you stay with us?' I told 'em I'd think about it.
That's how it all happened."[35]

Once he heard the hard-driving Garland play, Ory knew he had
his man. Moreover, Garland's violin-playing brother Johnny let it
be known that he was available to substitute for the band when
needed. Edward Garland would be in Ory's bands from the teens
through the fifties. He was the perfect bassist in Ory's estimation,
and his rhythmic drive became one of the band's calling cards.

With the bass role solidified, and a back-up violinist lined up,
Ory had to get the rest of the band on board about the move.

We were still playing for the ball games on Sundays in LaPlace
and the picnics afterward, and I would leave New Orleans

and go back home for our weekend engagements and play in the "big city" during the week. The ball teams from New Orleans gave me the final convincing advice that we had become too good for just country playing and were ready for the "big town." I put it up to the boys and they voted yes, for the move to the city. I went down a few days before they did and found a place for them to stay and they followed me down.[36]

With his days in St. John numbered, Ory could look back on a decade where he held his life together and found purpose after being cast adrift emotionally following his parents' deaths. Music had become his life. Ten years earlier he had played with a bunch of plantation kids on homemade instruments; now some of those same kids prepared to make the journey to New Orleans as professionals. As for Ory the musician and bandleader, he had kept his band together through personnel changes, performed in New Orleans, studied with Zue Robertson, played with the Pickwick Brass band, and bought what would become his signature instrument: a slide trombone. Finally, he had literally made a name for himself during his New Orleans apprenticeship. When he moved to the city, Kid Ory was a name people already knew. These were pieces to the puzzle that defined the young trombonist in 1910, as he waited on the platform at the LaPlace station to catch the Yazoo & Mississippi Valley train to his new home in New Orleans.

CHAPTER 6

1910–1916

NEW ORLEANS

The city of New Orleans was founded on a bend in the Mississippi River where it snakes along south of Lake Pontchartrain. It was settled by the French in 1718, ceded to Spain in 1762, returned to France in 1802, and sold to the United States as part of the Louisianan Purchase in 1803. In 1910 New Orleans was the fifteenth largest city in the country and the largest by far in the South. With a population of 339,075 it was a major port and railway hub. 89,262 of the residents were black.[1]

When Ory arrived in New Orleans, he stepped into a 192-year-old city already steeped in a diverse musical history. The city staged the first opera performances in North America no later than 1796, when a letter written by a member of the prominent Pontalba family references a performance of André Gentry's *Sylvain*. By the antebellum period the city was an opera center with Italian, French, and English opera companies. There was even a local publication, *Le Moqueur*, devoted entirely to opera news.[2] In 1837 one writer asserted: "We have now, in this place, what no city in America, and few cities in the world can boast of . . . strong [opera] companies in the English, French, and Italian languages, and what is more they are extremely well patronized."[3] The popularity of opera in New Orleans institutionalized European musical traditions there, providing a marketplace for classical musicians to perform and numerous venues for the public, of all stripes, to enjoy.

Still, opera, though significant, was but one cog in a diverse musical wheel, one that also included public dancing, singing, and drumming among the city's black population. There are references to slave dances as early as 1786, during the Spanish colonial period, when a law was passed restricting the hours of dances at public squares on Sundays till "the close of evening [church] service."[4] Public dances were still very much in evidence in 1808 when one writer described witnessing blacks making music and dancing on the city's outskirts: "They have their own national music, consisting for the most part of a long kind of narrow drum of various sizes, from two to eight feet in length, three or four of which make a band."[5]

In 1819 another writer noted blacks drumming and dancing in circular gatherings at Congo Square near Orleans Avenue and Rampart Street, but also noted the presence of other instruments: "The most curious instrument, however, was a stringed instrument which no doubt was imported from Africa. On top of the fingerboard was the rude figure of a man in sitting posture, and two pegs behind him to which the strings were fastened. The body was a calabash."[6] These intriguing stories of African dance and music making at Congo Square are snapshots in time of an evolving and variegated scene. Other observers witnessed the playing of fifes, fiddles, banjos, triangles, Jew's harps, and tambourines while participants danced jigs, Virginia breakdowns, and fandangos. Africans and their descendants "were borrowing rapidly from the culture around them."[7]

But the gatherings at Congo Square were a memory by the time Ory's father was born in 1850, much less by the time Ory came along. More relevant to the New Orleans traditions that directly influenced Ory are the emergence of dance bands and brass bands in the nineteenth century.

The popularity of brass instruments in New Orleans was well established by the antebellum period. In 1838 the *Daily Picayune* noted "a mania" in the city for "horn and trumpet playing." By 1853, musical funerals with brass bands had become immensely popular with militia units, firemen, and benevolent and fraternal societies.[4]

While it is not surprising that militia and firemen would hold military-style brass band funerals for their fallen comrades, what is interesting is the way this practice caught on with the general public through benevolent societies and fraternal orders. Benevolent organizations served as social safety nets for their members, providing sickness and death benefits. When a member died, the cost of the funeral was covered and a brass band was often part of the benefit. Dozens of societies, representing many ethnicities, existed before the Civil War; what is noteworthy is that they became immensely popular among freedmen after Reconstruction. These grassroots groups helped communities organize and pool collective resources for the benefit of their members in time of need. It was, in large part, these societies that funded the brass band music "movement" within the community of color in New Orleans.[8]

Brass instruments were also used for dance bands, often coupled with violin and guitar. Dance balls were popular to the point of obsession across all classes and ethnicities in New Orleans throughout the nineteenth century, providing work for a diverse collection of bands. "The story of music in New Orleans must begin with dancing. This was the earliest sustained musical activity there; it was always the greatest—in terms of effort and quantity; and it was the source and support of opera, concerts, and various other endeavors in the music-mad city." In 1804, Louisiana Governor William C. C. Claiborne wrote President Madison on the subject of dance balls in New Orleans, saying they "occupy much of the public mind." Frenchmen were apparently concerned that the Americans planned to ban the public balls. Ultimately, Claiborne let them go on as a sign of American goodwill.[9] Dance halls and ballrooms were the primary amusement in New Orleans at the time, catering to its entire population, black and white, slave and free, in many venues and contexts. A century later that enthusiasm was little diminished.

Between the brass and dance bands, Ory's new hometown boasted a healthy population of musicians fully integrated into the social celebrations and events of their communities. Within the confines of the city's music scene at the turn of the century and beyond, there was a division (as much social as musical) between the downtown Creole bands and the uptown non-reading, gut-bucket bands like Bolden's, and later Ory's. The Creole groups, including brass and dance bands, featured generally light-skinned musicians who played from written scores. By comparison, uptown bands like Bolden's were comprised largely of non-reading musicians who played by ear. By 1900, changes in national musical styles provided fodder for the New Orleans brass and dance band community. Ragtime emerged on the scene. With its emphasis on the second beat, this highly syncopated music would inform early jazz, and ragtime tunes made their way into the repertoires of New Orleans bands.[10] Around the same time, pioneers like Bolden injected the blues into the mix.

The dichotomy between the Creole and uptown bands of Bolden's day was still in evidence when Ory arrived on the scene. Ironically, Ory, the self-described "Creole," found himself at odds musically with the Creoles of New Orleans. Though he considered himself Creole ethnically and culturally, he was not a "Creole musician" in this context, as he did not read music and did not grow up in a historically Creole neighborhood like New Orleans' Seventh Ward. Ory had followed the uptown bands since his first visits to New Orleans, and it was of this musical school he considered himself a part. Still, he had developed his own style during the five years after he first heard Bolden. "Well they, they came here from LaPlace, a whole band from the country. They could play too," remembered bassist John Joseph of the Ory band's arrival on the New Orleans scene.[11] Future Duke Ellington band bassist Wellman Braud (1891–1967) recalled: "The Olympia was the best band at the time until Kid Ory and his band from LaPlace came to town, taking New Orleans by storm. The Ory band was smoother and more polished than the New Orleans bands."[12] Trombonist Earl Humphrey, (1902–1971), the grandson of music teacher Professor James

Humphrey said, "He was a smooth player with wonderful ideas about faking music. Wonderful."[13]

These early accounts of Ory and his band as "smooth" may offer a glimpse of what these musicians were doing that was different. Bolden's band is often recalled as being "rough." Ory liked Bolden but also appreciated the musicality of Robichaux's orchestra. Perhaps the Ory band, even at this early stage, had smoothed out the rough edges of Bolden's sound, and taken style points from Robichaux to play in a more polished way—thus Braud's recollection of Ory's band "taking" New Orleans.

Bassist George "Pops" Foster said, "His [Ory's] band could play a waltz and make it hot."[14] "Hot" is a term often applied to early New Orleans bands that played in an improvisational, gut-bucket style. That Ory would play a waltz hot suggests that his was a band that played hot all the time, unlike bands of a few years earlier that may have only played hot now and again.

From a personnel standpoint, Ory had the horses, and his New Orleans bands would benefit from the immense talents of future jazz stars like Johnny Dodds, King Oliver, Jimmie Noone, and Louis Armstrong. But these jazz greats would come later. For the time being, Ory plowed ahead with largely the same lineup that he had featured in LaPlace.

Ory's move to New Orleans in early 1910 was necessitated in part by his brother John's marriage to Cecile Tregre in 1909. John and Cecile had started a family and Dutt's room was probably needed to accommodate the growing clan. Although close to John's family (he was godfather to John's daughter Pearl), Ory was set on moving to New Orleans.[15]

In his first year there, Ory lived at a number of addresses with various family members who had also made the move to the city. These family members, including his sister Lena and her husband Warren Cotton's extended family, as well as cousin Leana Algere Robertson, lived in the uptown section of New Orleans today known as Central City. Though Ory moved there for this reason, it was a significant one musically. Within just a few blocks of Ory's 2135 Jackson Avenue home, numerous jazz legends resided over the years, including Jelly Roll Morton, Johnny Dodds, Mutt Carey, King Oliver, and Buddy Bolden. At nearby Lafayette Cemetery II on Washington Avenue, benevolent societies maintained tombs where countless brass band processions ended during Ory's residency. Central City was also home of the "holy roller" churches whose music, Ory said, had so influenced Bolden. Though Ory lived at many addresses in New Orleans in his nine years there, all were in the same general vicinity in Central City.

At first, Ory lived with Warren Cotton's brother, John, at 3201 Freret Street, near Washington Avenue. Then Ory and his younger sister, Annie, moved into Warren and Lena Cotton's house at 2823 Second Street. The Cottons had made the move to New Orleans from Baton Rouge a few years earlier.[16]

In 1910 the 2800 block of Second Street was an unpaved road occupied by five African American households and nine white ones.[17] Most of the homes were shotgun houses, that is, long narrow houses without hallways, where one room opens to the next in a straight line from front to back. Some houses were shotgun doubles, that is, a duplex with two shotgun apartments running down the length of the house. Some houses had plumbing, though most still had outdoor privies in modest backyards.

Among the white residents there were German immigrants and first-generation Americans. Many of the black neighbors worked as laborers and freight handlers. Ory's next-door neighbor at 2819 Second Street was Caroline Triche,, 50, a white seamstress. Living with her were a grown daughter, a teenage son, and a younger daughter. At 2825 was a German immigrant laborer Joseph Kieseler, 69. His wife Catherine worked as a midwife. Across the street at 2822 lived Nicholas Maugin, 38, a painter and his wife Viola. Living with them were their son, as well as two brothers-in-law who also worked as painters. The census lists them as mulatto.[18]

Through 1915 Ory also lived, off and on, at 2135 Jackson Avenue, where he rented a room from cousin Leana, and her common-law husband, Arthur Banks. Leana had married Ory's drummer Ed "Rabbit" Robertson in 1907, but left him and moved to New Orleans around 1909. Arthur Banks was a marble cutter and carpenter—trades he would teach Ory as they worked construction together in the coming years.[19] Joe Davis and his wife Virginia also lived in the three rooms on one side of the shotgun double house.

The Jackson Avenue neighborhood also was racially and culturally mixed. Ory's next-door neighbor was grocer Joseph Manino, 66, an Italian immigrant who ran a corner store at 2139 Jackson Avenue. One door down was Frederick Fisher, 48, a first-generation American of German descent who lived with his wife Octavia at 2129 Jackson Avenue. A couple of doors down the block at 2113 was George Patterson, 26, a black cook who lived with his wife, daughter, and stepdaughter; and at 2115 lived Thomas R. Scott, 56, a black laborer, with his wife, son, and grandson. Other neighbors' vocations included laundresses, a telegraph operator, a housekeeper, and laborers. In 1910, the street was paved with Belgian block, though the side streets were either unpaved or covered with shells.[20]

Though Ory's neighborhood was "mixed," it was not always harmonious. The Robert Charles Riot began July 23, 1900, when a black laborer named Robert Charles and his roommate had an altercation with New Orleans Police, which led to one of the policeman being shot by Charles in the 2800 block of Dryades Street. The ensuing riots led to the lynching of many black citizens and the burning of the Thomy Lafon school. Ultimately twenty-nine people died including Charles, who was shot dead and beaten post mortem by a mob.[21] In time, Jelly Roll Morton said, it became a thing people did not speak of.

Ory never once addressed the subject of race or racism on the record. If he had issues or suffered discrimination he kept it to himself. When asked if he was black he said he was Creole. He left it at that. Still, the segregated world in which he lived saw race in terms of black and white, and Ory, despite his Creole identification, was, by law, black.

Back on Jackson Avenue one night in 1910, it was not the sting of racism that was eating Ory, but the bite of bedbugs.

One particular night the cat was locked up in my room and, after I turned the light out, the cat got up against the shutters and started to scratch and I thought that someone was breaking in on me. I hollered to my cousin's husband, "Banks, they're breaking in back here on me." Banks said, "Yeah," and he called the guy in the next room whose name was Joe Davis and he said, "'Dave they're breaking in on Ory" and Davis said, "is he?" Nobody had time and the cat was still scratching and I was lying there afraid to move. The next thing, the bedbugs, which they called chinches, started biting me, just blistering me all over, and I was still afraid to move, even to try and knock them off of me. Later on my cousin got up and she said, "I'm going to see what's happening back there. There must be someone back there in the room with Dutt, or trying to get in." She lighted an oil lamp and came in. As soon as she entered the room, the cat saw the light and started to meow and everyone got up and made a big joke out of it but I was still all blistered from the bedbugs. I could see them in the mosquito bar, just crawling all around and I made up my mind that I would have to move out or they would have to clean up the place, if they wanted me to stay there.[22]

Storyville was one name given to New Orleans' legal prostitution district, which existed between 1897–1917. Prostitution was illegal in the city except in the area bounded by Basin, Iberville, Robertson, and St. Louis streets. There it flourished, sometimes in large, lavish mansions like Lulu White's Mahogany Hall but also in tiny "cribs," essentially small rooms that opened to the street.

The District, as it was also known, occupies a romanticized place in jazz history. As the story goes, jazz was created in Storyville; and when the red-light district closed down in 1917, the out-of-work musicians boarded the riverboats bound for Chicago, from whence the music spread around the world. This creation myth fails to recognize the vast musical landscape of New Orleans at large and the diversity of available music jobs including dances, funerals, lawn parties, parades, advertising wagons, baseball games, and carnival balls. As for musicians leaving as a direct result of work drying up in Storyville, it is worth noting that Louis Armstrong did not leave until 1922, and Jelly Roll Morton left as early as 1907. Conversely, some jazz histories have gone too far out of their way to disregard the import of Storyville. While it may not have been the sole early jazz incubator, the fact that there were clubs there and that Ory's bands played in them makes Storyville an essential part of Ory's history and, by extension, an essential part of jazz history. Still, Storyville was merely part of the New Orleans jazz experience, not the sum of it.

The reality is somewhere in between. The posh bordellos of Storyville featured pianists and occasionally string instruments, but generally no wind bands. The high-dollar side of the district was the corner of Iberville and Basin, closest to Canal Street. Four blocks between Canal Street and Iberville Street, including Basin, Franklin, Marais, and Robertson were not in the district proper. It was here in large part that the clubs and dance halls that became synonymous with jazz, and Storyville, would come into being. At various times these clubs neighboring the district included the Terminal Saloon, the Fewclothes Cabaret, John Lala's Big 25, the Shoto Cabaret, the Casino, Tournier's Saloon, and Pete Lala's, sometimes called the "Little 25."

Music clubs within the district proper included Billy Phillip's 101 Ranch (which was also known as the 102 and the Entertainers), the Tuxedo Dance Hall, Rice's Café, Abadie's Cabaret, and Groshell's dance hall. The Frenchmen's was a stomping ground for young pianists like Jelly Roll Morton. Another expansion of businesses stretched out behind the district on the Claiborne Avenue side, although the St. Louis Cemetery II lay in between. Still another entertainment district, called "the tango belt," ran from Rampart into the French Quarter down Iberville Street.

I'll try to describe Storyville to you. Parallel to Canal Street was Iberville, the main street of the section, which in earlier times had been named Custom House Street. The next street down from Iberville, was Bienville Street and the next was Conti Street. You were diminishing, as you were moving down, like the girls on the blocks. The next was St. Louis Street, right next to the water, the old stagnant water, infested with flies, bugs and everything poisonous. A man had to be very much in need to walk in that dark, dank miserable neighborhood, looking for a woman. Naturally, if he were broke, he couldn't choose. If he had dough, he could go to Custom House Street, but each degree less money led him to the street to fit his needs and his pocketbook. But, none of these streets, even St. Louis Street, could be compared with the poverty and degradation of Gravier, Howard and Basin streets. They were the end. When the girls landed there, they were at the bottom and there was no lower place to fall. On Gravier and Basin streets, drink of beer would usually suffice to pay off. [These streets were in "black Storyville," not the Storyville district.]

In Storyville, Custom House or Iberville was the street of the young and beautiful. As time went on and the girls grew older, their first freshness worn off, their desirability fading away, their first move away from their starting place was to Bienville Street. Bienville wasn't too bad a spot, they could still ask .75 cents there; but when they continued on down the line, in exact ratio to their looks and the rest of it, they'd go next to Conti Street and would be able to collect .50 cents there. When they hit the "Skid Row" of Storyville—St. Louis

Street, near the old basin—that was the end of the trail right there. Once out of Storyville, that wasn't the end of their downward slide. They'd hit Gravier, Howard, Saratoga and Perdido Streets, where the standard price was .25 cents and on slow nights, you'd get two for a quarter. That was rock bottom. Let's go back to Custom House Street or Iberville. There was a night club on every corner of the cross streets, such as Moray [sic, Marais] and Franklin and the rest. The nightclubs were often right next door to each other, about the same closeness as the houses in any clean city section of today. All that separated the houses on these streets was an alley that could accommodate only one person at a time to walk through. In each building, there were five or six "cribs," just room enough for a single bed, but no chair to sit down on. Everyone stood up. There was no time to lose. If they laid it down on the line, they had to move up. It was a pretty tough proposition, a going business . . . just like a barbershop . . . you're next my boy.

The only time anyone ever saw a chair in one of these cribs would be when a man would flash his money and somehow or other the girl would always produce a chair for him to hang his trousers on. Then when he was preoccupied, the door would softly open and a confederate of the girl would remove the trousers, take out the money and gently replace them on the chair and go about his business. The poor victim could go to the police and complain, and he often did, but when the police would ask the girl's name and address, he couldn't give the first and was always confused about the second because every crib looked alike from the outside and he would be left with the classic advice from the police, "Why you poor sucker, you should have had better sense in the first place."[23]

When Ory talks about women ending up on Howard, Gravier, and Basin streets, he is talking specifically about black prostitutes leaving the Storyville district, which catered to whites, and moving to the unofficial "black Storyville" on the other side of Canal Street, which served black clientele. This area did not enjoy the legal status of Storyville but it did share the music, and Ory played both districts through the years.

The district was full of characters. The "mayor" of Storyville was businessman Thomas C. Anderson. Storyville was known as "Anderson County," and he held tremendous sway within the district and without. Despite his connection to the district, or perhaps because of it, Anderson was elected to the Louisiana legislature. He owned the saloon considered the gateway to Storyville, Anderson's Annex, at Iberville and Basin streets. It sat at the bottom left corner of the district and glowed from the illumination of hundreds of electric lights and featured a bar that was a block long. Ory played at Anderson's on occasion and was familiar with the mayor.[24]

"Pete Lala" was the nickname of Italian-American businessman Peter Ciaccio. After Ciaccio's father died, his mother married her husband's former partner, whose last name was Lala. They were butchers, and Ciaccio and Lala was an ongoing business.[25] Lala ran several bars and clubs in his lifetime, most notably two in the vicinity of the Storyville district. His most famous club, at 1505–7 Iberville Street (on the lake side, uptown corner at Marais), was leased in late 1909 and began operating in 1910. Lala modernized the place, adding plumbing, heat, and electricity. Later he opened a theater at 425 N. Claiborne Avenue, on the backside of the district.

While playing at Lala's with George Jones in early 1910, Ory talked Lala into giving his own band a tryout. The Ory group apparently acquitted themselves well and by April had made the move to New Orleans.[26] Many musicians in New Orleans refer to playing at Lala's at one time or another; apparently it was *the* place to hear New Orleans' best vernacular musicians and bands.

Clarence "Little Dad" Vincent, a four-foot-tall mandolin player who hung around the district in this period, sat in with the Ory band occasionally when there was no violinist in the band. (He said Ory was often without one.) He enjoyed playing in the band and even worked out a routine with Ed Garland that became popular. When the rest of the band stopped, Vincent and Garland would continue playing the tune on just bass and mandolin. One by one, each of the instruments would come back in and take a hot solo. It was just this sort of improvisational risk taking that was behind the emerging jazz style. Take what you know and then try something different with it. In Storyville time was split between playing familiar tunes over and over, attempting to fulfill requests that the band might or might not know, and playing the blues. New Orleans bands were known for taking songs of the day and taking liberties with them. Bands often delighted visitors with the best version of a song they had ever heard. Taking liberties with the tune is at the heart of the blues. Jazz stands on its improvisational nature, one that flows directly from its blues origins. With its countless variations and interpretations, the blues was the nightly vehicle the Ory men employed to stretch out as musicians.

Besides the cabarets, the band was occasionally called upon to play sex shows in the district. Emma Johnson's studio was one regular venue for these spectacles. Ory remembered playing them in vivid detail:

> *Often they would have what they called contests. It would consist of three girls, nude, lying on the floor, and smoking cigarettes in odd fashions, and the fastest smoker would win the contest. The watchers would be betting on them as they would at the horse races. They'd number them one, two and three and the bets would be placed. Sometimes I bet myself. I very seldom won, but I'd take a chance, I'd bet a buck or so, picking the gal I thought had the best chance to win and once in a great while, I'd come out a winner. But, most of the time, it looked like I was just a sucker. I'd lose most of the time. I'd pick the "wrong horse." With all of these people watching, excited, some thrilled, it made you wonder how far some people would go to earn a few pennies.*

*Sometimes they would have men connected with the shows.
The one that could do the best job with the woman would win.
Then they'd go even further and form daisy chains, all of them
exhibiting their wares to the watching public and whoever put
on the best "show" was acclaimed the "winner."*

*After that they'd take a break and the house would start
selling drinks and making some money and we'd play and
they'd dance and we'd make some money from tips dropped
into the "kitty;" usually an old black, hard derby; the landlady would help us out by telling them that we weren't getting
paid that we were only in there hustling like they themselves
were. After each few numbers the hat would again be passed
around, and if we got enough money, we'd start playing again.
If we didn't get enough, the landlady would say, "There isn't
enough money for us to get any music, you boys had better
kick in some more into the kitty," and around would go the
derby again and you would hear the dollars falling in, they
would all be raring to go.*[27]

Ory said he also played Lulu White's at this time, and claimed
in his autobiography to have had an affair with Basin Street's Oc-
toroon Madam. Ed Garland, Ory's longtime bassist, said that was
not true. Apparently, though, White did help Ory at the start of his
career. For nine years Kid Ory played the district, appearing there
as late as 1919, two years after it was officially closed. His experiences there had an effect:

*As I worked in all the bad on through to all the good places in
New Orleans, I began to figure it out. I was really getting an
education in life. I was nothing but a boy from the country, living a clean life while I was growing up, not knowing what was
going on in the world, but I want to thank New Orleans and
Storyville for opening my eyes to how the rest of the world lived
and how people enjoyed themselves in that tough life. It looked*

as though the people were much happier down there, doing the things they did; which we would call wrong; more so than the people of today having a good time and living a clean life. They were much happier in New Orleans then. They enjoyed every-thing, the drinks, the entertainment, the music, everything that went on. They really got a kick out of it. It looked as though that was the way they wanted to live and they lived it.[28]

As alluring as the tales of the district are, Ory's staple work was as a dance band musician. He played as many country dances and picnics as he did nights in Storyville. "We played back and forth between New Orleans and LaPlace and on to Kenner and across the river to Gretna to Baton Rouge, on both sides of the Mississippi River—playing dances, lawn parties, picnics and house parties and, once in a while, we would play a fish fry, although we thought we had passed beyond that stage in our career."[29]

Ory continued playing music in the river parishes after mov-ing to New Orleans. He had grown up watching the bands play on payday during grinding season; now it was his band that played for the workers. One of his regular gigs was at the Godchaux Sugar Refinery in Reserve, but he played at a great many of the commu-nities between Baton Rouge and New Orleans. According to Gar-land, the band played most Saturday nights at plantations.

The band would travel by train upriver to get in the general vi-cinity of a small-town gig. Then they would be picked up by wagon to travel to the hall. Sometimes this involved crossing the Missis-sippi River by rowboat, always a dicey proposition. Once they ar-rived, they headed to the levee to ballyhoo the dance: "As soon as we hit town, we would always go out on the levee and play a couple of numbers to let people know we were in town and to advertise the dance. After that we came back to the house we were to stay in and had a big meal. Then the gang would line up in back of me and I would hold a lantern to lead them and we would all march down the sandy road to the hall."[30]

During a country dance the band would "play the cut"—a march that signaled the male dance partner to escort the girl to a table or booth and buy her a treat. This included a piece of fruit or a drink. Ory remembered just such a gig where Edward Garland (who was married at the time) was making time with a pretty woman and not paying attention to where he was walking. It was dark and Garland had one arm around his lady friend and another supporting the bass that was slung over his back. Garland stumbled over a cow that was sleeping under a tree. The cow gave out a loud moo and Garland was so startled he backed into another cow that rolled over his bass. "The rest of the boys gave him no sympathy whatsoever. They just laughed and laughed. We went right on to the hall and someone got hold of a bass in the loft that hadn't been played in years. It was missing two strings. [Garland] made a D and a G string with some rope and played them all night."[31]

Garland was apparently the brunt of a lot of jokes in this band. On a later trip to the country, Ory said Garland suffered another "fateful encounter."[32] The band was traveling by wagon to the gig and passed under a low-hanging tree branch. Garland's bass was standing upright in the wagon. As they passed under the tree it got caught in the branch and dragged out of the wagon. As the boys rolled on they looked back to see Garland's bass suspended over the roadway, swinging under the tree. From then on Garland said, he laid his bass down in the wagon.

It is unfortunate that many of the Ory band remembrances hinge on funny stories that offer few details about who was in the band and what they were playing. Still, they illustrate the variety of jobs the band played and bear out Ory's claim to have performed in "every hole that could be played" during his Louisiana residency.[33]

In New Orleans, Ory continued playing on advertising wagons for Lincoln Park, National Park, and various uptown benevolent societies. His band began to tangle regularly with Frank Duson's

Eagle Band, the Olympia Band, and Jack Carey's Crescent Band in impromptu musical competitions called bucking contests.

> *They used to have contests every time you'd get on the streets. Freddie Keppard's band whipped us good because he was a stronger trumpet player than we had at first. Then we started whipping everybody. The public was on my side. One chorus, that was all-right. When the other band was finished they'd tie the wagons together. The crowd tied them to keep them from running away from us. I used to say, "I'll let you go when I think you should go."*[34]

The competitions became neighborhood showcases for hot music. Rather than impede the Ory band, these cutting contests served as a major venue for the band to make its case. Ory relished his role as "the king of the street" and hit upon a way of marketing the band. "At the time, they used to advertise dances and picnics by hiring a wagon with a big sign on the side with band playing in the wagon. I decided to try a new idea and advertise my band that way. I rented a furniture wagon and told a fellow to make signs 'Kid Ory' with address and telephone number. After that, I got a lot of calls for jobs and began to get real well known."[35]

Before long Ory came upon another innovation in band advertising: "I was the first one to advertise in an automobile truck, you know. So we could catch the other bands, catch the horses. They couldn't get out of the way. It was lots of fun, you know."[36]

Betsy Cole's Willow Lawn parties were a regular gig for the Ory band in the uptown New Orleans community. Many musicians mention them playing there, including Louis Armstrong: "Many a night the boys would go to Mrs. Cole's lawn in my neighborhood where Kid Ory used to hold sway."[37] Most people remember the parties being held on Sunday evenings, though Sunday through Tuesday nights were popular. Musician "Wooden" Joe Nicholas (1883–1957) remembered the scene there: "They were out in the yard. Used kerosene and flambeaux to light the yard. They danced right on the ground, danced so frequently they had packed it into a good dancing surface."[38]

Betsy Cole's maiden name was Elizabeth Pickens, and she married Edward Cole in 1887. After Cole's death, she married Porter Jones, and in 1909 purchased a lot of property in Ory's uptown neighborhood, where Willow Street meets Josephine. This 30' x 159' parcel became the scene of the lawn parties. She was a spiritualist, according to Lillian De Pass, who suggested that Cole got rich by taking out insurance policies on people who met questionable demises.[39] Her favorite group, according to Ed Garland, was the Ory band. She said she wanted them to play her funeral.

During the band's tenure at Lincoln Park, a young woman named Elizabeth Davis Wallace began hanging around the bandstand whenever Ory performed.[40] Ory said he first met her when she was visiting his cousin Leana in New Orleans, before he moved to the city. "I first met my wife through my cousin she was visiting. She was in school at the time. I met her the first day I had long trousers. I was fifteen. Then she went back to school and we didn't see each other until she came back to New Orleans to live."[41]

Elizabeth began going with Ory, and they found they had much in common. Both were from the country, and Ory learned that she, too, was an orphan. She grew up with an aunt in Tangipahoa Parish, north of Lake Pontchartrain, and married a local man named John Wallace in 1907. They moved to New Orleans together, but she was unhappy in the marriage. Ory and Elizabeth, who her friends called Dort, stayed in touch, and Ory contacted her when he moved to town. In October 1911 they married and moved to 1906 Josephine Street, with Ory's sister Annie and her new husband Albert Anderson. Anderson worked for the railroad cleaning cars and had married Annie in January.[42] They had a child on the way and would soon move out to be on their own. Ory mentions his wife in a 1947 *Record Changer* interview, but she never comes up in his autobiography. (That the autobiography was dictated to his then-mistress Barbara GaNung in 1950–51 may be the reason.)

Ory said it was eighteen months after moving to New Orleans that the band began to drift apart. Lawrence Duhe, easily the best musician in the band, decided to quit over Ory's "big head." "His head began to swell," Duhe remembered. "We wanted an orchestra apiece. So he got his orchestra, I got one too." Duhe and his new band moved to the Fewclothes Café at 135 N. Basin Street and later played the 101 Ranch, both in Storyville. Filling in after Duhe's departure was Johnny Brown, a weak player who, according to "Pops" Foster, had such difficulty ending a piece that it was sometimes necessary for someone to pull the clarinet out of his mouth. Others are more charitable, but clearly Brown was wowing no one. Ory had a reputation for tolerating emerging players but not bad ones. The replacement was a twenty-year-old rice mill worker from Ory's uptown neighborhood whom he met in late 1911 or early 1912.[43] Johnny Dodds (1892–1940) remembered joining the Ory band: "I was practicing one day and Pops [Foster], whom I'd never met, walked by and heard me. Pops, always looking for talent, came in. I didn't go with Foster's group, Joe Oliver's Magnolia Band, but with Kid Ory who needed a clarinet then, and who gave me my first job in Algiers."[44]

Ory, often the protagonist in his recollections, said it happened this way:

> One day I needed a clarinet player and I heard about a guy who was working on the street around the corner that had a clarinet and was playing in his lunchtime. His name was Johnny Dodds. I went to see him. He just bought his clarinet, just playing the scale. I said, "Come to rehearsal on Tuesday." Saturday I called him to play, told him to play soft, if he was right to keep going, if he was wrong to stop. We played at Come Clean Hall at Gretna. I paid him $2.50, top salary in

those days. He didn't want to take it until he played better. I said, take it. You did all right.[45]

Edward Garland offers yet another twist on the story:

Johnny Brown had a furniture wagon, you know . . . and he used to haul different items you know that people buy furniture and stuff . . . Johnny Dodds used to work for him. And one day I come along, Johnny was sitting on the back of the tailgate and he was blowing his clarinet. I stopped and I stood at first and listened, you know he was just running over some things. So I walked up there to him and said "How would you like to play in a band." "I ain't playing with nobody" I said "how would you like to play with Kid Ory?" Johnny come on over there and fitted in alright with us.[46]

Johnny Dodds was born in New Orleans, but spent some of his early life in Waveland, Mississippi, along with his younger brother Warren "Baby" Dodds. Their home on Philip Street in New Orleans' Central City was a block from Buddy Bolden's 2309 First Street house. Everyone in the family made music, and Johnny sang tenor in the family quartet. His father Warren bought the clarinet for him while they were still in Waveland, before Johnny moved back to New Orleans around 1909.[47]

When Dodds started on clarinet in the Ory band, Brown kept his job by switching to violin but refused to speak to Johnny Dodds. It was not the only unusual personality dynamic in the band. Dodds and Garland fought every night about the pettiest of matters. Yet after work they went out for drinks and dinner together at the Eagle Saloon like it had never happened. The fights must have happened a lot, because many musicians mention the feuding. Adding fuel to the fire was the new nickname the band had saddled on Ed Garland. A regular customer named Montudi used to come into the district to hear the band. It became a joke in the band, and some nights members would refer to each other as "Montudi." The Ory men noticed that Garland was tiring of the joke so they hung the name on him. Johnny Dodds, in particular, would call Garland "Montudi" to the point of fisticuffs.[48]

The personality issues were small beer in light of Johnny Dodds's immense talent and potential. Though Duhe was a fine musician and reader, Johnny Dodds would develop into one of the most exciting soloists in early jazz. His feeling for the blues was so deep that his bandmates affectionately called him "Toilet."[49] Like the rest of the band, Dodds was barrelhouse: a gutbucket, non-reading musician who played by ear, or "head," as they used to say in New Orleans. Though he would later learn to read music, Dodds's New Orleans residency was one of an improvising ear player. He worked almost exclusively in Ory's band.

As he had done in LaPlace, Ory soon began looking at sponsoring his own events for the band to play. After a gig one night, Ory hung around the hall and watched the promoter count his money; that was all he needed to see. He proposed to the group that they put aside a portion of their earnings to save up enough money to book their own dances. The band had no interest in the Ory plan, so he set out to earn the money on his own through his day job cutting marble for a man named Johnny.

> I worked for Johnny about six weeks and worked four or five nights a week making pretty good salary, with my music jobs. I was getting $21 a week, a pretty good salary in those days, from Johnny. Living expenses weren't so great and I told myself, "I'm going to make this job a bank account." I put it away and I sacrificed. I didn't use any of it. The money I earned from my music, I used for my current expenses—living, rent, a little drink now and then, anything I felt I needed—but the rest I put away. I was building up a fund to put on my dance.

The first dance I promoted took place on March 11, 1912. I went down and rented a hall and I paid cash for it. After getting the hall, I went for my permit to operate the dance, then my permit for advertising. It cost only .50. I was all set for it and really wanted to do it. This was my own idea about to come true. The night of the dance came at last and it was a great success. The amount I invested more than paid off. In those days if a guy could knock out about $450 or a little more, for his one night, he had really had a success.[50]

The music business in New Orleans was cutthroat and bargain-basement. The bands played for pennies, and there was always another band that might come along and undercut the price or top you musically. The end result was losing one's job. Being the promoter and bandleader, on the other hand, insured that Ory would take home money one way or the other. With the success of his first dance at Economy Hall, Ory began to book other halls in town and promote his own events. These included Monday night dances and fish fries.

Then I made the announcement to the crowd that Kid Ory and his band would be playing there every Monday night and I wanted them to come and dance. My second dance was just as good as my first one. I kept thinking, however, of the hall about two blocks around the corner. And worrying about someone's taking that and hurting me. My next move was to rent that hall, Cooperators Hall, and fulfill my purpose. I wanted to keep it closed. The $17.50 wouldn't break me, and that way I'd be certain of no harmful competition. During the winter season, I rented Cooperators and Economy Halls and, as the spring and summer season opened I rented National Park.[51]

The Economy Society or, the *Societe d' Economie et d' Assistance Mutuelle* benevolent society, was founded in 1836 by fifteen free men of color.[52] In 1912 their large meeting hall stood at 1422 Ursulines Street in the Tremé neighborhood. It was used for club functions but it also served as a community center, where public dances were held. The hall was on the second floor, though the band played higher still, on a balcony above the dancers' heads. Kid Ory played Economy Hall on Monday nights until his departure from New Orleans in 1919. Over the years he became so successful at it that he hired other bands to play even as his band performed elsewhere. "Still later, I hired other halls and hired bands to play in them too, when I found I couldn't accommodate all the people trying to crowd into my dances. So, I made money right along, if they came to me fine, if they went to the other halls, I still made it."[53]

On Labor Day 1913, the Ory band was set to play for a parade that would travel through the Rampart and Perdido Street neighborhood. As the band took a break, dressed in their signature blue uniforms, they noticed a young cornetist playing with Captain Jones's Colored Waif's Home Brass Band. "The first time I remember seeing Louis Armstrong, he was a little boy playing cornet with the Waifs' Home band in a street parade. Even then he stood out."[54]

Louis Armstrong (1901–1971) was known as something of a local character. He was the son of William and Mayann Armstrong, though the first five years of his life he lived with his grandmother Josephine on Jane Alley at Perdido Street. He later moved with his mother and sister Beatrice to Perdido Street at Liberty Street, in the vice district sometimes referred to as black Storyville. With his mother working as a prostitute, young Louis was often left to wander the rough streets of the neighborhood. It was there that he befriended Ory brass band drummer "Black" Benny Williams, who acted as his protector. Armstrong ended up in the Waif's Home after firing a pistol in the air at the corner of Rampart and Perdido streets to greet New Year's 1913.[55] During his sentence, Armstrong learned cornet playing in the Waif's Home band. When he got out, "Black" Benny would bring him around to gigs with the Ory band.

In those days I had a brass band I used for funerals, parades and picnics. Benny, the drummer of my brass band, had taken Louis under his wing. One evening, Benny brought Louis, who had just been released from the Waifs' Home, to National Park, where I was playing a picnic. Benny asked me if I would let Louis sit in with my band. I remembered the kid from the street parade and I gladly agreed.

Louis came up and played Ole Miss' *and the blues, and everyone in the park went wild over this boy in knee trousers who could play so great. I liked Louis' playing so much that I asked him to come and sit in with my band any time he could. Louis came several times to different places where I worked and we really got to know each other. He always came accompanied by Benny, the drummer. In the crowded places, Benny would handcuff Louis to himself with a handkerchief so Louis wouldn't get lost.[56]*

The applause for Armstrong's cameos with the band won Ory over—despite the fact that young Louis only knew a couple of songs.

Unlike Ory, who came up when bands were just beginning to play hot and feature the blues, Armstrong emerged in a world where hot music was the norm. Just as Ory had followed Bolden, Louis Armstrong now followed the Ory band.

In late 1913 or early 1914, the Ory band was set to play a society function on St. Charles Avenue. The group had developed a good reputation in the uptown white circles because they were known for playing soft ragtime. Sometimes the band played so softly that the dancers feet could be heard shuffling on the floor. Ory guarded his reputation in these moneyed circles, so it must have been a shock when Joe Matthews showed up drunk at the uptown mansion. Ory fired him on the spot. A true brother's keeper, Lewis quit too.[57] Ory was swift in finding replacements.

Thomas C. "Papa Mutt" Carey (1890–1947) was a freak trumpeter, as the men then called it.[58] He used mutes and incorporated a driving style in his playing. Eventually he would develop into one of the city's hardest blowing horn men. And though he was still something of a neophyte in 1914 (he took up the horn only two years earlier), his abilities as a soloist outstripped Lewis Matthews. Preston Jackson said of Mutt Carey:

> *Most everybody has heard of Joe Oliver and Louis Armstrong, but few ever heard Mutt Carey in his prime. Mutt Carey, in his day, was equal to Joe Oliver. Mutt is the first trumpet player or cornetist that choked his horn. He used a drinking glass in the bell of his horn and how he did swing. Mutt had very mellow tone and a terrific swing. The softer the band played the better Mutt played. He was strictly gutbucket or barrelhouse. Nothing technical about his playing. Just swinging all the time, pretty diminished chords. He choked his cornet and made it moan just like Joe Oliver did later.[59]*

Carey's family was originally from St. Charles Parish, upriver from New Orleans, but they do not appear on the census between 1870 and 1900. He lived in uptown New Orleans with his brothers John and William at 2204 Eighth Street, before 1910. He was working as a cotton press operator by 1911, when he lived in the Lower Garden District at 604 Felicity Street.[60] Mutt Carey recalled his early life:

> *I was the youngest of seventeen children in my family. You know, my brother Jack had the Crescent Band in those days and was a pretty good trombone player as was my brother John and my brother Milton. Pete and myself played trumpet. I was twenty-two when I started playing trumpet. Lots of boys had a head start on me because they began playing earlier, but I caught up with them. You see, I first learned the drums*

*but got tired of packing those drums around, so I switched
over to trumpet. My brother, Pete, gave me my first lessons on
the horn. Later, John taught me also.*

*I got my first job with Jack's Crescent Band in 1912. They
had a lot of good bands in those days and a lot of fine musicians playing with them. I played with almost all of them during my years in New Orleans.*[61]

Jack Carey gave his brother a break and let him fill in on an
advertising wagon gig one Sunday with his Crescent Band. The
group ran into the Olympia band and were soundly defeated; but
the Olympia was a downtown band and Carey, and the crowd, was
from uptown. Despite Carey's defeat, the uptowners cheered him
anyway, shouting, "Go it, Papa Mutt! Go it!" From that moment on
he was Papa Mutt.[62] Though successful in Jack's band they did not
get along, so Mutt bolted for Ory's group. Hiring a hot horn player from under the nose of his rival thrilled Ory and steamed Jack
Carey. Jack Carey had no use for Ory, who remembered: "Mutt
Carey's brother (Jack) used to play trombone. I liked him but he
didn't like me. He was kind of jealous because Mutt came to play
with me. I gave him a spanking in a contest. He stopped me afterward on the corner and said, 'He can beat me playing trombone,
but he can't whip me!' I threw my arms around him and said, 'I
just love you Jack.'"[63] Mutt Carey would play with Ory off and on
through the 1940s.

Joining the band on guitar and banjo was Johnny St. Cyr (1889–
1966), who grew up in downtown New Orleans and began studying guitar around the age of 11. By the next year he was playing
fish fries with his teacher Jules Batiste. A reading musician who
labored days as a plasterer, St. Cyr met Ory through bassist Ed
Garland. He was a solid addition to the Ory lineup because of his
reading skills and his ability to improvise.[64]

Violinist Emile Bigard (1890–1935), the uncle of future Duke
Ellington clarinetist Albany "Barney" Bigard, started out playing

the Bungalow at the West End with bandleader Paul Chaligny. He then played with Sidney Desvignes before joining Kid Ory's band around 1914. He was a cigar maker by trade and operated a shop next to his house with six other rollers. Ory band rehearsals were often held at the Bigard family compound 1746 N. Villere Street in the city's Seventh Ward.

Though St. Cyr and Bigard were New Orleans Creoles who prided themselves on their musical education, they chose to play with Ory's gut-bucket band. His band was popular and, unlike those of a generation earlier, younger Creole musicians were open to the idea of playing in a non-reading, improvisational band.

The Ory band was still doing a significant amount of work in the rough clubs of the Rampart-Perdido area. Black Storyville was the area along Rampart and Perdido streets that featured night-clubs, theaters, and brothels for black clientele. Ory said the worst place he ever played was a bar in this district called Spano's on Poydras Street:

> It was just like an all-night market. It had no doors; just swing doors, never closed. The women were there drinking, sitting around, even sleeping on the tables just like the men who were sleeping on the tables. They weren't dressed neatly. They were very dirty. I didn't know any better at the time. I thought that was the way it was supposed to be. But, later, in visiting other places, I found out there was a little more class and that went on improving until I got up to the top, but it was still tough in its way. They wouldn't exactly talk the same, but life went on basically the same; everyone was hustling in the cribs. Some-times you'd find eight or a dozen men in there hustling as well as the women; the men would be looking for a man because they were freakish; and the women were looking for a man. Finally, there would be a great big argument; that's my man, let him alone; then you'd discover that that was supposed to be another man. I began wondering, what's going to happen

*around here; everyone is man and everyone is woman; who
is really the man and who is really the woman. Later on, I
found out there were different kinds of men; wearing trousers;
and different kids of women; wearing dresses, but they'd wind
up having arguments and you'd find a woman was fighting
about another woman and a man about another man. I still
couldn't realize quite what was going on until later someone
explained to me that they were freakish people. I said, "Oh, so
that's the way they do business." He answered, "yeah."*

*I was still just a youngster then, but with a little experi-
ence, and I began to understand what he was talking about.
I learned. After that I wasn't surprised in any place I went or
worked, I'd take it naturally; it didn't excite me. I wasn't surprised. I just ignored it, but I saw enough at Spano's place to
know that those things just weren't right.*[65]

Weary of dives, the band began playing regularly for affluent
white audiences, as the latter became acclimated to the type of hot
music that Ory offered. By 1915 much of his work during the week
was playing for white audiences, including two nights per week in
the district and at various clubs, hotels, and parties. "Word of us
crept into the moneyed and society circles and engagements followed in the homes of cotton brokers, society matrons, the yacht
clubs, gymnasiums, etc. and brought us more money for easier
work and in nicer surroundings too."[66]

Debutantes wanted the Ory band so they could dance the turkey
trot and the bunny hug. Ory courted this business, relying on his
good looks and charm to win people over. Ory played A-list parties
with such success that he cut into Robichaux's market. "Robichaux
asked me to play with him. I got all his work. We played at the
Gymnasium. The young kids liked my band better. He [Robichaux]
said, 'I like the way you play.' I said, 'I like the way you play too
but I'm not going to break up my band. It's too late. You had your
day.'"[67]

Dances at the New Orleans Yacht Club out at Lake Pontchartrain, and at the New Orleans Country Club off Metairie Road, became regular gigs. Ed Garland remembered playing hotel parties: "Ory's band worked several nights a week; they usually played Fridays nights for the Tulane boys, they played for parties on St. Charles Avenue and at the hotels including the Roosevelt, Grunewald, and St. Charles. During the week (we) played mostly for white people; on the weekend, and on Monday, they played mostly for colored."[68]

That Ory netted such jobs provides a clue to the cultural shift taking place with regard to the appreciation of hot music. Unlike Bolden a decade earlier, who played almost exclusively for black audiences, Ory helped the music cross over the racial and cultural threshold. Ory's group delighted whatever audience lay before them: a Saturday night in Storyville, a Sunday afternoon brass band parade or a Friday night hotel ball. The band traveled through different worlds, all existing in the same geographical space. This speaks to the wide appeal of the Ory band's music.

By 1915 the band was poised for another personnel change. The first to go was Johnny St. Cyr, who objected to Ory's making the band play overtime on advertising jobs. When the band, riding in a wagon, encountered another, they would take turns playing songs until one admitted defeat and left. Johnny St. Cyr remembered: "Kid Ory had a policy of trying to chase other bands away, by playing better. Sometimes he would have his band stay for so long trying to make another band leave first that the job would extend over the intended number of hours. The club officials would insist he finish the route. So the band had to work overtime for no money."[69] Johnny Dodds and Johnny St. Cyr both complained to Ory, who must have satisfied Dodds, but not St. Cyr, who quit the band. It was an amicable split, though, and St. Cyr would be a regular substitute in the Ory band.

Replacing him was as grizzled a veteran of New Orleans jazz as could be found. Lorenzo Staulz (1880–1928) had played in the

Bolden band and was a regular in Frankie Duson's Eagle Band. Staulz was known for singing obscene songs and was considered a good rhythm man. He wore diamond rings on his fingers and a towel around his shoulder when he played. His legitimate job was as a presser, though some said he also worked as a pimp. Punch Miller said, "He was a good banjo player."[70]

Drummer Ed "Rabbit" Robertson also departed. He would continue in music, playing an extended stay at the Iroquois Theatre on South Rampart Street and touring with Willie Hightower. Ory never mentioned why he left, but he always spoke well of him musically, calling him one of the best drummers he ever played with. Fortunately for Ory, he replaced Rabbit with the man he said was the best he ever played with: Henry Martin.

Martin (1893–1932) was born into a family that included his guitar-playing brother Albert "Coochie" Martin.[71] He grew up in the "back of town" neighborhood, along with other Ory drummers including James "Red Happy" Bolton and "Black" Benny Williams. A tall man, he lived with his parents well into his twenties. In addition to his exceptional skills as a timekeeper, Martin knew how to make sound effects and kept an array of noisemaking devices next to his drum kit. Ory said he was like a metronome, you could not get him to change tempo.

"Henry Martin was a great drummer," future Ory drummer Alfred Williams recalled. He followed him for miles during parades, when he would play snare drum with Ory's brass band. He would also tag along as a kid during Ory gigs at National Park. Martin would sometimes let Williams sit in around 1914. Drummer Alex Bigard (1898–1978) was dazzled by the playing of Martin and said he wanted to play like him when he grew up.[72]

"Black" Benny Williams (ca. 1890–1924) had a reputation as both a hell raiser and a sought-after drummer. "Black Benny was a wonderful drummer and a great showman. He played in dance and brass bands," remembered drummer Joe Watkins (1900–1969).[73] Benny's reputation on the streets extended from his role as a parade bass drummer and an enforcer. If anyone tried to mess with his band, Benny would respond with quick and decisive violence. Even the cops were scared of Black Benny. Benny became a regular member of Ory's brass band and was often on hand when the regular band played dances.

> *One night when we were playing a dance at St. Elizabeth's Hall, we saw we were going to run into some trouble with some of Frankie Duson's Eagle Band followers. While we were waiting for our money, we took the time to help ourselves to the knives and forks of the lady who had hired us, just as a means of arming ourselves for protection purposes only. We were joined by one Black Benny, a character who was noted for being able to accurately throw a rock a whole block and never miss his objective. This night, as we came out of the hall, ready to do battle with the gang waiting for us, we found to our great surprise, that the road was clear because old Benny and his trusty throwing arm had run them off all by himself before we even started out of St. Elizabeth's.[74]*

On one Sunday around this time, Ory's band bested Frankie Duson's Eagle Band while both rode around uptown in their respective wagons.

> *We backed up the wagons up as close as we could get together. We were nearly touching horns together. So, I wrote a number, "Old Frankie Died" and he (Duson) had my old trumpet player named Lewis Matthews. We called him Chif for short.*
>
> *We began to play and we start to sing that on the street. The tune "Old Frank Died" was to the tune of "The Old Cow Died" which was the lyrics at the time, "Old Frank Died and Little Chif Cried."[75]*

This really vexed Duson, who lived next door to Ory's guitar player, Lorenzo Staulz. Staulz reported to Ory that Duson had said, "You tell that little country guy I'm going take his horn from him today." The next day at the corner of Gravier and Rampart streets, the bands met again as both were engaged to play the same funeral. Ory drummer Henry Martin drew a picture of Frankie Duson running, followed by Kid Ory pounding him from behind with a trombone. Everyone who saw it laughed out loud. The last to arrive was Johnny Dodds. The Duson men had noticed the drawing and the howls of laughter rising from the Ory band as they looked at it. When Johnny Dodds saw it, he laughed out loud. "Johnny was a great guy to laugh," said Ory. Eagle bass player Dandy Lewis was so annoyed with Dodds's laughter that he punched him in the eye. Lewis yelled at Dodds, "Who wrote that?" to which a stunned Dodds replied that he had not. As Dodds's bandmates helped him off the ground, Black Benny arrived. The funeral progressed without further violence.[76] "So Johnny couldn't even see where he was going, just playing so, I give him credit for being a good sport and a good musician. He played just kept step. He didn't know where he was going, he was going uptown or downtown or back of town or front of town. He played the same as he always did."[77]

By 1916 Ory fielded an entirely different lineup from the band he had brought to New Orleans in 1910. Fortunately for him, his replacements were better than the men they replaced. Still, too much should not be made of the personnel alone. Having great musicians does not always translate into a successful band. Having an effective bandleader does. By 1916 Ory was certainly that. Constant playing in venues from National Park to Milneburg had burnished the Ory band's reputation as the premiere barrelhouse band in New Orleans.

CHAPTER 7

1917–1919

CREOLE JAZZ

At the dawn of 1917, Ory's was a successful and sought-after band. His clients included white bankers and black benevolent societies. They played lawn parties, Mardi Gras parades, Monday night dances at Economy Hall, and Sunday afternoons at Milneburg. Artistically, Ory's band refined a style of playing that bridged all these audiences while retaining the qualities that made the music "hot." He called it "soft ragtime." Soon there would be another name for it: jazz. And the Ory band would cement its legacy with the help of Louis Armstrong and Joe "King" Oliver.

The early biography of Joseph Oliver (1885–1937), jazz's first significant soloist, continues to be elusive. According to his wife, Stella, Oliver was born in Abend, Louisiana, on December 19, 1885. The year is contradicted by his World War I draft registration that says he was born on December 19, 1881. Other sources place Oliver's birth in New Orleans "in a house on Dryades Street in 1885." His mother was called Jennie, though her real name was Virginia. His father, Nathan Oliver, was a Baptist preacher. Stella Oliver said Oliver's father was a preacher, but said his name was Henry. By 1900 Joe lived uptown in New Orleans with his mother and stepsisters Fannie and Adel on Nashville Avenue. Virginia died shortly after this, and the Levy family she worked for "practically raised Joe," according to Stella. The family lived at Second and Magazine streets and Oliver did yard work.[1]

While still a teenager, Oliver joined a neighborhood brass band led by Walter Kenchen. Oliver traveled with the band to Baton

Rouge, where a dust-up with some local youth resulted in a scar over one eye. Over the years he suffered nicknames like "Monocles" and "Bad Eye." He eventually took to playing professional gigs with Henry Allen's Brass Band, the Onward Brass Band, the Original Superior Orchestra, and Frankie Duson's Eagle Band.[2] By 1916 his Magnolia Band held down a regular night at Pete Lala's.

Ory remembered Oliver hanging around his band, asking to be given a chance to play. Ory waved him off at first.

My old buddy, who was playing so loud and wrong, Joe Oliver, and he asked me to give him a chance. I told him I would think it over. He tried many times to organize a band and had had a few good musicians with him. But Oliver was all wet. His tone was bad and that is number one in playing cornet. His execution was a little too fast the way he blew it. It took a lot of patience and teaching to get him to the point that people agreed when I named him "King."[3]

Oliver became so frustrated on one occasion, after hearing Mutt Carey play in a parade, that he threw away his horn.[4] Oliver recognized his tone problem and worked on it, apparently for years. Preston Jackson remembered: "Later on, about 1914, I should say, Joe began to improve a lot. He used to practice very hard. I remember he once told me that it took him 10 years to get a tone on his instrument."[5]

Richard M. Jones recalled Oliver's arrival as top cornet man in New Orleans.

Freddie Keppard was playing in a spot across the street and was drawing all the crowds. I was sittin' at the piano, and Joe Oliver came over to me and commanded in a nervous harsh voice, "Get in B-flat." He didn't mention a tune, just said, "Get in B-flat." I did, and Joe walked out on the sidewalk, lifted his lips, and blew the most beautiful stuff I have ever heard.

> *People started pouring out of the other spots along the street*
> *to see who was blowing all that horn. Before long, our place*
> *was full and Joe came in, smiling, and said, "Now that _____*
> *won't bother me no more." From then on our place was full*
> *every night.*[6]

Ory relented. He remembered Joe Oliver joining the band in
1916 upon the departure of Mutt Carey. Violinist Manuel Manetta
(1889–1969) said Oliver was already in the band when he joined,
which was before the Original Dixieland Jazz Band records came
out in February 1917.[7] Ory remembered teaming up with Oliver:
"When Oliver came up with me, he and I got together and I told
Oliver, 'Let's work as a team because it's got to be one way or the
other. We're going to agree on tone and try to play together rather
than blast and try to force those notes. You can't do it.' Oliver said,
'All right, I'm willing.'"[8]

Ory was emphatic that it was Oliver who came up with "the
new style." He was speaking specifically about the divide between
what Oliver played and what Buddy Bolden and Freddie Keppard had previously done. Oliver's 1923 recordings reveal a musician who used many tricks of the trade, including, most notably,
his signature muted "wah-wah" effect. He would play into buckets, cups, hats and mutes to get a different sound from his horn.
Oliver's breaks—that is, where the rest of the band would stop
and he would play the fill—were also one of his calling cards. He
bent notes, executed flawless runs, and had a swing to his playing. He could imbue his horn with the sound of a crying baby or
the whinny of a horse. Oliver played with drive, power, imaginative phrasing, and emotion. Mutt Carey remembered: "Joe Oliver
was very strong. He was the greatest freak trumpet player I ever
knew. He did most of his playing with cups, glasses, buckets, and
mutes. He was the best gutbucket man I ever heard. I called him
a freak because the sounds he made were not made by the valves

but through these artificial devises. In contrast, Louis [Armstrong] played everything through his horn."⁹

With Oliver's horn laying down the melody, the Ory band continued to progress in the constantly evolving New Orleans jazz scene. By the time Oliver arrived, the Ory band had an established repertoire, a style of its own, and a reputation. People may have viewed Oliver as the leader of the band at times, but it was Oliver who joined Ory's band, one that had its own way of doing things. Oliver had to adapt. Ory's style involved using dynamics like changes in volume. He would get the band to play quietly to draw all the dancers close to the stage so they could hear, then bring the volume up on the next chorus. Oliver, who once got booted from a rich uptown gig because he played too loud, had to tone it down. Conforming to the Ory band's use of restraint and nuance served to melt away Oliver's "rough as pig iron" reputation while highlighting his immense skills as a soloist. Preston Jackson remembered:

> One of the best numbers I ever heard Joe play was Eccentric. He took all the breaks, imitating a rooster and a baby. He was a riot in those days, his band from 1915 or 16 to 18, being the best in New Orleans. The boys playing with Joe then were Johnny Dodds, clarinet; Edward Ory, trombone; Ed Garland, bass; Henry Zeno, drums; Eddie Polla(?), violin; and a guitar player whose name I have forgotten. How those boys could swing, and it was jazz they played, too, not ragtime music.¹⁰

Swing, jazz, and ragtime are, in their most common usages, words that refer to music in different historical periods; the ragtime era gave way to the jazz age, which was followed by the swing era. In this context, however, Jackson used the word swing not to denote a type of music, but how well the band played. He said they played jazz, but "could swing."

So the term "swing" serves to tell us that the Ory-Oliver band not only played jazz, but that they played it well. Some have argued that the music that came out of New Orleans did not become jazz until it reached the northern cities where it was recorded. Jackson makes it clear that Ory's was not a ragtime outfit, nor a near jazz group, but a hot New Orleans jazz band.

> *The band seems to have infused New Orleans dance band music with more of the African-American vernacular than had ever been done before. It presented the rough and beautiful tradition at its current best. It was from this band that one could hear, in its most sophisticated form, the texture of collective improvisation, as shaped by Oliver playing monkeyshines around Manetta's violin and by Johnny Dodds doing the same thing on clarinet when Oliver carried the lead.[11]*

Ory said a man who was friends with Oliver and used to run dances was the first to promote them as the Ory-Oliver band.[12] Ory and Oliver had followings independent of each other's. When they came together they reaped the rewards of their dual drawing power. Pete Lala jumped on the bonanza of the all-star lineup and also promoted them as the Ory-Oliver band.

While the band flourished and refined its dynamics with Oliver as its soloist, the inevitable happened: jazz was recorded. A group of young men from New Orleans, led by an Italian immigrant's son named Dominick "Nick" La Rocca, and calling themselves the Original Dixieland Jazz Band (ODJB), recorded several songs for Victor beginning in February 1917.

La Rocca (1889–1961) had played in Papa Jack Laine's Reliance Brass Band in New Orleans. Laine, sometimes called the father of white jazz, led or managed a half dozen bands and trained young musicians. The ODJB traveled to Chicago in 1916, went through personnel changes, and relocated to New York by winter 1917, when they recorded "Livery Stable Blues" and the "Dixie Jass Band

One-Step." Future standards "Tiger Rag," "Clarinet Marmalade," and "Fidgety Feet" would follow. The records, which sold in the millions, served to codify the jazz form for dissemination by a national audience. Once a local style, New Orleans jazz was now a hot commercial property. Back in New Orleans, Ory, Oliver, and Armstrong bought the records, too. Ory soon found himself emulating the ODJB by temporarily eliminating the violin chair in his band. Violinist Manuel Manetta recalled leaving the Ory-Oliver band:

> One band starts its business with six-pieces, that band sounds pretty good. They want everybody to follow suit then. Joe and them hated that because they got a little tangled with this [written] music. I could show them the division all the time. After the [Original] Dixieland [Jazz] Band came up using five pieces and things, well Joe and Ory got crazy about that. They wanted to organize on that and follow the style of the Dixieland Band. And they hated to lose me because I could play piano too.[13]

The ODJB's influence on Ory, and Oliver's decision to cut the band down, did not happen immediately. It happened before Manuel Manetta was drafted for World War I and left for duty the summer of 1917. He was still in the band as late as April, because he tells a story about the men in the band being worried about the draft.

In another bow to the ODJB, the Ory-Oliver band incorporated "jazz" into their name as early as November 1917, when "Ory and Oliver's Greater Jazz Players" are mentioned in the *Indianapolis Freeman*.[14] While Ory admitted the influence of the ODJB on his band, he and others suggest that it was a two-way street. Ory remembered seeing La Rocca in New Orleans before the bandleader left for Chicago. "Oh sure. You know they, La Rocca and those boys, used to stand on the walkways out at Lake Pontchartrain and pick up everything we were doing. I saw them."[15] Preston Jackson had similar memories: "The La Rocca boys of the [Original] Dixieland Jazz band used to hang around and got a lot of ideas from his [Ory and Oliver's] gang."[16]

Ory's band was known for its original material. Ed Garland said that, when he joined the band in 1910, they were playing made-up songs from the country. Stella Oliver had similar memories. "Ory would sing songs he had made up and the rest would then work them out. They would whistle and say songs they made up to each other." "Ory had a pretty good ear. That's why Joe liked him so much," Manuel Manetta recalled.[17]

While playing a gig in an advertising wagon, Ory began toying with the riff that would become his song "Do What Ory Say." Oliver's ears pricked up at the catchy ditty and he began to play along.

We were in a big furniture wagon, drifting along and when we came to a dull section, we weren't playing every corner, just the hot spots, the hot corners, so he said, "Keep playing it, play it again for me, please." So, he said, "I think I have it."

So, we got on a corner and he said, "Let's try it. Let's go." I stomped off and Oliver kept the melody and that quick I picked up the harmony. Oliver was pretty fast himself, as everyone knows, but that was a fast hand on the climax, my ideas. So we started playing it. We played it once or twice before we hit Toledano & Franklin where all the crowd was and there we met Jack Carey's band.

We started to play it and everyone wanted to know what number was it. It was so new, we didn't know it ourselves. We didn't have no title more than "Do What Ory Say." I didn't have no idea of no title so someone hollered and said, "What's the number you played, Kid?"

I said, "Oh, we're just playing." King Oliver said, "Do What Ory Say," and the word started spreading around.[18]

The chorus of the song went "if you don't like the way I do then kiss my f***ing ass!" The newsboys starting singing it and it caught on. "A lot of kids got spanked by their parents because they couldn't tell what did Ory say. Some of them would tell, but they had the wrong idea. They would tell it in the wrong way. It was very smutty, but still."[19]

The melody took on different names over the years. In 1917 Clarence Williams and Armand Piron published it with the title "Mama's Baby Boy." The writing credit went to Johnny St. Cyr, a former Ory band member, and Piron. Ory said Williams stole it: "Clarence Williams appeared at Economy Hall where we played it [Do What Ory Say] and he wrote it down and he was in the publishing business and stole an idea and he changed the title. He came to Economy Hall and had me play it a couple of times a night. I didn't know what they were up to. They were writing it down and got an idea for a title."[20]

Historian William Russell recorded bands in the forties that played the same melody with the title "Pork Chop." Whatever the name of the song or its origin, its popularity helped raise the band's profile.

Louis Armstrong remembered "Do What Ory Say," though not by name.

Kid Ory and Joe Oliver got together and made one of the hottest jazz bands that ever hit New Orleans. They often played in a tailgate wagon to advertise a ball or other entertainments. When they found themselves on a street corner next to another band in another wagon, Joe and Kid Ory would shoot the works. They would give with all that good, mad music they had under their belts and the crowd would go wild. When the other band decided it was best to cut the competition and start out for another corner, Kid Ory played a littler tune on his trombone that made the crowd go wild again. But

*this time they were wild with laughter. It was a cute little tune
to celebrate the defeat of the enemy. I thought it screamingly
funny and I think you would too.*[21]

The United States declared war on Germany on April 6, 1917,
and American men between the ages of 21 and 31 were required to
register for the draft. Oliver, Lorenzo Staulz, and Bob Lyons were
too old for the first call-up, but the rest of the band, particularly
Johnny Dodds, was nervous. The band played a gig for Mayor
Martin Behrman at Dixie Park around this time. The mayor's sec-
retary, Mike Rooney, informed them that Manetta would have to
serve, but that Dodds and Ory, who were married, could get a de-
ferment. The Ory men had been running around on their wives,
according to Manetta, no doubt fallen by the constant temptation
that surrounded them. So Ory moved out of the house he had
shared with Mutt Carey and back with Dort at 2330 First Street.
On June 5, 1917, Ory, Manetta, and Dodds went off to register.
Ory and Dodds got their deferments but Manetta went into the
army.[22]

In mid-1917 Pete Lala converted a building at 425 North Claiborne Avenue, between St. Louis and Conti streets, into a theatre. Lala pulled out the stops, advertising his new enterprise in
the *Indianapolis Freeman* in display ads featuring his picture. The
caption under his photograph read "Ol' Pete Lala." The theatrical
notices and advertisements ran from July 14 through December
22, 1917. The July 14 notice proclaims: "Mack and Mack are at the
First Class Theatre in New Orleans, Louisiana. Billy Mack is stage
manager and producer."[23]

Mack and Mack were a vaudeville duo comprised of Billy Mc-
Bride and his New Orleans–born wife Mary Thacker. Billy began
his career in 1908 in minstrel shows, then teamed up with Mary
after hearing her perform at Lincoln Park. They toured the vaudeville circuit as early as 1911, sometimes in other troupes but more

often in companies they led themselves. Many black musicians in New Orleans performed with the Macks over the years, highlighting the role vaudeville played in spreading the sound of New Orleans jazz.[24] In the summer of 1917 the Macks became the resident entertainers at Pete Lala's First Class Theatre, with Ory and Oliver's group serving as house band.

Members of the Mack and Mack company included Joe Lomas, or Loomis, a tenor who also played the straight man. The Metcalf sisters, Billie and Mary, were singers known for the tunes "Ain't You Coming Back to Dixieland?" and "Here's a Rose for You."[25] A notice in the *Freeman* of September 28, 1918, summed up a Mack and Mack performance in Cleveland:

> *Mary Mack and her merry makers of mirth are offering a show this week that is pleasing the patrons of theatre. The show is clean and free from vulgarity and is a good example of making an audience laugh without offending refined tastes. The jokes are good and there is plenty of action and humorous situations. The curtain rises on a four piece jazz band from New Orleans, the home of jazz. The audience compels several encores to "The Livery Stable Blues," which was played with a number of new variations.*[26]

Having the band on stage rather than in the orchestra pit put jazz front and center. This speaks to the continued novelty, and still emerging popularity, of jazz among audiences outside of New Orleans.

A November 10, 1917, "News of the Players" notice in the *Indianapolis Freeman* advances a tour planned by Mack and Mack including "Ory and Oliver's Greater Jazz players": "Billy Mack and Mary Mack are still on the boards at the 'First Class' Theatre in New Orleans, La. But will be seen in vaudeville soon through the South, North and East, with a new idea big act of fourteen people, namely the Metcalf Sisters, Molly Maddock, Jackson and Wynn, Ory and Oliver's Greater Jazz players, Joseph Lomas and Mack. Seeing is believing, so wait and see."[27]

Ory and Oliver chose not to tour, though Johnny Dodds did. The Macks were soon in Mobile and then on to Macon and Chattanooga. Ory and Oliver probably opted to pass on the tour because they were doing well in New Orleans and did not want to break up the group. The tour required only four men. It is probable there was more than business behind Oliver's decision not to go on the tour. According to Manetta and Ory, Oliver had fallen in love with Mary Mack. He took a job in another band backing her on nights the Ory band did not. Armstrong subbed with Ory on those nights. "She [Mary McBride] got a hold of that fast life. And I made Joe acquainted with her. Joe got crazy about her." Coincidentally, Billy Mack was arrested along with Oliver for disturbing the peace at Mack's home at 1877 Palmyra on August 1.[28] Other musicians and actors were arrested at the scene, so the gathering may have been a rehearsal.

By November 17 Lala was searching for new acts, though the Ory-Oliver band continued to play there. The buzz of activity at the First Class Theatre occurred against a backdrop of changing winds in the Storyville district. With the United States' entry into World War I, the Navy cracked down on rowdier ports of call like New Orleans. Houses of prostitution were banned within five miles of Navy bases. The district officially closed on October 10, 1917, but many houses, including Mahogany Hall, continued to operate. As late as March 1919 Lulu White declared, "New Orleans' district is not closed now, never has been closed . . . I can take you to fifty places that are running wide-open."[29] Ultimately she was made an example of and sent to Federal prison in 1919.

For the cabarets business carried on as it had before, and Ory continued playing the district well into 1919.

A staple with the band since 1912, Johnny Dodds had played with few groups outside the Ory band. He complained one day to bass player George "Pops" Foster that he had tied his fortunes too closely with one group. That is likely the reason that Dodds took a job with bandleader Fate Marable on the steamer S.S. *Sidney* upon his return from the Merrymakers tour in early 1918. He returned to the Ory-Oliver band in May 1918 at the end of the *Sidney*'s season, and was with Ory on June 19, 1918, when the band was arrested in a raid. Dodds left with the Merrymakers for another tour in July 1918 but returned by early 1919.[30] Ory went through a series of replacements, though it is hard to say in what order.

There is wide agreement that Jimmie Noone (1894–1944) "replaced" Dodds, but it was not a direct succession and his tenure with the band must have been short. Noone was on tour with the Creole Orchestra from December 1917 through at least early March 1918, and he left New Orleans again in the summer. Early in his career Noone played with Freddie Keppard in the district, and later led a band with cornetist Buddy Petit (1887–1931). His big break came when he traveled to Chicago in 1917 to join Keppard and the Creole Orchestra.[31]

The Creole Band, as they were often called, was a pioneering early New Orleans group. The original band began touring the vaudeville circuit nationally in 1914, playing New Orleans jazz to audiences who had never heard it before. The band received positive notices and clearly made an impression on people who heard them.

Noone was an inventive, fluid clarinetist with imaginative, melodic phrasing that must have been a contrast to Johnny Dodds, his stylistically rougher predecessor.

Ory and others mention various substitutes, apart from Noone, that played in the band through Johnny Dodds's absences in 1918 and 1919. Some became regular members of the band, while others filled in on occasion. Ory said these men included "Big Eye" Louis Nelson Delisle, Sidney Bechet, Wade Whaley, and George Lewis.[32]

Sidney Bechet (1897–1959) became one of the most celebrated figures in jazz. An amazing soloist, he played with power, swing, and endless melodic variations. Ory says he played with Bechet, but it could not have been in this period, as the clarinet virtuoso left New Orleans in 1917.[33]

Wade Whaley (1892–ca. 1968) was born in Jefferson City, Texas, but was a regular in New Orleans during the 1910s.[34] His playing was not that of Johnny Dodds or Jimmie Noone; he was at best a placeholder in the band. Drummer Abbey "Chinee" Foster, who played in the Ory-Oliver band around 1918, remembered Whaley being in the band.[35]

"Big Eye" Louis Nelson Delisle (1885–1949) trained under Lorenzo Tio Jr. and played in the Eagle Band. In addition to clarinet, he played banjo, bass, and accordion. He had replaced George Baquet in the Creole Band and toured with them before returning to New Orleans in 1917.[36]

Clarinetist George Lewis (1900–1968) is best known as a leading figure in the New Orleans jazz revival movement of the forties and fifties.[37] An amazing non-reading clarinetist, Lewis's style often made the clarinet sound as if it were singing.

"Chinee" Foster also remembered Albert Nicholas (1900–1973) playing in the band.[38] Nicholas was another student of Lorenzo Tio Jr. and a nephew of jazzman "Wooden" Joe Nicholas. He went into the navy in 1916 but returned to New Orleans at the end of his service. That would probably mean he played with the band no earlier than late 1918. Ory would play with Nicholas again in King Oliver's band in 1927 and his own Creole Jazz Band in the forties.

There were also personnel changes in the rhythm section. Longtime bassist Ed Garland departed by August 1917. He hooked up on a tour with the Tennessee 10, backing blackface singer Mabel Elaine in vaudeville. Ory's old clarinetist Lawrence Duhe was also on that tour. Replacing Garland on bass was about as old a jazzman as could be found in 1917. Bob Lyons (1872–1949) performed with Buddy Bolden and Frankie Duson playing guitar and banjo.[39] He operated a shoeshine stand at 323 South Rampart Street but played music by night. .

Ory featured two notable drummers while Oliver was in the band. Henry Zeno (1880–1918) had played in the Buddy Bolden band and later worked with Frankie Duson and Manuel Manetta. He was in King Oliver's band at Pete Lala's before Oliver joined Ory. "Red Happy" Bolton (1885–1928) was another favorite of Oliver's and had been a member of his Magnolia Band.[40] He joined when Oliver did.

> At the Winter Garden, which was a new spot about a block from the Roof Garden very near the jailhouse . . . right across the street from it. In fact the prisoners could hear the music all night. When it opened I was hired and business got so good that it took all the business away from the Roof Garden. The owner of the Roof Garden was very unhappy about this and did the usual thing. He called the cops. One night, the wagons backed up and we saw the sergeant and about 9 or 10 cops come out and come into the hall. It was very early for those days, just about 11 o'clock at night. The sergeant told us that no one was to move and added this is a raid. All the people were very quiet and stood there like statues as the policeman rounded up everyone . . . except the few who managed to escape. Then along came the sergeant and the policeman asked him, "What about the band?" He said "Oh I guess you better run them in too." So we all went to jail and then through night court and everyone who had it or could get it paid $2.50 bail.[41]

The Winter Garden raid took place at 11:45 p.m. on June 19, 1918.[42] Oliver, for one, was furious. Unable to placate his star cornetist, Ory instead offered him a way out. Ory had received a telegram promising work in Chicago. He passed it along to Oliver, who talked Jimmie Noone into going along. "I received an offer to take my band to Chicago, but I was doing too well in New Orleans to leave. Joe, however, along with Jimmie Noone, who was my clarinetist, decided to go up to Chicago."[43]

In other tellings of the story, it was Mutt Carey who told Oliver about the vacancy. Carey had been playing with Lawrence Duhe's band in Chicago but left because he hated the cold. The two tales are explained by the fact that Oliver took two jobs in Chicago: Oliver and Noone joined Bill Johnson's group at the Royal Gardens, while Oliver doubled in Lawrence Duhe's band at the Dreamland Cafe.[44]

It must have been a blow to Ory to loose Oliver. On a personal level, Kid Ory and Joe Oliver were the best of friends. Despite Ory's statements about Oliver's formative years as a musician, he genuinely respected Oliver and credited him with innovation and imagination. He called him "a natural" who came up with "the new style" and that was why he named him "King." When Ory gave Oliver his nickname is uncertain, but it must have been before Oliver departed New Orleans for Chicago in 1918. The next time they met, in Oakland, California, in 1921, he was billed as King Oliver.[45]

Before he left, Oliver discussed the band's future with Ory. "Joe told me before he left that he could recommend someone to take his place. I told him I appreciated his thought but that I had already picked out his replacement."[46]

It might seem obvious, particularly in hindsight, that Kid Ory would select Louis Armstrong to replace Oliver, but he had reasons not to. Louis, who everyone then called Dipper, was only sixteen years old, younger by far than anyone else in the band. Ory had already "auditioned" Louis by letting him sit in in Oliver's place; Ory said the crowd was thin and stayed outside during Louis's set, and when Oliver made his entrance the place filled up. That alone might have given Ory pause.

Further complicating matters, Armstrong did not own a cornet. Still, Ory decided to place his faith in Armstrong. Armstrong remembered running into Ory when he went to the train station to see Oliver off.

The minute the train started to pull out I was on my way out of the Illinois Central Station to my [coal] cart—when Kid Ory called to me. "You still blowin' that cornet?" he hollered. I ran back. He said he'd heard a lot of talk about Little Louis. "Hmmm . . ." I pricked up my ears. He said that when the boys in the band found out for sure that Joe Oliver was leaving, they told him to go get Little Louis to take Joe's place. He was a little in doubt at first, but after he'd looked around the town he decided I was the right one to have a try at taking that great man's place. So he told me to go wash up and then come play a gig with them that very same night. What a thrill that was! To think I was considered up to taking Joe Oliver's lace in the best band in town![47]

Ory was furthered swayed by his estimation of Louis's potential and enthusiasm. "There were many good, experienced trumpet players in town, but none with of them had young Louis' possibilities. I went to see him and told him that if he got himself a pair of long trousers I'd give him a job. Within two hours, Louis came to my house and said, 'Here I am. I'll be glad when eight o'clock comes. I'm ready to go.'"

Ory bought a horn for Louis to play and he used it to it full effect. Armstrong proved the perfect understudy for Oliver, as he knew many of the band's tunes and arrangements. Armstrong makes Ory out to be a benevolent figure in the telling of the story.

The first night I played with Kid Ory's band, the boys were so surprised they could hardly play their instruments for listening to me blow up a storm. But I wasn't frightened one bit. I was doing everything exactly the way I heard Joe Oliver do it. At least I tried to. I even put a big towel around my neck when the band played a ball down at Economy Hall. That was the first thing Joe always did—he'd put a bath towel around his

neck and open up his collar underneath so's he could blow free
and easy. And because I'd listened to Joe all the time he was
with Kid Ory, I knew almost everything the band played, by
ear anyway. I could catch on real fast.

Kid Ory was so nice and kind, and he had so much pa-
tience, that first night with them was a pleasure instead of a
drag. After that first gig with the Kid I was in.[48]

Ory's instinct about Armstrong's potential proved correct. He
was emerging as a musician in his own right and it was paying div-
idends for the band. "After he joined me, Louis improved so fast it
was amazing. He had a wonderful ear and a wonderful memory.
All you had to do was to hum or whistle a new tune to him and
he'd know it right away. And if he played a tune once, he never forgot it. Within six months, everybody in New Orleans knew about
him."[49]

Armstrong knew what he had playing in the Ory band, which
was to play the music he loved and get paid well for it. At the time
he viewed his membership in the Ory band as his arrival, calling
the band "the cream of the crop."[50]

I was looking forward to bigger things, especially since Kid Ory
had given me the chance to play the music I really wanted to
play. And that was all kinds of music from jazz to waltzes.

Then Kid Ory really did get a lot of gigs. He even started
giving his own dances, Monday nights downtown at the Econ-
omy Hall. Monday night was a slow night in New Orleans at
that time, and we didn't get much work other places. But Kid
Ory did so well at the Economy Hall that he kept it up for
months and made a lot of dough for himself. He paid us well
too.[51]

Armstrong took in a kaleidoscope of jobs working for Ory,
from the New Orleans Country Club to brass band parades. Louis

relished his new gig, saying, "Yea I was a proud youngster playing in Kid Ory's band."[52] To that end, Armstrong recalled one instructive tale of a funeral where he and Ory played as substitutes with John Robichaux's brass band. Unlike the gut-bucket Ory band, the Robichaux men read music. Some had been slow to warm to the new hot style of playing and looked down on non-reading musicians like Ory and Armstrong. Armstrong recalled:

After we reached the cemetery, and they lowered the body six feet in the ground, and the drummer man rolled on the drums they struck up a ragtime march which required swinging from the band. And those old fossils just couldn't cut it. That's when we Ory boys took over and came in with flying colors.

After that incident those stuck-up guys wouldn't let us alone. They patted us on the back and just wouldn't let us alone. They hired us several times afterward. After all, we's proved to them that any learned musician can read music, but they can't all swing. It was a good lesson for them.[53]

While the old divisions between the downtown Creole bands and the uptown gut-bucket bands continued, by 1918 they had become irrelevant because Creoles born in the mid-1880s and after—like Jelly Roll Morton, Sidney Bechet, Jimmie Noone, and the members of the Original Creole Orchestra—fully embraced jazz as their music. Whatever stylistic variations may have remained between this young generation of Creoles and the uptown musicians were now in the context of a common music and, ultimately, common bands. Ory's group regularly featured both Creole trained, reading musicians, like Emile Bigard, Manuel Manetta and Johnny St. Cyr, and gut-bucket players like Johnny Dodds, Mutt Carey, and Louis Armstrong. In this context, the old labels lost their significance.

With the Armistice in Europe November 11, 1918, Ory was sent home from his day job working at a shipyard on Poland Avenue in the Ninth Ward. Shipyard workers had been exempt from the draft, and that may have been one of Ory's reasons for working there. Ory said he was so happy that the war ended that he jumped atop a streetcar. He had cause for joy. The music scene, particularly at the cabarets, had been shut down for much of the summer due to the war.[54] That joy was no doubt tamped down by the arrival of the Spanish Flu pandemic. It raced through the population of New Orleans in the fall and early winter, killing hundreds of people, including Ory's sister Lizzie, who passed on New Year's Day 1919. Eventually the flu subsided, and New Orleans' music scene came back to life.

When Ory's former violinist Manuel Manetta mustered out of the army in early 1919, he stopped by Pete Lala's First Class Theatre to check up on the band. He said it was a cold night and Armstrong was on the stand freezing wearing a straw hat to try and keep warm.[55] He exchanged greetings with his old bandmates and regaled them with tales of army life that never took Manetta further than Arkansas.

When trumpeter Ernest "Punch" Miller returned to New Orleans after his army service, he heard the Ory band at the Big 25. Punch sat in and played two numbers, including the war's anthem "Over There," which the Ory men were oddly unfamiliar with. The boys kidded Armstrong about Punch's outstanding playing and Louis got mad and threatened to quit. As it was, Louis was looking to move on anyway.[56]

On a Monday night in early 1919, bandleader Fate Marable dropped in at a dance in New Orleans at the Cooperator's Hall and heard Kid Ory's band playing "Honky Tonky Town." Marable led the orchestra on the Streckfus steamer *Sidney*. The boat wintered in New Orleans but spent the summer months up north. Fate asked who was playing the trumpet.[57] Armstrong remembered: "Fate's (band) had a wide range and they played all the latest music because they could read at sight. Kid Ory's band could catch on a tune quickly, and once they had it no one could out play them. But

I wanted to do more than fake the music all the time because there is more to music than playing just one style."[58]

The musical education Armstrong enjoyed in the Ory band cannot be underestimated. It was the right band at the right time in Louis's development as a musician. Being a member of the band opened to a larger world for Louis, giving him an opportunity to nurture and develop his talent. Playing with Fate Marable was the next logical step. Ory helped make that possible. In May, Louis left Kid Ory's band and traveled by train to St. Louis to join Marable and play the summer season aboard the S.S. *Sidney* up north. Ory filled the trumpet chair with "Punch" Miller and Henry "Kid" Rena.[59]

Ernest "Punch" Miller (1894–1971) was born in Raceland, Louisiana, and started playing in New Orleans after his discharge from the army in 1919. He knew the men in the band, and when the chair opened up he joined Kid Ory. Kid Rena (1898–1949), who Ory said was his last cornetist in New Orleans, spent time at the Colored Waif's Home with Louis Armstrong and later studied with Creole cornetist Manuel Perez.[60]

While the artistic heyday of the Kid Ory band of New Orleans was now behind it, it remained a successful band. This begs the question: why did Ory leave? Ory had received offers to go to Chicago or on the road and, so far, had passed.

Writers have opined that the migration of New Orleans musicians, most notably to Chicago, was a result of everything from Jim Crow to higher wages to the closing of Storyville. With regard to musicians, the impending federal enforcement of Prohibition in New Orleans probably factored in as well.[61] Hundreds of bars would be raided by year's end, and it was clear that change was coming to the city's night scene. The freewheeling days of the honky-tonks and cabarets were over. The New Orleans *Item* carried stories of longtime Storyville proprietors like Anthony Martin of the Gem Saloon and L. A. Abadie of Abadie's Cabaret being forced to close in the fall of 1919. "The flow 2.75% beer throughout the

United States must stop Oct. 26. And in New Orleans 967 saloons which survive out of the city's original 1200 must either close their doors or confine their sales to (soft) drinks."[62]

Still, Ory may have survived the crack-down given the variety of jobs he had around the city. Certainly his work at hotels and private clubs, as well as the dances he sponsored, would have been enough to sustain the band. Ory's final undoing in New Orleans came when he crossed Pete Lala, his longtime benefactor, in a business deal.

Lala, impressed with Ory's success at sponsoring dances, and facing reduced revenue because of the closing of the district, decided to go into business with him sponsoring dances. After some time, Ory, dissatisfied with the deal, quit and returned to sponsoring his own dances claiming Lala's place was too small to turn a profit. Lala, who apparently had influence with the police, got Ory's dances raided. While there are no records of the police actions in 1919, Manuel Manetta confirmed that the police shut Ory down. Speaking of Lala, Ory said, "He had the power."[63]

> Pete got a little peeved with me because I had left him. Evidently he was more than just peeved I found out later. One night after I went back to Cooperator's Hall I had a big dance going full swing. The place was packed, jammed. About 25 cops came in, not saying a word to anyone. They just walked in and stood around. In about 10 minutes there was none left but me and the band. That made it tough. I said to myself "this is it." I knew who had sent the police, no one but Pete Lala would have bothered. In fact, right after that, I found out that he said that anyplace I opened; he would see to it that I was raided.[64]

Eventually, Ory's life must have been threatened, as he recalled his reason for leaving New Orleans was, "I was afraid I going to lose my health." In a hurry to get out of town, he asked his wife

Dort if she wanted to go to Chicago or California. She picked California.[65]

The night before he left, Ory and the band gathered around a long table at Ben Mulligan's Saloon on Perdido Street. They drank whiskey, beer, and Sweet Lucy and made great plans for the future.[66] After a few drinks, Kid Ory, Johnny Dodds, Louis Armstrong, who had returned to New Orleans after a summer with Fate Marable, and Joe Lindsay, the band's most recent drummer, fell to their knees and swore they were going to California. The plan was Ory would go first, secure work, and then send for the band.

On a Friday evening in mid-August 1919, Kid Ory and his wife boarded the train for Los Angeles.[67] "With the nightmare of constant raids staring in my face, I knew I'd never make it and decided not to operate anymore and it wasn't long after that I made up my mind to leave New Orleans for the West Coast."[68]

CHAPTER 8

1919–1925
CALIFORNIA

∞∞

Edward and Elizabeth Ory stepped off the train in August 1919 into a Los Angeles already brimming with transplants from Louisiana. Ads in California's black newspapers like the *California Eagle* and *Western Outlook* carried notices and ads for the Louisiana Commercial Association, the Creole Human Hair Company, and the Louisiana Creole Club. There were even groups that celebrated Mardi Gras with formal balls.

Many African Americans from the South pulled up stakes and moved to California around the same time Ory did. Why Los Angeles? During a short visit somewhere between 1908 and 1910, Jelly Roll Morton had found that not much was happening musically in California except in Oxnard, which he called "a very fast-stepping town."[1] Ory's move may have had less to do with music and more to do with a massive exodus of people from the South to the country's major population centers. Ory's move, and those of Oliver, Armstrong, and many other musicians in the so-called "New Orleans musical diaspora," were all part of the Great Migration of 1915–29, when southern blacks moved to major urban areas, particularly Chicago and New York but also Los Angeles. The reasons included education and employment opportunities, and a chance to escape Jim Crow.

Set against the background of the Great Migration, the travels of New Orleans jazzmen "takes on epic proportions at times, in the sense that it is the embodiment of the story of the African-American people at that time, moving relentlessly from place to place, trying to make a new life—trying to find a voice for a tradition that began on the shores of west Africa with the slave trade and arrived in the twentieth century with a migration that was itself an odyssey."[2]

Their new communities did not always greet the new arrivals with open arms. Restrictive neighborhood covenants, social discrimination, and segregated facilities were all familiar relics from the South that were very much in evidence in California when Ory arrived. Darker-skinned women were refused service at clothing stores, and some restaurants insisted blacks use the back entrance. In 1920 a third of "employed males worked as janitors, porters, waiters, or house servants. Los Angeles did not have as many industrial jobs as northeastern cities, and blacks were largely relegated to the position of laborer." "Blacks were virtually absent from retail trade and non-professional white-collar jobs—the largest area of employment in the city. In 1920 Los Angeles had 11,341 salesmen, 28 of whom were black."[3]

By the 1920s African Americans had expanded into previously white areas, most notably the Central Avenue area, where "older residents in [this] community moved southward, displacing over half of the white residents and leaving their old houses to the new arrivals." Ory and his wife settled in this neighborhood, living first at 1533 E. 21 Street in 1920, then at 919 E. 32 Street by 1922. They later bought a house a block off Central Avenue at 1001 E. 33 Street, which they owned until the forties.[4]

Soon after his arrival, Ory ran into a man named Pops Saunders who offered him a job cooking for transit workers. Ory had often worked jobs outside of music in New Orleans, so it was not unusual that he would seek employment. Los Angeles was in the throes of a transit strike, which was threatening to shut down the city, and the company had hired replacement workers to keep the buses and streetcars moving. The workers were being housed for their safety, and Saunders was looking for someone to feed them. Ory, as anyone who knew him would confirm, was a celebrated cook who in later years included recipes in the liner notes of his records. He was something of a rube when it came to organized labor, though knew he would be viewed as a strike-breaker. Still, he agreed to the job.

He [Saunders] was quite a politician here at that time and he was looking for men to work. They were having a big strike in Los Angeles and were looking for cooks, waiters and dishwashers plus pantry boys and everyone that belongs in a kitchen unit. He said to me, "Young man, you're all dressed up there. Are you looking for a job?" I said, "No, not exactly, I just arrived here last night." He said, "Well, do you care to work?" I said, "It depends on what kind of work." I thought to myself, it might be something good and I can pick up a few bucks right quick. Mr. Saunders told me, "There's a big strike coming off tomorrow and we need some men." Naturally I didn't know anything about a union, as I had never been a member of a union and I asked him what he had to offer. He said, "I want a chef on down to the eighth cook" in the one particular place he had in mind. I told him, "I'd rather be a chef. What do you pay?" He told me, "Eleven dollars a day, but remember, you have to stay on the premises." I asked him, "Why?" "Well," he said, "you may get hurt if you leave the building alone." I said, "You mean I'd be a strikebreaker." He answered, "Yes, that what you would be called." He added, "Lots of them are going to break it. They're going to work. I've plenty of them signed up already. The streetcars have to run." I thought it over and finally decided I might as well make that money . . . it was right there for me . . . and I accepted the job as a chef and went to the building at Seventh and Central Avenue. There we were feeding fourteen hundred people a day. I was the chef all right. I had seven cooks under me and just the steward over me. I had a man to cut each different kind of meat. At breakfast, I had one cook who fried only eggs and another who only did potatoes, one for bacon and the others right down the line with whatever we served for breakfasts. I stayed on the job until the strike was nearly over and someone told a promoter that I was in town and the promoter asked where he could locate me. His informant also told him that I had taken the job merely because it was some quick money that I felt I should pick up. The promoter secured permission to enter our building and he came to see me.[5]

Promoter Lee Locking set up Ory at the Cadillac, a cabaret and nightclub, which was down the street from the Texas and Pacific railway station at Fifth and Central avenues. Various other entertainers were employed there, and bands likely played for the floorshow.[6]

He asked me if I would send for my orchestra when the strike was over. We could do business. I asked him what he was offering for the band and he told me, and I answered that it wasn't enough money and, naturally, he came to my terms. I said to him, "By the way, you want me to send for and get my boys here? There's a little matter of some transportation money." He said, "All right", and planked down five hundred dollars. I got off that night and deposited the five hundred dollars in an all-night bank.[7]

Ory sent for pianist Manuel Manetta and paid for tickets for Armstrong, Dodds, and Joe Lindsay. After all, they had sworn on their knees at their meeting at Ben Mulligan's that they were going to California together. However, it was not to be. Johnny Dodds's wife pitched a fit about the trip and would not let Manetta deliver the tickets. The porters at the train depot may have furthered Dodds's trepidation by saying he would be sent home in disgrace because he could not read music. Joe Lindsay's wife reacted the same way as Dodds's wife, and that doomed the trip. Both Dodds and Armstrong said they would not go without Joe.[8]

Vexed and worried about how Ory would react, Manetta secured Mutt Carey, Wade Whaley, and Alfred Williams—all alumni of the Ory band in New Orleans—and caught the train with them to Los Angeles.[9] A nervous Manetta was the first to grab his bags and disembark so that he could explain the band situation to Ory. Manetta had not told the boys that they were not Ory's first choices, and he wanted to make sure Ory did not either. Before Manetta could reach him, Ory spotted Mutt's familiar face and figured out what had happened.

The timing for his band's arrival was perfect; the group played that very night to a packed house. When the New Orleans folks heard Ory was in town, he was an instant draw. Manual Manetta said, "We played and played." "We really did very well there. Business was good," Ory remembered. Drummer Alfred Williams said of the band's performance, "They [the Ory band] played the same thing they were playing here [New Orleans]—jazz. They [the California audiences] went wild over it. They had never heard that." Mutt Carey concurred, saying, "People could sit down—they saw that what they'd been listening to was a lot of tin cans rattlin', and they fell for our music like a baby falls for milk."[10]

To advertise the band's arrival and its gig at the Cadillac, Ory resorted to the promotional device that had served him so well in New Orleans: the advertising truck. The band, complete with piano, rode a truck down Central Avenue past the train station and ultimately to the front door of the Cadillac, playing the old New Orleans favorite "Brown Skin Who You For?" Manual Manetta remembered people busting open their doors to get out and see the band. Ory said, "We didn't get to Hollywood, but news got out there, you know? The movie stars came."[11]

One of the attractions of the Cadillac was that it was a black and tan (mixed-race) club. This social progression attracted the attention of the Los Angeles police, who were apparently willing to tolerate the club so long as black men did not dance with white women. The club owner, Rich Baker, ignored the warning, and the police raided the Cadillac shortly after the band's opening. Baker managed to get it open again, only for it to be raided a second time in early 1920 and shut down completely. Manuel Manetta, who had come from New Orleans specifically for the Cadillac gig, left after the second raid, which he said was four months after he arrived in the fall of 1919. Manetta's mother was ailing back in New Orleans and she wanted her son home.[12]

Prior to Ory's migration, the most successful jazz group in Los Angeles was the Black and Tan Orchestra, which played the Cadillac as early as 1916. Jelly Roll Morton recalled the band, which he played with on occasion: "Previously [they] had a band playing there when I went to the Cadillac. The band was named the Black and Tan Band—that's the name [they] had taken. They had no fame at all—juss a band consisting of four pieces: trumpet n trombone n drums n piano. But they didn't have a regla piano player; they picked up anybody that could halfway [play]."[13]

The leader of the group was trombonist Harry Southard. The band apparently formed in Texas around 1914 or 1915, and added "Jazz" to their name in 1917. Despite the group's longevity, it was apparently behind the curve when it came to playing hot jazz. Ory drummer Alfred Williams recalled, "The Black and Tan was the best band there. They tried to play New Orleans style but they just didn't have the style."[14] Williams also observed: "They [Black and Tan] was a reading band. It was a puzzle to them to see how Ory played different numbers in different keys even though he didn't know music. One night Ory went to a place where they were playing. The people there asked Ory to sit in. Harry Southern [the band's leader] took his trombone and put it in his case at intermission. Wouldn't let Ory play it."[15]

Manetta remembered another episode a while later at the Dreamland Club, when the Black and Tan Orchestra invited Ory to sit in: "So one Sunday night Ory was in the Dreamland, a little high or something, and they got him on the bandstand. The first number Ory was supposed to play with them was unfamiliar, both the key and the arrangement, and they went into it so quickly that Kid Ory was lost. But the next number was 'Tiger Rag' and that was it!"[16]

By early 1920 Ory secured a regular job at the Dreamland, a black-owned establishment at Fourth and Stanford run by a man named Hite. Eventually the Spikes Brothers acquired the club. Johnny and Reb Spikes were a musical and entrepreneurial force on the scene at Los Angeles's Central Avenue in the 1920s. Hailing from Muskogee, Oklahoma, they operated an open-air playhouse there in the mid-1910s employing musicians like Jelly Roll Morton. After their move to Los Angeles in 1918, they opened the Spikes Brothers Music Store at 1703 Central Avenue, which became the center of black musical activity for over a decade.[17] Musicians would go there to line up gigs and find out about tours and casting calls for the movies. Reb Spikes recalled:

> At the time we had no colored union. Whenever someone wanted a band, they would call the store. We always could get a band together for them because most of the musicians in town spent a lot of time in the shop . . . we always knew who was available. We had as many as seven or eight bands working at a time. Johnny did most of the arranging for our bands—in addition to teaching piano, trumpet, and sax."[18]

As musicians the Spikes brothers were nothing, special according to the often-critical Jelly Roll Morton, who dismissed them as "corn fed." As men in the music business, they "wisely conceded the preeminence of those [New Orleans] musicians as musicians, and took over everything else." To this end the brothers employed Jelly Roll Morton, Ory, and other New Orleans musicians on the scene in Los Angeles. Ory first met the Spikes while playing at the Cadillac.[19]

The band did a good business at the Dreamland until about March 1921, when the police raided it for race-mixing. Alfred Williams recalled that the police told the Spikes brothers to cut out the dancing between black men and white women. When Reb said it was not against the law, the cops handcuffed him and closed the place."[20]

With the Dreamland gig over, the Ory band reconstituted in Oakland to perform at the Creole Café at 1740 Seventh Street. Mutt Carey had gone into business with drummer Curtis Mosby selling instruments at a storefront location a block from the Creole Café. He likely pushed for Mosby to replace Alfred Williams, who was sent packing to New Orleans that spring. Mosby had been born in Kansas City, Missouri, in 1895 and had moved to California about the same time as Ory. In the twenties he would tour with Mamie Smith and record with his band the Blue Blowers. Later he worked as a California music promoter. Despite his relationship with Mutt Carey, Mosby was not with the band for long, and soon drummer Ben Borders joined the group. Borders was born in 1893 in Waxahachie, Texas, south of Dallas, and moved to Los Angeles in the late teens or early twenties after performing in circus bands. He worked with New Orleans native and Creole Band member Dink Johnson before joining Ory.[21]

A succession of pianists filled in after Manetta's departure, including New Orleans native Fred Washington; L. Z. Cooper, a Los Angeles theatre pianist; and Madeline Carey, Mutt's wife whom he met in Los Angeles. Wade Whaley remained on clarinet.

Sidney Deering was the proprietor of the Creole Café and Major Smith was general manager. The venue offered "Dancing every afternoon, including Sunday from 2–7 pm. All refreshments .25." Reb Spikes said the club opened about 1920, remembering that it was not open in 1919 when he played downtown Oakland. Conversely, drummer Charlie "Duke" Turner recalled: "The Creole Café opened about 1918 or 1919, and . . . at that time, it was supposed to be one of the prettiest places this side of the Rockies."

Turner continued, "Ory was big stuff when he was playing trombone at the Creole Café." Indeed a report in the *Western Appeal* said the club was crowded nightly.[22]

Meanwhile, Ory secured a gig for his old friend King Oliver at the Pergola Dancing Pavilion at 949 Market Street in San Francisco. The owner liked the Ory band and wanted to hire them, but Ory's group had a full schedule at the Creole Café and the Iroquois Theatre in Oakland. Ory sent for Oliver, who left Chicago May 21, 1921, with a band that included Lil Hardin, piano; Jimmy Palao, violin; David Jones, saxophone; Minor Hall, drums; Johnny Dodds, clarinet; Honore Dutry, trombone; and Ed Garland, bass. Oliver and his wife Stella moved into an apartment at 45 Garden Avenue in San Francisco.[23]

The band opened at the Pergola on June 12, 1921, and the job lasted until early 1922. Minor Hall quit by August, but elected to stay in California and played with Ory. Oliver sent to St. Louis for drummer Warren "Baby" Dodds to replace Hall, resulting in a fine from the union since he did not first seek permission before making the move. Baby Dodds would also play in Ory's band.

By year's end, Dutry, Palao, and Lil Hardin had quit the Oliver band and returned to Chicago. Ory became a regular substitute in the Oliver band. One of the gigs Ory played with King Oliver was a Mardi Gras Ball held by the Louisiana Commercial Association at Oakland Municipal Auditorium on February 28, 1922. The event was advertised on the front page of the *Oakland Sunshine* newspaper. After this, work slowed down for Oliver; he relocated to Los Angeles, but was not able to establish a regular residency—bouncing instead from country club dances to fraternal halls. By June, Oliver was back in Chicago, though without bassist Ed Garland, who opted to stay in California with Ory.[24]

Beginning in the spring of 1922, Kid Ory's career is traced in great detail by columnist, vaudevillian, and promoter Ragtime Billy Tucker in the pages of the *Chicago Defender* via a column called

"Coast Dope." Tucker's column follows Ory through his live appearances, radio broadcasts, and the making of his first records. There was no line between journalist and promoter, and Tucker served in the role of both for the Ory band—writing up the very gigs that he himself was promoting. Be that as it may, for the first time there is consistent, contemporaneous coverage of Ory's career, his band, and its activities. Through Tucker's column, Ory's local performances received a national spotlight. At the very least, Tucker provides a window into the steady work of a band at the height of the jazz age.

One prominent place the Ory band played was Leak's Lake, also known as the Wayside Amusement Park, in Watts. Reb Spikes said he opened Leak's Lake in the summer of 1921 a few months after the Dreamland was closed.[25] Spikes remembered: "I went out to Watts and bought some lots, I built a dance hall on those lots and called it Leak's Lake. The lake was nothing but a frog pond; a guy named Leak raised bull frogs there. The hall was built about 1921. It was about 100 feet long; the band stand and refreshment bar took up twenty feet and left about 80 by 50 feet for dancing."[26]

The site was an amusement park with a dance hall connected to it. During the day it catered to private parties and promoted the recreational side of the park. On Saturday and Sunday nights, it was a dance hall. An ad dated June 24, 1921 in the *California Eagle* shows that Spikes thought of Leak's Lake as a hall for rent, encouraging those needing a location for "Church picnics, lodges or private parties" to call for bookings. Another ad mentions a labor union picnic that was to be held there.[27]

Reb Spikes recalled: "I had a merry go round out there for the kids, and I had concessions—drinks and souvenirs and things on the outside that a couple of fellows rented for—you know, they sold souvenirs and things on the outside. Was going to have a regular little park out there but it didn't pan out so good." Jelly Roll Morton recalled playing Leak's Lake:

> *The man who ran Leak's Lake out in Watts [Spikes] used to
> hire me to play piano. Watts was an after-hours place; they
> didn't open until 11 o'clock. There was gambling and they sold
> whiskey [during Prohibition]. They had tables and a place to
> dance. All the sporting class of people from Los Angeles and
> Hollywood came out there after one o'clock at night. It would
> be loaded with white people and black people and stayed
> open until five or six in the morning.*[28]

These two remembrances paint a very different picture of the
same place. Though Spikes sought to emphasize his dream for
what the place might have been (a full-scale amusement park), in
the end, it was primarily a dance hall.

Ragtime Billy Tucker announced the Ory band's arrival from
Oakland to play at Wayside Park: "Kid Ory's Original Creole Orchestra is also among the new arrivals in the city, and were a great
attraction in Oakland. They are here for an indefinite stay and open
tonight at Wayside Amusement Park, formerly, Leak's Lake."[29] Apparently the Ory band continued to live in Oakland as late as July;
a notice in the *California Eagle* mentions Mr. And Mrs. Ory of
Oakland visiting the Zanders of Los Angeles on July 1, 1922.[30]

In the spring of 1922, the Spikes Brothers hatched a plan with
Hollywood Bowl manager, opera tenor, and recording studio
owner Arne Nordskog to make a series of records. Nordskog had
opened his Santa Monica recording studio in 1921, initially to record classical artists he was introducing to West Coast audiences.
The Spikes brothers' idea was to make records that would feature their compositions and sell them in their store. Reb Spikes
recalled: "Back in those days our store was the only place in Los
Angeles where recordings by black artists could be purchased. As
a result we did a huge record business. We decided to make our
own records to sell in the store."[31]

The Spikes decided to try and get Ory's band to accompany
two local singers—Roberta Dudley and Ruth Lee—singing Spikes

brothers compositions. An early notice in Tucker's column in the *Chicago Defender* said one of the singers would be Caroline Williams, but she is not mentioned in later notices. The session probably took place in May 1922, as this notice in the *Chicago Defender* on May 27 bears out: "Last week they [the Spikes Brothers] sent to Oakland for Kid Ory's Famous Creole Jazz Band to make their first records."[32] Ory recalled the session, saying: "They were made out on Santa Monica near the beach. The studio was just a small room. Nothing fancy. We made them all in one day—one afternoon."

Though he had no previous experience with audio engineering, Frank Lockwood (Nordskog's father-in-law) built the recording machine that Ory's band played into on that spring day. It was an imperfect contraption that broke down throughout the session. To make the record, musicians stood in front of a series of megaphones stationed in cubicles that transmitted the music to a vibrating needle, which cut directly into a spinning wax disc while a technician cranked the machine throughout.

Arne Nordskog remembered meeting Kid Ory the night before the session and playing a prank on him: "I met Kid Ory and his band at a nightspot to arrange Ory's first recordings in 1922. The date was set for 8:00 am the next morning. 'How should I dress?' asked Ory. 'Tux!' cried his trumpet player. Sure enough, came Ory and his tuxedo at 8:00 am sharp, just ahead of the milkman, to play into the horns that could not see, and to no end of kidding by his fellow players."[33]

A hitch in the recording session was that Ory's regular clarinetist, Wade Whaley, was not able to make it. Pianist and former Creole Band drummer Dink Johnson was pressed into service on clarinet. The Spikes had co-composed "Krooked Blues" with Johnson, so that might have had an influence on his presence at the session; and he apparently made his presence felt, tapping his foot so loudly during recording that they put a mattress under his feet.[34]

The other members of the band were Mutt Carey, trumpet; Ben Borders, drums; Fred Washington, piano; and Ed Garland, bass.

Ben Borders was relegated to playing wood block, as drums did not record very well on the primitive recording gear. Likewise, Ed Garland's bass is inaudible. Garland later complained, "There wasn't room for me near one of those large [recording] horns. Ben Border's drums were too loud and you can't hear the bass."[35] Ory, Carey, and Johnson come through very clearly, as does the piano at times, particularly on the vocal performances.

The musicians recorded six songs, four of which were backing the singers. These included Roberta Dudley singing "Krooked Blues" and "When You're Alone Blues," and Ruth Lee doing "Maybe Some Day" and "That Sweet Something Dear." Billy Tucker's column mentions that the band would record the Spike brothers' "Someday, Sweetheart"—a tune Jelly Roll Morton also claimed. he Spikes and Morton had been in a row over the song, and the Spikes may have decided to skip it to avoid a problem with Jelly over royalties.

To Arne Nordskog, the session offered a chance to check out his equipment and maybe make a little money for his fledgling enterprise. He saw the Spikes as talent agents who agreed to buy his product wholesale for distribution at their store. To the Spikes brothers, they were the producers and investors in a project meant to highlight their song publishing and boost record sales at their Central Avenue store. They likely also appreciated the prestige factor in producing the West Coast's first jazz records, as evidenced by their fictitious press release announcing they were building a phonograph factory.

Ory had other ideas. Fearing the singers were drowning out the band, he convinced the parties to let him make two instrumental recordings. The Spikes, knowing the popularity of the Ory band, probably figured it was a good move; and it likely did not matter to Nordskog. The band recorded Ory's composition, "Ory's Creole Trombone," and a Spikes brothers tune, "Society Blues."[36]

In later remembrances, it is clear Ory was very proud of having made the Sunshine/Nordskog sessions in 1922. And while he may have not understood the import of his recordings at the time, he certainly understood the influence and reach that musical recordings could have. He had, after all, watched as the jazz craze swept the country in the wake of the Original Dixieland Jazz Band recordings of 1917.

When the session was over, the Ory men boarded the train back to Oakland, each $20 richer. The wax master recordings were then sent back east to be electro-plated, to produce a nickel stamper from which the records would be pressed. The finished 78 RPM records would be just weeks away.[37]

On June 2, 1922, the Spike brothers put on a major jazz and blues show at the Gaumet Auditorium in Los Angeles on a Friday night, featuring Ory's band, Ruth Lee, and Roberta Dudley. The show was meant to highlight the recording of the Sunshine records. Ragtime Billy Tucker wrote: ". . . Kid Ory's famous Creole band, which made the first records for Spikes Brothers. The band offered a number from the pen of Mr. Ory, entitled, 'Ory's Creole Trombone.' Then they played 'Maybe Someday,' which was successfully featured by Ms. Ruth Lee. Who is after the laurels of Mamie Smith, and who in a manner of speaking has as much chance as anyone else that I know."[38]

The hype surrounding the recording sessions, the Ory band's emerging popularity in celebrity circles, and the Spikes brothers' contacts combined to get Ory's Sunshine Orchestra, as they were being called, a shot at a series of live radio broadcasts beginning on June 27, 1922. The *Los Angeles Examiner* operated radio station KWH and was promoting the new technology—even giving away radio sets for every ten new newspaper subscriptions sold.[39]

Ory's Sunshine Orchestra, a Negro organization famous for original productions of Negro melodies, jazz, blues and instrumental numbers will entertain radio fans from the Examiner *station KWH this afternoon beginning at 5:30 p.m. This organization, together with other Los Angeles Negro talent, is*

producing phonograph records, which have won wide popu-
larity, especially with motion picture and theatrical people,
and promote to make Los Angeles a center of this typical
American music.

Aside from the orchestra, made up of expert players, there
are other artists on the program today, Miss Ruth Lee and Ro-
berta Dudley, singers who have made many hits in the past.

The music to be played and sung this afternoon is original
being composed by Spikes Brothers. The numbers are "Some-
day, Sweetheart," "When it's Too Late," "Krooked Blues," "May-
be Some Day" and many other hits composed by the Spikes
Brothers.

The Spikes Brothers Phonograph Company [at] 1203 Cen-
tral Avenue is turning more records, which will be released at
an early date.[40]

Ory said he found broadcasting intimidating: "We all got up
there and started trembling. We thought that everybody was hearing us all over the world. We played three or four sessions. The
second time we started playing pretty good. I guess we were the
first New Orleans style band to make a radio broadcast too."[41]

Reaction to the broadcast was positive, as carried in the *Examin-*
er's pages. "Ory's Sunshine Orchestra was wonderful and was heard
very distinctly and loudly on our radio," wrote Mrs. J. D. Coles of
Covina, California. C. H. Lieby of Los Angeles wrote the *Examiner,*
saying: "The colored band from Central Avenue on your radio the
other evening were just splendid. Could hear every instrument as
plain as if in the next room."[42]

By early July, 5,000 pressings of Ory's records had been cranked
out. A few went on sale in Chicago and there was moderate interest. But back in Los Angeles they flew off the shelves. "Every
Sunshine record passed over the counter of our shop. When the
5,000 were gone, we didn't order any more," Reb Spikes remembered. In comparison to the Columbia Record Company, it was a

respectable run of records. For example, a 1925 Columbia recording of "Fo' Day Blues" by the Original Jazz Hounds stamped 4,400 copies on the first run, and 2,500 on the second.[43] Ethel Waters's "Go Back Where you Stayed Last Night"/"Down Home Blues" had an initial printing of 5,275, followed by 2,000 more. Both would be considered successful records, as they outsold their initial runs.

Seen in this context, it is noteworthy that a little independent record label in Los Angeles had a print run that was equal to or exceeded a typical pressing of the country's second largest record company. Of course, the six Ory recordings were issued as three distinct records. The assumption about the Ory records has always been that they were distributed in such small numbers that they had little influence, but to have 5,000 records by one band distributed primarily in one city meant that the Sunshine records qualified at least as a local hit.

To whom the recordings belonged became a point of contention between the Spikes and Arne Nordskog, who asserted: "The Spikes Brothers . . . arranged for Kid Ory's band to make the recordings at the Nordskog Laboratories in Santa Monica. They were released under the Nordskog label throughout the world, with the Spikes ordering a great number for sale in their own store, where they sold like hotcakes to the Negro trade."[44] Indeed, all the pressings of Kid Ory's 1922 Sunshine sessions are on the Nordskog label, which strangely identifies the band as Ory's Seven Pods of Pepper. From Nordskog's point of view, the band had recorded for his company and it was appropriate that they be affiliated with his label. That is not how Reb Spikes appreciated the session. He thought Nordskog was making the records for the Spikes brothers. "For some reason Nordskog put his label on our records. He called Ory's Sunshine Orchestra The Seven Pods of Pepper . . . he had no business doing this—they were our property! We had contracted for 5,000 pressings that should have had our Sunshine label. We had to paste our label over his. They had to be oversize and almost covered the last grooves!"[45]

The Spikes brothers' Sunshine label proclaims "Manuf. By Spikes Brothers Phonograph Co. Inc. Los Angeles." This is in line with a notice in Ragtime Billy Tucker's column of May 20, 1922, which announces, "Spikes Brothers building phonograph factory." This bit of fiction was nothing more than self-promotion as the brothers never built a phonograph company and certainly did not manufacture the Sunshine Records themselves.

Though Nordskog and Reb Spikes agreed that the record sold out in Los Angeles, there was ultimately a disagreement over money. Nordskog contended that the Spikes failed to pay for their records and won a judgment in Los Angeles Superior Court.[46] The Spikes' refusal to pay may have grown out of frustration over the label issue.

The Kid Ory recordings of 1922 are, at the very least, a milepost in the continuum of New Orleans jazz band recordings that began in 1917 with the Original Dixieland Jazz Band, and would continue with King Oliver's Creole Jazz Band in 1923. "Ory's Creole Trombone" is significant, in part, because it is an ensemble piece from beginning to end with all the players engaged throughout. A performance for the ages? No, but an instructive snapshot in time to have of an important jazz figure and his band. In this light, "Ory's Creole Trombone" presents the very essence of Ory the bandleader; ensemble passages framed by solo breaks resolving through a series of strains. The out chorus of "Ory's Creole Trombone" is an outstanding example of New Orleans jazz polyphony, comparable to the recordings of the ODJB. Unlike the ODJB, Ory's band turns in a nuanced performance while still retaining plenty of pep and vigor.

Inspired in part by stunt or novelty, trombone pieces like "Lassus Trombone" (1915), and perhaps lifting a section of the piano rag "Carbarlick Acid" (1903), "Ory's Creole Trombone" highlights his tailgate playing—a hallmark of New Orleans–style jazz. The breaks throughout the piece and its multiple themes are exactly the kind of music one would expect to hear from a group of musicians who spanned the musical eras from ragtime to jazz. "'Ory's Creole Trombone' is a simple, 'down-home,' swinging piece from start to finish. Its melody is, indeed, Creole in flavor. The trombone is shifted back and forth from lead to countermelody. Its first strain is a 'smear' strain and in its third strain are some 'breaks' where the soloist [Ory] performs some simple but demanding pyrotechnics."[47]

Ory was correct to suggest the band would be lost beneath the singers on the four other sides and to request that the band record without them. It is not that the band does not turn in good performances, particularly on the instrumental passage of "Krooked Blues," but that the restraint the band has to exercise backing a singer leaves it in a supporting role. Further, the material was not part of the band's regular repertoire. Still, these vocal recordings offer a hint of what the band sounded like backing singers at the Cadillac, Dreamland, and Creole Café.

The Kid Ory recordings were significant at the time to the band in that afterwards, they could say that they had "made a record." The fact that the records served as a successful promotional device is borne out by the Ory band's inclusion in the *Examiner* radio broadcasts, which mentioned the recordings. In turn, these appearances, as much as the record itself, spread word of the band beyond Los Angeles. The fidelity of the performances, as reported by the listeners, was certainly better than that of the records.

With radio broadcasts and Hollywood folks buying his record at the Spikes brothers' store, Ory's role as a bandleader at predominantly black establishments was about to end. Just as Ory's band crossed over the racial divide in New Orleans, it crossed over to playing country clubs, Hollywood parties, and A-list functions in Los Angeles. One admirer of the Ory band was silent film star Mae Murray. Known as "the girl with the bee-stung lips," all of her movies featured elaborate dance numbers, and on occasion she hired the Ory band to play off-screen for the on-screen dancers when they performed their numbers. In his recollection Ory said the year was 1919, though he mentions drummer Ben Borders being in the band. Borders did not join the band until after its move to Oakland in 1921. In 1921–22 Murray made *The Gilded Lily, Peacock Alley, Fascination,* and *Broadway Rose.*[48] These silent films no longer exist; Ory was likely off screen anyway.

Ory and the band spent much of July 1922 playing in San Diego and on railroad excursions to San Diego and Tijuana, sponsored by Ragtime Billy Tucker and his business partner, M. T. Laws.[49] Ory's Sunshine Orchestra played in a special train car set up for dancing. The Tijuana excursions were especially popular, as it was the closest "wet" city to Los Angeles during Prohibition.

At the same time, they made regular appearances at Ragtime Billy Tucker's dances at the Hiawatha Dancing Academy, as Tucker himself explained:

> *The Hiawatha Dancing Academy is running along in smooth shape with two bands in evidence, the All-Star Syncopators and Kid Ory's Sunshine Orchestra. The latter has the distinction of being the only jazz band of the Race to play for the radio in this city, likewise the only jazz band of any race to make records of any kind. They have recorded several numbers for the Spikes Bros. and are slated to record some more in the near future.*
>
> *The orchestra is comprised of the following: Kid Ory, Manager and trombone; "Mutt" Carey, leader and cornet; "Slockem" [sic], clarinet; Buster Wilson, piano; Ben Borders, the drums; Earl [Wade] Whaley, saxophone and a Mr. Davis, bass violin. What I mean, they put out some really wicked tunes and are a hit wherever they play.*[50]

A correction later ran saying that Ed Garland was the Ory band bassist. Adam "Slocum" Mitchell was a clarinetist originally from New Iberia, Louisiana, who had played with Jelly Roll Morton in California. He had been out west since the late 1910s, when he was photographed as a member of Sid LeProtti's So Different Jazz band.[51]

Buster Wilson (1897–1949) was originally from Atlanta, but grew up in Los Angeles where he became a protégé of Jelly Roll Morton. Ory said that ultimately Buster Wilson was a better pianist than Morton.

> *Ory's Sunshine Orchestra (the record makers) are featured every time the door opens at the Hiawatha Dancing Academy. They are now playing at the popular dance palace two nights a week and two matinee dances. Every Saturday afternoon and evening finds them there, likewise every Monday night and Thursday afternoon. Besides playing the Hiawatha they are featured along with a white orchestra at the Perluss Dancing Academy the balance of the week. The Perluss is an "ofay" dance hall. Whenever these boys play they prove a "riot" and are always in demand.[52]*

Another Tucker notice proclaims: "I can boast of record crowds every time the doors open. Ory's Sunshine Orchestra deserves a great deal of the credit. They are featured every time the doors open. They play for me at every dance and really deliver the goods."[53]

Sonny Clay (1899–1973), a California bandleader in his own right who would later record under his own name, joined rival Ory's band in August of 1922. Clay was a native of Arizona who moved to Los Angeles around 1916. He played with Jelly Roll Morton and the Spikes brothers before joining Ory in Oakland. Clay is quoted by Ragtime Billy Tucker as saying: "He wants the world to know he is with them [Ory] and says that if anyone doubt that it is the hottest jazz outfit in existence to lay down some jack and they are ready to back the statement."[54]

At the end of 1922, the doings of the Ory band drop from the pages of the *Chicago Defender*. The band's last notice on December

23 states that Ory will sponsor dances at the Normandie Dance Hall. Tucker had a reputation for stiffing musicians and there was likely a parting of the ways over money.

Ory's disappearance from Ragtime Billy Tucker's column coincides with Ory and the Spikes brothers parting ways. The summer had been filled with promotions and activity surrounding the record with mixed results. Despite the success of the Sunshine record (inasmuch as it sold out), the Spikes got out of the music recording business because of debts to Nordskog and because artists at Black Patti—an African American–owned record company—had recorded some of their compositions. Since Black Patti was already established, it was easier for the Spikes to just sell their records instead of making their own.

The Spikes also sold their interest in Leak's Lake to Jelly Roll Morton and other musicians. The brothers blamed the hours of upkeep, having to run bootleggers off, and an attack of rheumatism. "It got so rough out there I sold it to the musicians," Reb Spikes recalled.[55]

This did not mean the band was not busy. Though the notices are fewer, there are still enough mentions in the *California Eagle* to prove that the Ory band had plenty of gigs. Performances at the Panama Social Club, Los Angeles Creole Club, Moose Hall, the Blue Lantern, and Assembly Auditorium kept the band busy in 1923 and 1924. One telling notice in the *Eagle* on December 12, 1924, notes that Ory will play at the Assembly Auditorium after playing primarily for white audiences the last year. This may explain fewer notices about the band in black newspapers.

Ory recalled playing "taxi dances" from 1922 until 1924 with an incarnation of his band that featured eight pieces including two saxophones and Pops Foster, a former New Orleans bandmate, on sousaphone. Taxi dances were for male patrons who would buy tickets to dance with a so-called "dime-a-dance girl" for one tune. The dancers earned a partial commission with each ticket, which also went to pay for the band and the venue. Taxi dancers, while only working a few hours an evening, frequently made two to three times the salary of a woman who might work in a factory or a store.[56]

For a band playing a taxi dance, it meant countless renditions of tunes that were cut short so that the dances did not last too long and there would be turnover. The grind of playing taxi dances left Kid Ory dissatisfied with his band.

Since his arrival in 1919, he had met great success in California. The Sunshine recordings, live radio broadcasts, movie work, and Hollywood parties kept the Ory band busy throughout its five-year residency in the state. By 1925, however, Chicago had emerged as the premiere showcase for jazz; Los Angeles was a backwater by comparison. The sheer amount of recording work alone could keep a man busy in Chicago. With the help of two old friends, Ory would get the opportunity to try his fortunes in the Windy City.

CHAPTER 9

1925–1933
CHICAGO SIDEMAN

Louis was in New York then, playing with Fletcher Hender-son. I remember getting a letter from him. I was in California then with my own band. Louis said he had the offer of a job for a band at the Dreamland in Chicago, and also the offer to record for Okeh. He said we'd both make some money, so I decided to give up my own band, and go back East to Chicago. That was the end of 1925. I thought the world of Louis, so I was glad to go with him.[1]

Through most of his career Ory was a dance bandleader, seldom playing in the bands of others. The exception was, ironically, a period that was perhaps his most fabled—the late 1920s in Chicago. There he backed up Louis Armstrong, Jelly Roll Morton, and King Oliver, making classic recordings that crystallized the sounds that defined the jazz age.

Both Louis Armstrong and King Oliver contacted Ory in California in 1925, asking him to come to Chicago. Armstrong was looking for a steady trombonist for his inaugural recording group under his own name—Louis Armstrong and his Hot Five—and a man for his Dreamland Ballroom band. Oliver, meanwhile, wanted to replace trombonist George Filhe in his new band the Dixie Syncopators. Oliver apparently made the request first, but Ory waited until Louis's offer was in hand before embarking on the train to the Windy City.

"Louis wrote to me, told me he was going to leave Fletcher (Henderson), he heard I was coming to Chicago, would I record with them, you know," Ory recalled. Louis probably "heard" that Ory was coming from Oliver. Ory remembered arriving in Chicago "a few weeks" before Louis, who returned from New York no later than November 9, when he waxed a Chicago recording with Bertha "Chippe" Hill.

The Great Migration led to the relocation of 65,000 blacks to Chicago from Louisiana, Mississippi, Alabama, Arkansas, and Texas between 1910 and 1920. The attraction was, in part, northern industries including railroads, steel mills, stockyards, and slaughterhouses that "actively recruited non-unionized black laborers." By 1920 the African American population of Chicago stood at 109,894.[2]

With the influx of those newcomers, and the added dollars they made working in the North, a market was created for entertainment. "Economic opportunity in a growing market for leisure time entertainment drew African-American musicians north from New Orleans into competition for the dollars that urban workers could devote to recreation in Chicago."[3] In terms of real dollars and cents, there was no comparison between what a musician could make in New Orleans as opposed to Chicago. New Orleans musicians could expect between $1.50 and $2.50 per gig, plus tips. By the time Ory got there, Chicago cabarets were paying sidemen $40 a week plus tips. Further, Chicago had emerged as a major music capital featuring live bands, recording studios, and music publishing. It was also a hub for touring companies on the vaudeville circuit. A musician looking for work had a good chance of finding it in Chicago. Hot Five member Lil Hardin could not believe her good fortune when she settled in Chicago, saying, "I made it my business to go out for a daily stroll and look this 'heaven' over. Chicago meant just that to me—its beautiful brick and stone buildings, excitement, people moving swiftly, and things happening."[4]

Many New Orleans musicians had traveled there including Jelly Roll Morton, King Oliver, Sidney Bechet, Johnny Dodds, and Louis Armstrong. Oliver had coaxed Armstrong out of New Orleans in 1922 to join his Creole Jazz band; in 1923 a series of recordings were made that are considered classics today. Likewise, Jelly Roll Morton recorded his fine piano solos for Gennett Records, waxing his compositions like "The Pearls" and "The Wolverines" while based in Chicago.

Along with the opportunity to record, Chicago offered "the Stroll"—a series of nightclubs on the Southside on 35th Street around Calumet that employed many New Orleans jazzmen. Over the years Ory would play at many of them, including the Dreamland Café, the Plantation Café, and the Sunset Café. Other clubs on the Stroll included Elie Café No. 2, DeLuxe Café, and the Apex Club. Chicagoans danced to jazz at a variety of venues: cabarets, roadhouses, vaudeville and movie theaters, dance halls, excursion boats and trains, and private parties, with white, black, and "black and tan" crowds.[5] Throughout his Chicago residency, Ory worked in multiple bands at clubs, cabarets, and theatres—all the while participating in recording sessions for other artists.

Ory and Dort settled into an apartment on the South Side at 444 E. 48th Street in an area known as Bronzeville. The label was placed on the community by a newspaper editor in reference to the color of its residents. A city unto itself, Bronzeville had its own bustling downtown, with parks and commercial, shopping, and theater districts. The 400 block of 48th Street, where the Orys lived, is a wide thoroughfare lined with trees and brownstone townhouses and apartment buildings. Their home was a recently constructed, three-story brown brick apartment building with a center entrance framed by rounded corners. The Stroll, where Ory would perform, was several miles away, so he likely rode one of Chicago's new motorized buses up and down Michigan Avenue to work.[6]

On November 12, 1925, the Louis Armstrong Hot Five with Kid Ory on trombone convened at the Okeh studios in Chicago and tore into Armstrong's composition "My Heart"—thus beginning a recording series that documented jazz as it was in 1925 and foreshadowed what it would become. The Hot Five was a recording group created by Okeh Records to tap the growing "race" record market. Okeh had been founded in 1916 as the Otto Heinemann Phonograph Corporation by Otto K. E. Heinemann (1877–1965)— a German-American manager for German-owned Odeon Records in New York. Heinemann set up a studio and pressing plant in New York and issued his first 78 RPM records in 1918.[7]

Okeh first issued foreign-language records in Swedish, Polish, German, and Yiddish in an attempt to market to immigrant communities. But in 1920, Okeh caught lightning in a bottle when its recording of Mamie Smith's "Crazy Blues" sold over 100,000 copies. New Orleans pianist and composer Clarence Williams was hired as director of "race" records at Okeh to better help the label exploit the African American market with blues and jazz records. Another New Orleanian, Richard M. Jones, was put in that role when Okeh expanded its operation to Chicago. It was Jones who oversaw the recording of the Hot Fives for Okeh.

I don't know who got the idea for the Hot Five record. It may have been Richard M. Jones, who worked for the Okeh company at that time. He worked for them in Chicago as a pianist for different blues singers and writing and selecting tunes, and it may have been through him that the Okeh company approached Louis. We made our first records in Chicago at the Okeh studios, and of course when we made them we didn't have any expectation that they would be as successful as they became. The time was something like today, with people crazy about jazz and the Charleston, and our kind of music went over very well. Times were good, and people had money to buy records.[8]

Louis Armstrong recalled E. A. Fern, the president of Okeh, being behind the recordings. "The minute Mr. Fern gave me the go sign, I hit the phone and called the musicians' union, and asked permission to hire Edward 'Kid' Ory, Johnny St. Cyr and Johnny Dodds."⁹

Before the Hot Five, jazz was a source of entertainment for dancing. When Armstrong and the Hot Five were done, it was an art form. At their best, the Hot Fives are a high water mark for New Orleans–style polyphony and collective improvisation. For the tongue-in-groove nature of the form—where each player listens to the other and strives to produce music that will fit the music played by the other while still defining one's individual style—*E pluribus unum* could be the motto of New Orleans jazz. Yet in some circles, the value of the Hot Five is that they mark a departure from the collective, New Orleans-based sound. This school of thought believes that the Hot Five are important because they herald the arrival of the lone soloist, standing apart from the others. That the recordings stand the test of time in both camps speaks to their influence and import—not only as historical documents of New Orleans men defining the jazz style that was theirs, but as a significant artistic statement as well. Armstrong's trumpet pyrotechnics do not need extolling here. He defined the vocabulary of the style with his growls, slurs, and imaginative phrasing while maintaining a constant grip on the melody. In one context, the other musicians are bit players in Louis' drama and emergence as an artist.

Oddly enough, the jazz music of the Hot Five that so encapsulated the zeitgeist of the Chicago nightlife was often recorded at nine or ten in the morning, as the musicians rolled in from the previous night's work with other bands. Ory recalled the scene in the studio.

> Our recording sessions would start this way: the Okeh people would call up Louis and say they wanted so many sides. They never told him what numbers they wanted or how they wanted them. Then Louis would give us the date,

and sometimes he'd call me and say, "I'm short of a number for this next session. Do you think you can get one together?" I'd say, "All right," and that's the way Savoy Blues came to be composed, two days before we recorded. We would get to the studio at nine or ten in the morning. We didn't have to make records at night, with the lights out, or get drunk like some musicians think they have to do before they can play. In the beginning we made records acoustically, and there was a separate horn for each man. The recording engineer would motion to us if we were playing too loud or too soft, and then we'd know to move back or to move in closer. Then later, of course, we made records electrically.

When we'd get in the studio, if we were going to do a new number, we'd run over it a couple of times before we recorded it. We were a very fast recording band; in fact the records I made with the Hot Fives were the easiest I ever made. We spoiled very few records, only sometimes when one of us would forget the routine or the frame-up, and didn't come in when he was supposed to. Even then, we'd try to cover up. After we'd make a side, Louis would say: "Was that all right?" And if one of us thought we could do it over and do it better, why Louis would tell them we wanted to do it again, and so we would do it over.

We usually made 8 sides at one session, and we made them so quickly that all the Okeh people were amazed . . . Most of the other bands took all day to make a couple of sides. We would make eight in three hours. Often we didn't know the tunes when we got to the studio: one of us would suggest a melody; we'd run through it once and then record it. We never used any kind of arrangement. All we needed was a lead sheet and everybody would figure out his part.[10]

The easy repartee between the former Ory bandmates, now Hot Five members, certainly was conducive to efficient use of studio time. Over the course of the recordings, the band would wax a mix of popular tunes and original compositions by Lil, Louis, and Ory. Members of the band were encouraged to contribute ideas and, to their credit, the Okeh people stayed out of the way and let the band work.

> *I think one reason those records came out so well was that the Okeh people left us alone, and didn't try to expert us. Another reason was we all knew each other's musical styles so well from years of working together. And then of course, there was Louis, himself. You couldn't go wrong with Louis. I always liked his style the best. That's not to take anything away from Oliver, but I always thought Louis was the greatest, and I still think so.*[11]

There are dozens of Hot Five records, more than will be addressed individually here; further, there are books specific to this topic.[12] Still, there are particular recordings and songs that figure largely in Ory's story both as a musician and composer, none more so than the band's February 26, 1926, recording of the song most identified with Kid Ory: "Muskrat Ramble."

As a performance, "Muskrat Ramble" is arguably Ory's best on record. If not, it is clearly his most emblematic. Ory is all over the place with growls, smears, and all the glissando he can muster. Here he is the consummate ensemble player, performing material he knows well in a style conducive to his strengths. The record is a joyous testament to jazz as good-time music, and to Ory as a musician. Unlike some Hot Five recordings, the arrangement and performance are crisp, suggesting the band members may have been familiar with the tune prior to its recording.

While the status of "Muskrat Ramble" as a classic jazz record is a given, the origin and authorship of the composition has been the subject of disagreement and conjecture. Ory said, "I wrote it back around 1921 when I was playing [saxophone] in a taxi dancehall at Third and Main in Los Angeles. It had no name then."[13] Gene Anderson in *The Original Hot Five Recordings of Louis Armstrong* notes the obvious ragtime origins of "Muskrat Ramble," particularly its 16-bar chorus and "saw-toothed" theme. To Anderson, "Muskrat Ramble" echoes, to varying degrees, Scott Joplin's "Maple Leaf Rag" (1899) and the Original Dixieland Jazz Band's "Tiger Rag" (1918). This makes perfect sense in that Ory's musical awakening happened around 1899 and his ride at the top of the New Orleans music scene was at its peak in 1918. It was between these two mileposts that Ory matured as a musician. But did he write it, or was it a tune that he picked up?

Sidney Bechet suggested that "Muskrat Ramble," or at least the second strain of the piece, was based on a tune he heard as a kid in New Orleans called "The Old Cow Died and the Old Man Cried." There are many songs with the title "The Old Cow Died," including nursery rhymes, so it would be difficult to say to which song Bechet is referring. Interestingly, Ory recalls a story where his New Orleans band played a song called "The Old Cow Died." If "Muskrat Ramble" is "The Old Cow Died" and Ory's band played it in New Orleans, then why his story about writing it on saxophone in 1921?[14]

At times Armstrong claimed authorship, as in a *Down Beat* article in 1965 when he told Dan Morganstern, "I wrote 'Muskrat Ramble.' Ory named it, he gets the royalties. I don't talk about it." Ory said that Lil named the song at the end of the session.[15] The name of the song was the subject of confusion as well: the original Okeh label carried the misprint "Muskat Ramble." This would make it seem to be a song about Old World wine and not Louisiana swamp creatures. Still, Ory, Louis, and Lil all agreed that the name of the song was indeed "Muskrat Ramble." Whatever the origin of the song or its title, "Muskrat Ramble" will forever be linked to Kid Ory. In later years he would perform it several times a night, and he earned royalties until the day he died from the many recordings of the song by other artists.

The "Muskrat Ramble" session also produced one of the Hot Five's most enduring and successful recordings, "Heebie Jeebies." "The records were very successful by this time, and 'Heebie Jeebies' was what today would be called a hit record. That was the record where Louis forgot the lyrics and started scattin'. We had all we could do to keep from laughing. Of course, Louis said he forgot the words, but I don't know if he intended it that way or not. It made the record, though."[16] Kid Ory flubs the timing of his spoken line at the extended ending of the song. He says "What ya doin with the Heebies?" a few beats early, but the band recovers. Whether the story about forgetting the lyrics is apocryphal or not, Armstrong's nonsensical scat singing staked sales of "Heebie Jeebies" to the tune of 40,000 copies in just a few weeks. It was the Hot Five's first commercial success, and the Heebie Jeebie dance was promoted into a craze by the Okeh company itself.[17]

On June 23, 1926, the band returned to the studio and recorded "The King of the Zulus." The record features a vaudeville routine in the form of spoken banter by Richard M. Jones and Clarence Babcock, and boasts what might be Kid Ory's best solo on record. After a collective introduction, Ory takes over with a slow, bluesy solo that is tone perfect. Lil may have written the piece out and played it for Ory to follow; however if this is true, the recording makes clear it was written with Ory in mind, as it sounds like a part he would have played on his own.[18]

On September 2, 1927, the Hot Five recorded "Ory's Creole Trombone," the tune Ory had once played in New Orleans and had recorded for the Spikes brothers and Arne Nordskog in 1922. This more realized version of the song has Armstrong taking a solo and some of the breaks originally played by Ory. Though a solid performance, the piece sounds dated compared to other Hot Five material. Perhaps this is why this side was not issued in the twenties; it was issued in 1940 after being rediscovered in the Columbia vault by then student, later producer George Avakian.

"Struttin' with Some Barbeque"—easily the most popular tune by the group apart from "Muskrat Ramble"—was recorded on December 9, 1927.[19] It features a magnificent multi-chorus solo from Armstrong, soaring collective playing, and a split solo chorus by Johnny Dodds and Kid Ory. Ory turns in a noteworthy performance that is marked by restraint. It is an instructive contrast to his more athletic playing on "Muskrat Ramble." "The stop-time accompaniment energizes Ory's solo by throwing its melodic simplicity into sharp relief. Like his earlier Hot Five solos, Ory here constructs improvisations around triads, often with blue thirds, relying on smears and syncopation for variety."[20]

The band's December 10, 1927, recording of "I'm Not Rough" was a deliberate attempt by Armstrong to recapture the sound of the Ory band of New Orleans and its soloist Joe Oliver. "I can see King Joe Oliver, right this minute, blowing his cornet, and playing this tune in the advertising wagons on Sundays . . . He was in Kid Ory's band at the time . . . And they played an arrangement to 'I'm Not Rough' which we tried to remember the idea when we recorded it."[21] The performance is a mid-tempo blues with breaks, stop-time passages and collective playing that could certainly be evocative of the Ory-Oliver band of New Orleans. Armstrong said the band was trying to get in the "New Orleans groove" on this recording, and it is fascinating to ponder how close they came.

On December 13, 1927, Ory gathered with the Hot Five for the last time, recording his composition "Savoy Blues." Ory wrote the song two days before it was recorded and named it after Chicago's Savoy Ballroom, where he played with violinist Clarence Black's orchestra. The track also features guitarist Lonnie Johnson, who had been a featured soloist on the band's recording of "I'm Not Rough." While much of the song is a vehicle for Johnson, it is Armstrong who ultimately puts his stamp on "Savoy Blues," rendering a solo that is counted among his best.[22] Ory plays a klaxon-like sliding part that transitions from the solo passages to the final movement of the song.

The Hot Five recordings are representative products of their time; they were created to fill a niche market but found success beyond this purpose, becoming historical and artistic documents of a music.[23] With little practice and without the advantage of actual music jobs to hone its repertoire, the Hot Five invested much time with arrangements and details in each recording. There are flubs and miscues throughout, but this does not diminish the power of the music. Ory summed up his Hot Five experience this way:

> *Those days in Chicago were very happy. We had all played together before, and were friends from the old days. Louis, Lil and Johnny Dodds played together in the Oliver band in 1923, so they had good experience together. And of course, I had played with Louis, Dodds and St. Cyr in New Orleans when they were in my band. The only one of the Hot Five I hadn't played with was Lil, but that made no difference. She was a fine piano player, and from the first we all worked together very easily.[24]*

That Ory was afforded the opportunity to play with musicians he was comfortable with, in a style that was his own, was his good fortune. While the Hot Five sessions were a vehicle for Louis Armstrong, they provided Ory with a platform as both a performer and composer. The collaborative nature of the Hot Five, and the fact that it was a small group, meant it had to strive to bring all its creative guns to bear. Here Ory's contributions are significant. Ory's tailgate—some would say throwback—style of trombone was a perfect counterpart to the work of Armstrong and Dodds. His trombone part—particularly the tag ending—of "Muskrat Ramble" is still de rigueur for traditional jazz trombonists. That tune, and Ory's "Savoy Blues," have become classics in the jazz canon and are still performed by bands around the world.

Gene Anderson offers a fair assessment of Ory's Hot Five legacy:

> *As a recent reviewer aptly put it, Ory's "rawness, even at times crudeness" forms part of this music's charm. . . . Ory fulfills ably the multiple roles of quasi-bassist and quasi-drummer in addition to his duties as trombonist. More rhythmically than melodically inventive, Ory renders his best solo in this set in "King of the Zulus," for whose "primitive" style and limited harmonies it is perfectly suited. Bursting energy suffuses all of his solos and breaks, however, while his copyrighted "Muskrat Ramble" endures as the most famous of the Hot Fives, and his "Savoy Blues" stands among the best.*[25]

Apart from the Okeh recording sessions, the complete Hot Five band made three sides for Vocalion in April and May 1926. "After I Say I'm Sorry," "Georgia Bo Bo," and "Drop that Sack" were recorded under the name Lil's Hot Shots.

The group, minus Louis, recorded as the New Orleans Wanderers and the New Orleans Bootblacks for Columbia, waxing the jazz classic "Perdido Street Blues" on July 13, 1926. Other recordings included "Papa Dip" and "Gatemouth," the latter of which prominently featured Ory.

Conversely, Armstrong's expanded group, the Hot Seven, did not feature Ory, as he was in New York with Oliver when the recordings were made. Likewise, a later version of the Hot Five—the so-called Chicago Hot Five—featured a different trombonist.

The Hot Five was a studio band that only played "a few benefits," according to Ory. "The Hot Five never played together as a band outside of a few benefits. We'd all take a short time off from the regular jobs we had and play for a half hour or so at some affair. We always would break it up, and then go back to our jobs."[26] Still, Ory makes it clear that when he first arrived in Chicago he did play in a band with Louis at the Dreamland and that Johnny

Dodds, Johnny St. Cyr, and Lil were in it. "The idea was that we would have a regular band at Dreamland, and then that five of us from the band would make records together. I got to Chicago a few weeks before Louis, and played around at different clubs. Then Louis got there, and we rehearsed the band for a few days before we opened at the Dreamland. We had Johnny Dodds, Johnny St. Cyr and Lil with us."[27]

The Dreamland was a black and tan club on Chicago's Stroll at 3520 South State Street. By Ory's recollection it was a "big band" at the Dreamland, one that featured the members of the Hot Five but not in that format. Lil's Dreamland Syncopators, a six-piece unit, played for the club's reopening in October 1925 without Louis, and it is possible that Ory was in this band, too. Armstrong was successful at the Dreamland, but when he asked for more money the club owners balked. By December 1925 Louis had moved on to the Vendome Theatre and Erskine Tate's orchestra, while the Hot Five fanned out to find other live music jobs.[28]

> *Everything was fine for a while, making the records for Okeh, and playing at Dreamland with the big band. It was a good sounding band, and very popular. People line up in the snow to get in to hear us. But they didn't pay very well, and when Louis asked for more money for the band, they wouldn't come across and so we left. After that, Louis went with Erskine Tate, and I joined Oliver. Johnny Dodds had his own outfit at Kelly's Stables and Johnny St. Cyr played in Cook's band. Lil was married to Louis then, and she didn't play with any band, as I remember, but just recorded. Even though we were working in different clubs, we kept the Hot Five going.*[29]

Ory's old friend King Oliver had a new band, the Dixie Syncopators, and had secured a long-term deal performing at the Plantation Café at 35th and Calumet streets beginning in February 1925. That summer Oliver wrote to Ory and offered him the trombone chair in the band then occupied by George Filhe (1872–1954). Filhe was getting old and his musical ear, by his own admission, was not what it had been. Still, Ory apparently held off joining until late 1925 when the Dreamland Cafe gig with Armstrong went bust. Ory said, "Louis went with Erskine Tate, and I joined Oliver." While Filhe played out his six-week notice, Ory manned an alto saxophone, an instrument he had picked up playing taxi dances in California.[30] Ory remembered the Plantation Café where the Oliver band performed:

> It [the Plantation] was one of the finest clubs in those days. That was on 35th and Calumet, you know between South Park and—what was that Calumet? One block from South Park. The Nest was right across the street. The Sunset was over this way. Three clubs right together. . . . The atmosphere was fine in there, the acoustics was good. Everything. Nice bandstand, everything. They had nice rugs on the floor. Floor show and everything.[31]

The Plantation was a popular, white-owned, black and tan cabaret along the Stroll on Chicago's South Side at 338 East 35th. It was opened by Edward Fox and Al Turner, but came to be controlled by the Al Capone gang.[32]

The King Oliver band of this period was a fine unit, though it was not a New Orleans–style jazz band, despite the fact that it was full of New Orleans players including Barney Bigard, Albert Nicholas, Luis Russell, Bud Scott, and Paul Barbarin. Oliver followed trends in music, and being divorced from the Crescent City for nearly a decade, his style had changed. Be that as it may, the group made many recordings in 1926 and 1927 that are the pride of any 78 RPM record collector. In *King Joe Oliver*, Brian Rust and Walter C. Allen suggest that the Dixie Syncopators may have been Oliver's last great band, and that the records they made prove this to be true.[33]

In March 1926, Oliver secured a recording contract with Bruns-wick-Balke-Collander Company for their new series of Vocalion race records. "From then until the end of 1928, the Dixie Syncopators contributed to jazz a number of discs which, if they lack the ensemble brilliance of those of the Creole Jazz band, show a wide range of tone colors, and feature some splendid musicians. For the first time Oliver's horn is realistically recorded, and it hits out of the grooves across the years as fiercely as the day it was put to wax." Oliver does all of the solo trumpet work and Ory is heard to employ the mute for the first time, perhaps taking a tip from Oliver himself.[34] Ory's studio work with Oliver kicked off with a recording of "Too Bad" and "Snag It" on March 11, 1926. By the time of Ory's last session with them in April 1927, they had recorded seventeen issued sides, including "Black Snake Blues," "Sugar Foot Stomp," "Wa Wa Wa," "Willie the Weeper," "Dead Man Blues," and "Deep Henderson."

The Dixie Syncopator recordings show a side of Ory not found on the Hot Five sessions. Belonging to Oliver's band meant there were written trombone parts, though Ory had never really learned to read music with any aptitude. To better handle this challenge, and to improve his tone, Ory sought out lessons from Chicago trombonist Jaroslav Cimera, who he recalled as "Schemmery." A native of Bohemia, Cimera (1885–1972) had played in John Phillip Sousa's band, toured the country in tent shows, and would eventually become an executive with C. G. Conn Musical Instruments. He was a noted composer and wrote method books for the trombone. One of his students remembered, "The lessons were a half hour long. The charge was $3, reasonable for the day; less than that of other well-known teachers. He had a large class of students and he had a lot of endurance. I think he preferred a large class as he would have a better chance of discovering someone with real talent who would help his reputation. Cimera was a self assured man, possessed of strongly held opinions which he rarely changed."[35]

At that point, Schemmery asked if I had studied with anyone before and I told him that I had taken lessons from a man named Bouncer in Los Angeles but after about 6 lessons with him, I had felt that I really could outplay him and therefore it was rather foolish to be paying him money for lessons. So Schimmery gave me a number, which seemed very simple to me, to play for him. However, he wanted it played in a certain way in a legato movement and when I tried it, I found it was really tough. He gave me this to take home with me as my lesson for the week and after practicing it every day, I was able to run through it easily and perfectly on my second visit to the professor. When I got there, he asked me to play it over for him, which I did, and he listened very carefully then, he said, "that sounds fine," and I thanked him. So he left the room and went into the next room and he kind of scared me because I thought he was bringing something else for me to play but he came back carrying his horn and he had the harmony part of the same number that I had just played for him and he said "Let's try it again." Then we played a duet with him on harmony and I was playing just as I had before and to me it sounded just like two voices blending so easily and beautifully and when we finished Schimmery said he thought it was great.

During this time I was working with King Oliver's orchestra at the Plantation and some of the boys in the band noticed, especially on sweet numbers, that I was changed and asked me what was happening as I had told no one what I was doing. Then a friend of mine, Gerald Reeves asked me who are you taking lessons from. I said "Why?" and he said he's like to get in touch with him and I gave him Sch's telephone number and address and after he had had a few lessons from him he told me that he thought Sch was one of the greatest trombone soloists he ever heard and was well pleased with his lessons.

I kept on with Schimmery for eight months that took in the latter part of 1926 and the beginning months of 1927 and then

we left for St. Louis with the Oliver band and went on to New
York from there. I've always been grateful to Schimmery for
what he did for me and I can never forget the man.[36]

Ory would never be a great sight-reader, but his lessons brought
him to a higher level of musical understanding than he had previously enjoyed, as evidenced by his performances on the Oliver
recordings, particularly "Willie the Weeper" and "Black Snake
Blues." His solos on these tracks are his best with the band and
rank among his finest recorded work as a sideman.

Gangs and violence were all part and parcel of the Chicago Prohibition era experience, and Ory had a few encounters with the
underworld. Most notably, he recalled Al Capone at the Plantation, a club the gangster allegedly controlled: "Yeah I knew him,
knew Al. Knew all his boys, yeah. He used to come in the club, the
Plantation all the time. The guys, they were very nice to me. Prohibition time, they used to have the best liquor, better than we're
drinking now. They gave me a fifth."[37]

The summer Ory moved to Chicago, a bomb harmlessly det-
onated on the roof of the Plantation, but it succeeded in driving
business away.[38] It may have been part of the feud between Capone's Southside gang and that of Northside boss Earl "Hymie
Weiss" Wojciechowski. "Two bombs were exploded late last night
on the Southside. The first was thrown on the roof of the Plantation Café, a 'black and tan' resort at 338 East 35th Street. Nearly
100 guests on the dance floor were panic-stricken by the blast, but
were soon quieted. The damage was about $200."[39]

On September 20, 1926, Capone was the subject of an assassi-
nation attempt, one that led him to sue for peace. When he could
not come to terms with Weiss, the war continued. The Plantation
remained open despite the war, which ended when Capone's men
gunned down Weiss on October 11. The Dixie Syncopators continued there until about February 1927, when the café closed for
repairs. The place was set to reopen on April 5 of that year with

Oliver headlining, but a mysterious fire gutted the Plantation on March 31.[40] The fire destroyed everything, consuming all of Oliver's photographs and publicity materials. "Mystery Fire Causes Big Loss in Plantation Café: Fire early this morning wrecked the interior of the Plantation café, 338 East 35th street, notorious in the past as a 'black and tan' resort. The place has been closed for a month for repairs according to James Keyes, assistant manager of the place. He was unable to give a cause for the fire, which he said resulted in damage of $50,000."[41]

Whether the fire was a fluke or a continuation of Chicago's gangland violence is unclear. Ory also remembered a shootout later at the Sunset Café: "Once in the Sunset . . . start shooting. I don't know who it was, it was a gang or . . . I found myself behind the stove in the kitchen. All I could smell was fried potatoes."[42]

Ory also recalled being stopped while carrying his trombone case the night of the St. Valentine's Day Massacre, when members of Bugs Moran's Irish crew were gunned down in a garage on February 14, 1929: "So, I got off the train to go take a lesson that night. During that night this thing happened. I got off the train and they grabbed my [trombone] case, thought I had a machine gun in it, in Cicero [Illinois]. Plainclothesman, must have been a cop. So I opened it up and let him see it."[43]

The fire at the Plantation Café left the Oliver band without steady work. Oliver resorted to the old Ory trick of hiring a truck to promote the band, and drove his eleven-piece outfit around town playing "Dr. Jazz," his latest number. On Easter they performed opposite Louis Armstrong's Stompers at his regular gig at the Sunset Café. Oliver followed this with trips to Milwaukee to play the Roof Garden and St. Louis. Ory's last recording with the band. The trip did not go well and the band ended up broke.[44]

In May 1927 King Oliver got an offer from promoter Jay Faggen to take the Syncopators to New York to play at Harlem's Savoy Ballroom. Apparently the band arrived tired and disheveled for their first appearance, prompting Oliver to offer an apology to the audience. During the gig Oliver's teeth began to give him trouble, making it difficult to play; so New Orleans native Henry "Red" Allen did most of the soloing. Still, reports in the *Chicago Defender* declared "Oliver takes New York by Storm."[45] After two weeks at the Savoy, the band played a series of one-nighters before being offered a long-term contract at the new Cotton Club in Harlem. Incredibly, Oliver turned it down, and the job went to Duke Ellington. Ory remained in the band until June 11, 1927. By then he could see the writing on the wall, and he made the decision to leave his old friend's band.

> *That was when I was working at the Savoy Ballroom [in New York]. And he owed me $100.00 for a recording, you know, told me he didn't have no money. I said "That's all right. You need any more money?" He said, "No, I need it but you're too nice, you didn't protest me against the union." I said, "Did you pay all the other guys?" He said, "Yeah." I said, "If you need anything, I'll help you out." He said, "Thanks for naming me 'King,'" and shook hands.*[46]

Ory never saw Oliver again. Ory returned to Chicago to work for Dave Peyton, whom Oliver had replaced at the Plantation back in 1925.[47]

In late 1926, while he was playing and recording with King Oliver and making the Hot Five discs with Louis Armstrong, Ory made three recording dates as a member of Jelly Roll Morton's Red Hot Peppers.

Morton (1890–1941) is an enigmatic figure in early jazz. Though his oft-derided claim to have invented jazz is an overstatement, he was nonetheless a mover and shaker as a composer, piano soloist, and recording artist. Morton was born Ferdinand Joseph Lamothe and grew up in a Creole neighborhood in New Orleans' Seventh

Ward. He heard the French opera, street parades, and Buddy Bolden while growing up in a family that saw musicians as "tramps." He moved to Central City as a teenager, where he encountered Mamie Desdunes and learned his first blues composition, the "2:19 Blues." He was further influenced by pianists Porter King and Tony Jackson, and played in the Storyville district before leaving New Orleans in 1907. In the 1910s he performed in vaudeville troupes in blackface, and at other times assumed the role of pianist in the house band. In 1915 his composition "The Jelly Roll Blues" was published; and by 1917 he had settled in Los Angeles. There he performed at the Cadillac and Leak's Lake for the Spikes brothers, while composing songs like "The Pearls," Kansas City Stomp," and "Someday, Sweetheart."[48] He moved to Chicago in 1923.

By September 1926 when Morton convened the first rehearsal session of his new recording group the Red Hot Peppers at Chicago's Webster Hotel, he was a studio veteran, having made numerous recordings for Gennett, Paramount, and other labels. Like Armstrong, when it came time to put a studio band together he relied on old friends, including Kid Ory.

How long Morton had known Ory is unclear. The only mention Ory ever made about Jelly Roll in the context of New Orleans is that he never played above (that is, uptown of) Canal Street. This is a reference to Jelly's Creole pride, in that the area above Canal Street was considered the "American part of town." Morton does not mention Ory in any of his stories about New Orleans and it is possible they were not on the scene at the same time. (Morton left the city as early as 1907 while Ory did not move there until 1910.) Ory and Morton certainly crossed paths in California and played at many of the same venues.

In addition to Ory, Morton favored New Orleans natives including drummer Andrew Hilaire, clarinetist Omer Simeon, guitarist Johnny St. Cyr, and bassist John Lindsay. Simeon described the rehearsals on the north side of Chicago in the Webster Hotel.[49]

We had rehearsals for the recordings and [Walter] Melrose [Morton's publishing partner] always came down to the rehearsals to get an idea of what it sounded like. Walter Melrose published most of Jelly's tunes, and he would bring down some of the stock orchestrations from his publishing house. We used them merely as a guide until we got familiar with the tune and didn't need the music anymore. We improvised the ensembles, and we would always play the solos and ad-lib.

Jelly would set a routine for each number, and they all had to be timed to be no more than three minutes playing time. Jelly arranged special introductions that he had in mind and then Ory, George Mitchell, and myself got together and harmonized it and tried it out. Jelly set a routine so the order of the solos was decided. We always placed an ensemble, and the melody was going at all times until probably the last chorus, the take out chorus, you know. Then everybody would give out, but the melody dominated most of the time.[50]

George Mitchell, the group's non–New Orleanian, also remembered Jelly Roll's arrangements: "Jelly would write out parts for all the guys to play. Some of those boys like Simeon and Ory could just sit down, go through a thing and play without music, but I'd have to have something as a guide."[51]

Ory remembered both the rehearsals and arrangements:

We had two rehearsals for the recordings, down at the union local in Chicago. When we recorded, we had all good men there and most of the records came out perfect the first time. Jelly paid me more than the union scale to record, sometimes I'd get double. You know he had the best musicians and treated them with respect.

Yes we had rehearsals, and yes he wrote things out for everyone. He'd write something out for me, but after I played what he wrote for me he said, "That doesn't sound like you, so forget it; play your own way." There wasn't enough in his parts, you know. After he wrote out what he wanted, the boys would add on to it. That's just what I did. He didn't have nothing but bass notes and I wanted to put some harmony and legato and you know, other stuff in it, mix it up. And he told me, "Don't worry about your music; I can't write your music."[52]

Despite Jelly Roll Morton's reputation as someone who was hard to get along with, St. Cyr, Mitchell, Simeon, and Ory all enjoyed working with him. Ory got a kick out Morton, recalling, "At one recording session, I remember Jelly pulling his pants leg way up; he had a diamond on his leg garter." Omer Simeon recalled, "But with all of us—The Red Hot Peppers—we got along very well with him."[53]

As Mitchell, Simeon, and Ory all agree, Jelly Roll's records featured a balance between arrangement and improvisation.

Several of the musicians who worked with Morton . . . have described his methods as a leader. These statements are quoted in a number of sources, but they all attest to the fact that Morton rehearsed carefully—he even paid for rehearsals; that he shaped the arrangements either in written-out or dictated form; that he discussed with his players where breaks and solos would fit best, although he retained a final veto; that he rarely if ever interfered with the solo work; that he knew what he wanted over-all and often worked until he got it.[54]

In *Chicago Jazz*, William Howland Kenney also praises the Morton recordings:

Morton's Red Hot Pepper recordings blended a remarkable precision in the performance of the leader's arrangements with relaxed polyphonic ensembles. Morton fashioned an unprecedented compositional and textural originality out of the seven-piece jazz band tradition, which had moved from

New Orleans to Chicago. Although he had used saxophone as a lead instrument before 1926, Morton avoided the two-saxophone section; he arranged however, lovely harmonized passages for clarinetists Darnell Howard and Barney Bigard on "Sidewalk Blues" and "Dead Man Blues." He even had Omer Simeon double on bass clarinet, an unusual instrument in jazzband music.[55]

The first side recorded was "Black Bottom Stomp"—a recording that put "the world on notice" about Morton's claims as a jazz musician.[56] "First of all the piece is superbly recorded. The tremendous exuberance and vitality of this performance are captured perfectly with a live, roomy acoustical presence. 'Black Bottom Stomp,' one of Morton's finest compositions, was probably written expressly for this recording date."[57]

Ory is all over this record, which is full of pep and vigor. In many ways it harks back to the energy of the Original Dixieland Jazz Band, but with nuance. One commonality between these bands is that both feature tailgate trombonists (in the case of the ODJB, Eddie Edwards). Jelly Roll Morton and ODJB leader Nick La Rocca were born a year apart (1890 and 1889, respectively), and came of age musically as tailgate trombone began to dominate the scene; to them, the term would be redundant. That is why Ory's talents were so well utilized on the Red Hot Peppers sessions. Morton, a man of Ory's generation, embraced Ory's musicality to the point of allowing him to play his own way without a written part. Ory was the perfect trombonist for these records; his style fits naturally with Morton's sense of what a jazz band should sound like. Among Morton's recordings, Ory stands out on records like "Cannon Ball Blues," "Black Bottom Stomp," and "The Chant." Here, he is perfectly at home playing in collective passages with occasional breaks and solos.

Because Ory left for New York with Oliver in May 1927, he missed later Red Hot Pepper Sessions. Ory said that he made a record in St. Louis with Morton, though the titles and fate of that date are unknown.[58]

Over his years in Chicago, Ory recorded with other artists including Luis Russell, Irene Scruggs, and Butterbeans and Susie. Some discographies name other recordings; however, Ory discographer Sid Bailey dismisses many of these, including Lovie Austin's Serenaders, some of Johnny Dodds' Blackbottom Stompers, Louis Armstrong's Hot Seven, some Chicago Footwarmers, Jimmie Noone's Apex Club Orchestra, Bennett's Swamplanders, and Ma Rainey and her Georgia Band. (Albert Wynn—a trombonist who sounded very much like Ory—was apparently the player on the Austin and Rainey recordings for Paramount.)

On July 2, 1928, Kid Ory made his last recordings of the 1920s, when Johnny Dodds's Chicago Footwarmers waxed "Get Em Again Blues," "Brush Stomp," and "My Girl," three unremarkable sides that do not begin to tell the story of Ory's amazing though brief career as a Chicago studio musician. By this time, Ory had played on at about thirty recording sessions with some of the top stars of the era. The Hot Five's "Muskrat Ramble" and "Savoy Blues"; The Red Hot Peppers' "Black Bottom Stomp" and "Grandpa's Spells"; King Oliver's "Black Snake Blues" and "Sugarfoot Stomp"; and the New Orleans Wanderers' "Perdido Street Blues" are all classic recordings that have in common the presence of Kid Ory.

When Ory arrived in Chicago, he could make the claim to having been with the first recorded New Orleans jazz band of color and of having led the city's hottest jazz band through the teens. Had his career ended there, Ory's legacy would have been very different. But it did not, and as a result this pioneer of jazz has left a body of work that speaks to both his strengths and limitations as a musician. That he had the benefit of playing with the other giants of his idiom in the styles he was comfortable with means the collective recorded work is indeed a fair assessment of his abilities.

Assessing his legacy can be to compare apples and oranges. The Hot Five and Red Hot Peppers were recording bands only. By contrast, King Oliver's band was an ongoing affair with tight ar-rangements and much nightly practice in performance. The Mor-ton and Armstrong recordings retain classic New Orleans polyph-ony. The Oliver recordings are largely afield of the New Orleans style, and sometimes Ory gets bunched up between the brass bass and the saxophone section. The added instrumentation, as com-pared to the Hot Five and the Red Hot Peppers, was not condu-cive to tailgate trombone playing, and moved Ory out of his com-fort zone. But this, too, is telling: Ory performs nimbly with this band, demonstrating that he continued to evolve as a musician. He was most at home, however, playing tailgate trombone. His performances in standard New Orleans–style polyphony—best expressed in the Hot Five's "Muskrat Ramble," the New Orleans Wanderers' "Gatemouth," and the Red Hot Pepper's "Black Bottom Stomp"—are emblematic of his musicianship.

Some critics deride Ory's musical abilities. In his book *Louis Armstrong's New Orleans*, Thomas Brothers writes of Ory, "He never learned to read music and covered up his weak command of the trombone by smearing over missed notes with glissandi." In *Chicago Jazz: A Cultural History*, William Howland Kenney offers a left-handed compliment, calling Ory a "technically limited but emotionally powerful polyphonic ensemble player." In *Jazz Mas-ters of New Orleans*, Martin Williams notes the soul of Ory's play-ing, stating that, "when Ory plays, all the emotion, all the warmth, the joy and humor and pain, all the things he usually hides, come out. As a bandleader, he is a boss and many of his sidemen have ac-tively disliked him. But as an ensemble player, Ory is all discretion, deference, support and soulful cooperation."[59]

To pillory Kid Ory's musicianship, particularly his solo skills, is to forget who Ory is at heart. Ory, no matter what other type of music he learned to play, was at his core an ensemble trombon-ist. He sounded best in that type of band, and the bands he was in often sounded better with him in them. Still, in the context of jazz evolution, the trombonist that emerges from these recordings is a pioneer jazz musician playing a style that is already passé. Yet, this is instructive in placing Ory in the jazz continuum of which he is very much a part.

> *Although [tailgate] players like [Eddie] Edwards, Ory, [George] Brunis and [Roy] Palmer were all active through-out the 1920s, the tailgate style was no longer reflected in the currently printed dance music. The "modern" trombone part of the early 1920s was a more streamlined, elegant part. The countermelodies were less complicated and pitched in a higher register. By comparison, old style countermelodies were heavy and lumbering.[60]*

Ory's reasons for returning to California may have had some-thing to do with the music business (particularly recording) slow-ing down. His last recording session had been in the summer of 1928. By the next summer, recording work had not picked up. 1929 found Ory in Boyd Atkins's Chicago Vagabonds, perform-ing at the Sunset Café.[61] Atkins was the composer of the Hot Five hit "Heebie Jeebies" and had a large orchestra in keeping with the current trend toward bigger bands. It was a type of music far afield of the style that Ory, now 42 years old, had played when he left New Orleans in 1919. Ory gave his two weeks notice, and Atkins told Ory he had to give four weeks notice. It turned into a squabble and the union president got involved. Why he was in such a hurry to go may have had its roots in marital discord in the Ory home. His wife Dort wanted to move home to California. Her ultimatum took the form of a June 15 newspaper notice in the *Chicago Defender*:

> *Friends of Mrs. Edward Ory 4816 Michigan Avenue regret to learn that she is leaving Chicago soon to be away indefinitely. Mrs. Ory will go first to the old home at New Orleans, La. where she will visit with relatives and friends for a month,*

making brief visits to nearby parishes. She will be the home
guest of Dr. and Mrs. C. C. Haydel, her nephew and his wife.
    Her ultimate destination is Los Angeles, Cal where she re-
sided for more than 10 years. Mrs. Ory owns property in both
New Orleans and California and it is to look after her inter-
ests that she feels obliged to leave at this time.[62]

Ory is not mentioned in the article. The driving force behind Mrs.
Ory's urgent need to go home to New Orleans and then on to California, may be rooted in Ory's philandering, which extended back
to his days in New Orleans. In her 1954 divorce filing, Mrs. Ory
cited numerous affairs and bad behavior on Ory's part through the
years.

And so it was that the jazz age ended for Kid Ory, not with a
bang but a whimper. He left Boyd Atkins's band and Chicago and
returned to in California.

Not long after the Orys arrived home, the stock market crashed
and the Depression began to take hold. For four years Ory struggled on in California, performing in a series of bands, again as
a sideman. In San Francisco he played in Louisiana native Clem
Raymond's Orchestra; in Los Angeles he played with Mutt Carey's
taxi dance band, Freddie Washington's group, and Emerson Scott's
band. By 1932 he was in Charlie Echol's Ebony Serenaders, followed in 1933 by a stint in the Pantages Theatre show *Lucky Day*.[63]
After that, Ory's constant musical activity, dating back over thirty
years to his childhood in LaPlace, came to a halt. And though Ory
would return to music a decade later—and again taste success, in
the jazz revival of the forties and fifties—the accomplishments
that etched his place in history were behind him.

Assessing Ory's legacy requires consideration of the diverse
facets of his career. As a composer he scored a hit with "Muskrat Ramble" and enjoyed royalties until his death in 1973. He was
a recording pioneer whose 1922 Sunshine records were the first
by a black New Orleans jazz band. His work in Chicago with Jelly

Roll Morton, Louis Armstrong, and King Oliver produced classic records that captured the spirit of the jazz age. As a trombonist he was, if not the creator of the tailgate trombone style, its most faithful and imitated proponent. And while he lacked the skill of a virtuoso, he understood perfectly the role of the trombone in a New Orleans jazz ensemble.

Most significantly, Ory was an early, hot, successful New Orleans bandleader who provided work and stylistic direction for future stars like Louis Armstrong, Joe Oliver, and Johnny Dodds, among others. In return Ory's sidemen assured his success through their immense talents and long-term associations. Their common musical experiences, forged in the Ory band, played out not only in the confines of New Orleans in the 1910s but in the clubs and recording studios of Los Angeles and Chicago in the twenties.

But by 1933 this was all a memory. Ory, then 46, called it quits and took a job as a janitor with the Santa Fe Railroad in Los Angeles.

CHAPTER 10

1933–1973

EPILOGUE

As Kid Ory swept up the mailroom at the Santa Fe Railroad office in Los Angeles, the jazz age must have seemed an era long past. With money short, Dort also worked as a maid and seamstress.

In 1937 Ory's brother John and his wife Cecile and family moved from St. John Parish and joined him in Los Angeles, where they found a home a few blocks away. According to Johnny Ory's son Harold, the family passed the time at home playing bridge into the wee hours, cooking, and visiting. Though times were tough, he said the family stuck together and was very close. Johnny and Ed threw in their lots together and raised chickens for family consumption and as a side business to make a little extra money. The venture was short lived, as Johnny Ory died of a heart attack on May 24, 1939.[1]

A magazine article on Ory in the UK record collectors' monthly *Tempo* in April 1938 finds him at his home at 1001 East 33rd Street. Though there are no direct quotes from Ory, it is clear the writer had spoken with him. It mentions that he lives in a nice little home and has become more active in music lately, writing down his old songs and composing new ones. He copyrighted a number of songs beginning in 1940 including old numbers like "Ory's Creole Trombone." Other tunes penned by Ory in the early forties included "Jaywalk," "Are You Selling Songs Mister," and "Mussolini Carries the Drum for Hitler."[2]

In 1940 Jelly Roll Morton, who had returned to Los Angeles, rehearsed a band at the Elks Hall that featured Ory and many of the men he had played with over the years, including Ed Garland, Bud Scott, Mutt Carey, Ram Hall, Wade Whaley, and Buster Wilson; but Morton had no work for the group, so Ory dropped out of the rehearsals.[3] A year later when Jelly passed away, Ory stood as a pallbearer.

Still Ory worked to get back into music. By September 1942 he was playing in Barney Bigard's band at the Club Capri in Los Angeles, in a group that also featured Charles Mingus on bass. Meanwhile, Ory was leading a band of four musicians at the Tip Toe Inn in East Los Angeles, sometimes doubling on bass.[4] Around this time he enjoyed a financial windfall when Bigard took Ory to his publisher's office to find out about the royalties from composing 'Muskrat Ramble.' Bigard assumed that Ory had been living well off the proceeds from the hit song and was shocked to learn otherwise:

> *One day we were sitting in his house preparing these craw-dads when out of the clear blue sky I asked him "How much royalties do you get out of 'Muskrat Ramble?'" I don't even know why I asked. I guess more out of conversation than curiosity. "I don't get nothing" came his reply and I almost fell off the chair . . . His publisher years ago had been Melrose Publishing Company, and they had sold the song to another publishing company and Ory had never gotten nickel one from the song. I had some friends in the music publishing business on Vine Street in Hollywood so I called and asked them who published "Muskrat Ramble." These friends looked it up and said that the Levy Company had it. I took Ory down to this Levy publishing next day . . . "Hello Mr. Levy, I said I'd like to introduce you to Kid Ory and he has never gotten a dime in royalties" . . . Anyhow, this Mr. Levy turned over a check to Ory for around $8000 right there and then, and furthermore he got royalty checks of $600 or so every quarter from then on.[5]*

Proceeds from his publishing, particularly "Muskrat Ramble," would support Ory for the rest of his life. He and Dort bought a big new house at 3715 Arlington Avenue.

By this time, there were rumblings of a revival of interest in 1920s hot jazz. Some fans, put off by the form's stylistic shift toward bebop, clung to the jazz style that had proceeded the swing era. Jazz researchers and fans sought out long-forgotten musicians, sponsoring concerts, radio broadcasts, recording sessions, and books. One fan of New Orleans jazz was filmmaker and radio host Orson Welles. He wanted a New Orleans–style band for his radio show and in March 1944 hired Kid Ory. Ory had no idea who Welles was. The Welles broadcasts opened up many opportunities for Ory, and the band would soon be in the recording studio and playing extended residencies at the Jade Palace in Los Angeles and the Dawn Club in San Francisco.[6]

Nesuhi Ertegun, a Turkish-born ambassador's son, founded Crescent Records in 1944 specifically to record the Ory band. Ertegun produced four sessions in 1944–45 that captured the essence of Ory as a bandleader and trombonist in a way that none of his recordings from the twenties had. Sessions with major labels Decca and Columbia followed as well as a small private label named after its owner, Dr. Frederick B. Exner. By 1950 Ory's comeback from janitor to jazz legend was complete.

Buoyed by composing royalties from "Muskrat Ramble," recording dates, two European tours, and extended residences at the Beverly Cavern in Los Angeles and the Hangover Club in San Francisco, Ory lived the high life during the fifties. He was featured in the film *The Benny Goodman Story* and appeared on radio and television.

His personal life had a second act as well. Though Ory remained married to his wife Elizabeth, or Dort, he was an adulterer going back to their days together in New Orleans. Despite this, Dort supported Ory in the lean times, working as a seamstress and maid. That changed after Ory took up with a serviceman's wife named Barbara GaNung in 1949. The affair was ultimately discovered and in April 1954, a short time before GaNung gave birth to Ory's daughter Babette, Dort sued for divorce. Things were going well for Dort in court until Ory's lawyers pointed out that she had never gotten a divorce from her first husband, John Wallace. Dort claimed that she had asked Ory about that before they were married in 1911, and he had told her there was no need because John Wallace was dead. When the defense threatened to call John Wallace to the stand, Dort's case fell apart. The marriage was annulled and she died in 1965.[7]

Ory and GaNung married in November 1955 and moved in together in Marin County across the bay from San Francisco. GaNung's children by her previous marriage, Arthur and Donald, also lived with the Orys. GaNung was a demanding and abusive woman, according to Babette. Arthur GaNung recalled cryptically in 2002, "They lock people up for the things she did."[8]

GaNung, who was white, was instrumental in getting Ory to deny any African American heritage. She made racial comments about members of his band and was behind the falling out between Ory and his longtime friend and bassist Ed "Tudi" Garland in 1955. She fed Ory's paranoia about money and told him not to give interviews lest someone write a book about him and undercut Ory's attempted autobiography. When interviewers managed to get to him in 1957, GaNung often interjected her own opinions and ideas to the point that Ory himself had to correct her.

Longtime friends of Ory, as well as members of his family, say that when Barbara came into the picture they were cut out. After 1955 Ory socialized almost exclusively with whites. Ory became a man his old friends no longer recognized. Barney Bigard, a longtime friend, saw the changes: "He was just a different guy."[9] He lived in fine homes in Los Angeles and the San Francisco Bay area, drove a Lincoln sedan, and sent Babette to private schools. He briefly operated his own club, Kid Ory's On the Levee, in San Francisco.

Ory broke up his band in 1961 after returning to Los Angeles from the Bay Area. There he relaxed into the role of jazz elder statesman. He made cameos in other groups and played one last time with Louis Armstrong on the Disneyland riverboat *Mark Twain* in 1964. He retired to Diamondhead, Hawaii, in 1966 and enjoyed occasional visits from jazz fans from around the world.

He traveled to New Orleans one last time in 1971 to appear at the Jazz and Heritage Festival. Ory led the opening parade through Congo Square Thursday afternoon to kick off the event and was slated to appear that weekend. Ultimately, he was so frail that his performance was practically inaudible. During the visit, he saw relatives and reconnected with old friends. There were tears and hugs at nephew Dr. C. C. Haydel's home as Ory embraced his sister Annie, who he had not seen since leaving New Orleans in 1919.

Ory returned to Hawaii and died there of pneumonia on January 23, 1973, at the age of 86. A funeral, complete with a brass band, was held in Culver City, California, at Holy Cross Cemetery, where Ory was buried near the top of a hill. As the brass band descended the incline at the end of the service they struck up "Muskrat Ramble" and "Ory's Creole Trombone."[10]

1850–1901: Ozeme "John" Ory, Kid Ory's father. Courtesy Babette Ory.

The Woodland Plantation House, LaPlace, Louisiana. 2001. Ory was born about a mile behind the main house next to the Woodland sugar mill. Photo by John McCusker.

Kid Ory's band, ca. 1910: Ed "Rabbit" Robertson, Kid Ory, Lewis "Chif" Matthews, Johnny Brown, Joseph "Stonewall" Matthews, Foster Lewis. Courtesy of the Hogan Jazz Archive, Tulane University.

1910–15: Kid Ory lived with relatives at this house at 2133–35 Jackson Avenue between 1910–15. His was the first home of a New Orleans jazz pioneer saved from demolition, renovated, and marked with a plaque by the Preservation Resource Center. Photo by John McCusker/*Times-Picayune*. Used with permission.

ca. 1917: Kid Ory in New Orleans.
Courtesy Babette Ory.

ca. 1919: Edward and
Elizabeth Ory in California.
Courtesy Babette Ory.

GRAND MARDI GRAS BALL

at

THE MUNICIPAL AUDITORIUM ARENA

Tuesday Evening, February 28, 1922

Under the Auspices of the

Louisiana Commercial Association

Music by King Oliver's & Ory's Celebrated Creole Orchestra.

Prince R. D. Clark, President; Count H. O. Whaley, Earl Chas. Songy, Marquis A. D. Lawrence, Duke S. S. Boucree, Earl A. K. Martin, Baron S. O. Villa, Sir Knight John Craig, Count E. R. James, Grand Duke Emille Martin, Marquis M. D. Broadnax and Duke Charles Baker.

PRINCE F. H. BURRILL, SR., Chairman.

Grand Duke A. B. MARTIN, Sec.   Lord G. INGRAHAM, Treas.

GENERAL ADMISSION, $1.00 (And War Tax)

1922: Ad in the newspaper *Western Appeal*, February 18, 1922.

1922: A Kid Ory band in California including Warren "Baby" Dodds, Ory, Mutt Carey, Edward Garland, and Wade Whaley. Courtesy of the Hogan Jazz Archive, Tulane University.

THE ONLY RACE JAZZ BAND THAT HAS MADE PHONOGRAPH RECORDS ON THE COAST

1922: Another Ory California band. Ory is second from right. *Chicago Defender.*

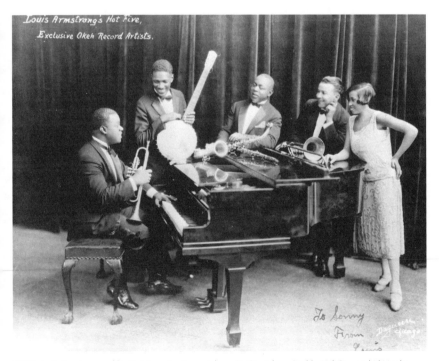

1925: Louis Armstrong and his Hot Five: Armstrong, Johnny St. Cyr, Johnny Dodds, Kid Ory, and Lil Hardin. All but Hardin were alumni of the Kid Ory band of New Orleans. Courtesy of the Hogan Jazz Archive, Tulane University.

1927: Handbill advertising King Oliver's arrival in New York. Ory is far left.

Edward and Elizabeth Ory's Chicago home at 444 East 48th Street. Photo by Alexandra Johnson.

1926: Jelly Roll Morton's Red Hot Peppers: Morton center, with Omer Simeon, Andrew Hilaire, John Lindsay, Johnny St. Cyr, Kid Ory, George Mitchell. All but Mitchell were from New Orleans. Courtesy of the Hogan Jazz Archive, Tulane University.

1946: Kid Ory's Creole Jazz Band at the Jade Palace with Bud Scott, Mutt Carey, and Joe Darensbourg. Courtesy Babette Ory.

1947: Kid Ory at his home on Arlington Avenue in Los Angeles. Photo by George Fletcher. Courtesy of the New Orleans Jazz Club Collection of the Louisiana State Museum.

1950: Elizabeth "Dort" Ory and Edward Ory. Courtesy of the New Orleans Jazz Club Collection of the Louisiana State Museum.

1950: Barbara GaNung and Kid Ory in Los Angeles. Courtesy Babette Ory.

1956: Kid Ory in Europe with Alvin Alcorn and Phil Gomez. Courtesy Babette Ory.

1971: Kid Ory's return to New Orleans to play the Jazz and Heritage Festival at Congo Square. Courtesy *Times-Picayune*. Used with permission.

1972: Kid Ory's last birthday, Honolulu, Hawaii. Courtesy Babette Ory.

AUTOBIOGRAPHY

This is an excerpt from Kid Ory's "autobiography," most of which is loose pages recalling a story or event. The presence of Mutt Carey and Emile Bigard suggests this story happened around 1914–15.

A PIT-A-PAT TALE
9 AUGUST 1951

While my band and I were still living and working in New Orleans, I signed up for a little tour we were going to make between the Crescent City and Baton Rouge, and received deposits from the various spots we would hit. This money came to about $35 or $40. For the first time in my life, I did something I had never attempted or thought of before . . . I fooled around and spent the deposit money. This wasn't mine to spend . . . it was the band's money. I was really in a fix.

The first stop on the tour was in St. James Parish at the Beehive Hall. The dance was a great success, but when we got though playing, I still didn't have the money to pay the boys off. I didn't say anything, just got on the train with them. The boys, using what money that had had with them, started a pit-a-pat game, but I didn't get into it. When they got to the hall after the dance, they started another game. I had about a buck or so, and I decided to invest that in the game, thinking maybe I'll be lucky. I lost that money and told them, "Boys, I'm broke." I kept wondering where I was going to get the money to pay the boys for their night's work.

Papa Mutt Carey spoke up. He said, "I'll put you in the game." And gave one dime and I started to pay. I won all the money that I had spent so foolishly and wrongly, too, and still had about $15 left for myself. Barney Bigard's uncle, Emile, said to Papa Mutt, "Anyone who would give that lucky guy a dime to get in the game is crazy. He was out of the game, why didn't you keep him out?"

Papa Mutt told him, "He would give me a dime or a dollar to put me in a game and I would have given him more than a dime, but we were betting a dime to start with, so I gave him a dime. There's nothing wrong with that."

Emile Bigard said, "Now I haven't got any money."

I came in at that point and the discussion and said, "Here, Emile, I'll pay you for your night's work."

And I did, partly with his own money, though, because he had been one of the biggest losers in the game.

AUTOBIOGRAPHY

It is unclear where and when this story takes place. The presence of Edward Garland, Joe Oliver, and Roy Palmer strongly suggests New Orleans before 1917 when Garland left for Chicago. No record has been found of the arrest. "Leggo" Caldwell is a mystery and may be a transcription mistake by Barbara GaNung.

14 AUGUST 1951

One night after we finished working, we all went to the house of a trumpet player named "Leggo" Caldwell. I remember that Joe Oliver and Ed Garland and another trombone man, Roy Palmer, were along, as well as many others. We were having a pretty gay time and a policeman knocked at the door. He said he wouldn't do anything to any of the party that time, but we had to cut down the noise before he was forced to do something about it. We thanked him and assured him we'd do better and the party went on again.

We had more drinks and finally forgot all about the warning. The next thing we knew was the police arriving again. This time they brought the wagon and backed it right up the door. The trombone man, Roy Palmer, said to them, "I'm just an old trombone boy. Can't you let me slip through?"

The cop said, "Yeah, we'll let you slid right through here," and showed him into the wagon.

Ory's Sunshine Orchestra, "Maybe Someday," on the Spikes Brothers' Sunshine label, 1922.

SELECTED DISCOGRAPHY

Hearing Ory's signature tailgate growls on record tells the story that lies between the lines of this book and can only serve to enhance one's appreciation of the musician, bandleader, and composer. This list is designed with the jazz neophyte and today's digital music consumer in mind. Rather than suggest expensive compact disc box sets, I have chosen to offer a list of individually available recordings that the reader can find on iTunes and other digital music sites. Be warned that in the digital music marketplace, which is free from the extensive liner notes of yesteryear, it is often hard to know which version of a song you are buying. With that, as well as the 78 RPM record collector in mind, I have listed individual recording dates, labels, and matrix and issue numbers to try and make sure that you buy the right version of "Muskrat Ramble" (There are dozens available). Another hint: since Ory was a sideman in the twenties, it is helpful to search under Louis Armstrong, King Oliver, or Jelly Roll Morton to find his recordings. Band name, session date, record label, song, personnel, matrix number, and issue number are listed for each song. For the most complete Ory discography available, see Sid Bailey, *Greatest Slideman Ever Born: A Discography of Edward "Kid" Ory*, 3rd ed., September 2000.

SELECTED DISCOGRAPHY: THE TWENTIES

Ory's Sunshine Orchestra/Spikes' Seven Pods of Pepper Orchestra
ca. May/June 1922

Nordskog/Sunshine Records
Kid Ory, trombone; Mutt Carey, trumpet; Dink Johnson, clarinet; Fred Washington, piano; Edward Garland, bass; Ben Borders, drums.
Ory's Creole Trombone NORDSKOG 3009/SUNSHINE 3003

Louis Armstrong and his Hot Five
November 12, 1925
Okeh Records
Louis Armstrong, cornet; Kid Ory, trombone; Johnny Dodds, clarinet; Lil Hardin, piano; Johnny St. Cyr, banjo.
Gut Bucket Blues / 9486-A/ OKEH 8261

Louis Armstrong and his Hot Five
February 26, 1926
Okeh Records
Georgia Grind 9533_A / OKEH 8318
Muskrat Ramble / 9538-A / OKEH 8300

King Oliver's Jazz Band
March 11, 1926
Vocalion Records
Joe Oliver, trumpet; Kid Ory, trombone, Bob Schoffner, trumpet; Albert Nicholas, Billy Paige, Barney Bigard, reeds; Richard M. Jones, piano and vocal; Bud Scott, banjo; Bert Cobb, sousaphone; Paul Barbarin, drums.
Snag It / E-2634W / VOCALION 1007

King Oliver and his Dixie Syncopators
April 21, 1926
Vocalion Records
As previous entry except Luis Russell replaces Richard M. Jones on piano.
Deep Henderson / E-2892W / VOCALION 1014

King Oliver and his Dixie Syncopators
May 29, 1926
Vocalion Records
Sugar Foot Stomp / E-3179W / VOCALION 1033

Louis Armstrong and his Hot Five
June 16, 1926
Okeh Records
Dropping Shucks / 9731-A / OKEH 8357
Who's It / 9732-A / OKEH 8357

Louis Armstrong and his Hot Five
June 23, 1926
Okeh Records
Add Clarence Babcock and Richard M. Jones, speech on "King of
the Zulus"
The King of the Zulus / 9776-A / OKEH 8396
Sweet Little Papa / 9779-A / OKEH 8379

New Orleans Wanderers
July 13, 1926
Columbia Records
Kid Ory, trombone; George Mitchell, cornet; Johnny Dodds, clari-
net; Lil Hardin, piano; Johnny St. Cyr, banjo.
Perdido Street Blues / 142426-1 / COLUMBIA 698-D
Gatemouth / 142427-2 / COLUMBIA 698-D

Jelly Roll Morton's Red Hot Peppers
September 15, 1926
Victor Records
Jelly Roll Morton, piano; Kid Ory, trombone; George Mitchell,
trumpet; Omer Simeon, clarinet; Johnny St. Cyr, banjo; John Lind-
say, bass; Andrew Hilaire, drums.
Black Bottom Stomp / 36239-1 / VICTOR 20221
The Chant / 36241-3 / VICTOR 20221

Jelly Roll Morton's Red Hot Peppers
September 21, 1926
Victor Records
Marty Bloom, effects.
Steam Boat Stomp / 36285-3 / VICTOR 20296

Jelly Roll Morton's Red Hot Peppers
December 16, 1926
Victor Records
Grandpa's Spells / 37255-3 / VICTOR 20431
Canon Ball Blues /37258-2 / VICTOR 20431

King Oliver and his Dixie Syncopators
April 22, 1927
Vocalion Records
Tick Gray, trumpet replaces Bob Schoffner; Omer Simeon replaces
Albert Nicholas and Billy Paige, reeds.
Willie the Weeper / E-5168W / VOCALION 1112

King Oliver and his Dixie Syncopators
April 27, 1927
Vocalion Records
Bert Cobb or Lawson Buford, sousaphone; unknown, banjo.
Black Snake Blues / E-5170W / VOCALION 1112

Louis Armstrong and his Hot Five
September 2, 1927
Okeh Records
Ory's Creole Trombone / 81310-D / COLUMBIA 35838

Louis Armstrong and his Hot Five
December 9, 1927
Okeh Records
Struttin' With Some Barbeque / 82037-B / OKEH 8566

Louis Armstrong and his Hot Five
December 10, 1927
Okeh Records
Add Lonnie Johnson, guitar.I'm Not Rough / 82040-B / OKEH 8551

Louis Armstrong and his Hot Five
December 13, 1927
Okeh Records
Add Lonnie Johnson, guitar.
Savoy Blues / Okeh 82056-B / OKEH 8535

With the exception of the 1922 Sunshine sessions, all of Ory's recorded work in the twenties was as a sideman. When he returned
to the recording studio in 1944, it was as a bandleader. All of these
recordings, with the exception of a Louis Armstrong session, are of
the Kid Ory's Creole Jazz Band. The band played a mix of marches,
rags, popular songs, original tunes and a number of Creole French
songs ("Creole Song," "Eh La Bas" and "Blanche Touquatoux") that
hark back to the songs Ory heard as a boy in St. John the Baptist
parish, Louisiana. Though Ory would record into the sixties, it was
the work of the original Ory come-back band, featuring long-time
sidemen like Thomas "Mutt" Carey, Edward "Montudi" Garland
and Minor "Ram" Hall among others, that best tells the story.

SELECTED DISCOGRAPHY: THE FORTIES

Kid Ory's Creole Jazz Band
August 3, 1944
Crescent Records
Kid Ory, trombone; Mutt Carey, trumpet; Omer Simeon, clarinet;
Buster Wilson, piano; Bud Scott, guitar; Ed Garland, bass; Alton
Redd, drums.
Get Out of Here and Go Home / CPM-10-32-1A / CRESCENT 2
Creole Song / CPM-10-35-2A / CRESCENT 1

Louis Armstrong and His Hot Five recording of Kid Ory's "Savoy Blues," Okeh Records, 1927.

Kid Ory's Creole Band
February 12, 1945
Exner Records
Joe Darensbourg replaces Simeon on clarinet.
Dippermouth Blues / EX5-3A / EXNER 3

Kid Ory and His Creole Band
March 21, 1945
Decca Records
Minor Hall replaces Alton Redd, drums; add Cecile Ory (Johnny's wife), vocals.Blanche Touquatoux / L3757 / DECCA 25134
High Society / L3755 / DECCA 25133

Kid Ory's Creole Jazz Band
August 5, 1945
Crescent Records
Same personnel as first Crescent session but add Minor Hall, drums.

Panama / 1006 / CRESCENT 7
Do What Ory Say / 1010 / CRESCENT 5\

Kid Ory's Creole Jazz Band
September 8, 1945
Crescent Records
Darnell Howard replaces Omer Simeon, clarinet.
1919 / CRE 1013 /CRESCENT 4
Maryland, My Maryland / CRE1015 / CRESCENT 3

Kid Ory's Creole Jazz Band
November 3, 1945
Crescent Records
Maple Leaf Rag / CRE1023-4 / CRESCENT 8

Kid Ory and his Creole Jazz Band
October 12, 1946
Columbia Records
Barney Bigard, clarinet.
Tiger Rag / HCO 2089-1 / COLUMBIA 37274

Louis Armstrong's Dixieland Seven
October 17, 1946
Victor Records
Louis Armstrong, trumpet; Kid Ory, trombone; Barney Bigard,
clarinet; Red Callender, bass; Charlie Beal, piano; Bud Scott, gui-
tar; Minor Hall, drums.
Do You Know What It Means To Miss New Orleans / D6VB2192 /
VICTOR 20-2087

Kid Ory and his Creole Jazz Band
October 21, 1946
Columbia Records
Bucket's Got a Hole In It / HCO2106-1 / COLUMBIA 37274
Eh La Bas / HCO2107-1 / COLUMBIA 37275

LOST COMPOSITIONS

In the 1940s Kid Ory composed a number of songs that he never recorded nor, to the author's knowledge, performed. They include four songs he copyrighted, "Jaywalk," "Mussolini Carries the Drum for Hitler," "Why the Blues Was Born" and "Don't Forget the Santa Fe Train and Bus," and one he composed with Bud Scott but did not copyright, "Calling the Children Home". Of these, the latter is probably the most interesting musically and historically, since both Bud Scott and Ory heard Bolden "call his children home."

"Don't Forget (the) Santa Fe Train and Bus" May 21, 1941

"Jaywalk" January 3, 1942

"Mussolini Carries the Drum for Hitler" March 4, 1942

AND KEEP YOUR SELF RIGHT ON THE DOT IF YOU MO VE

WE WILL LO SE THEN WE'LL BE TWO GREAT BIG FOOLS, BUT

GREATE WAS NOT AND HE HAD TO STOP THEN HE TURNED RIGHT AROUND AND

THEN HE FLOPPED So NOW HE'S NOT EV-EN PLAYING THE BULL FID-DLE

HE JUST CARRIES THE DRUM FOR HIT- LER

FIFE & NICHOLS MUSIC COMPANY
1407 VINE STREET   HO 0534

"Are You Selling Songs Mister?" February 9, 1942

WONT IT TO   SLOW   I DONT WONT IT TO   BLUE

BUT I   WONT - A - GOOD SUG— ME   CUE YOU JUST

GRAB YOUR HORN AND GET   ON   THE SPOT   AND LAY YOUR MOUTH PEACE

ON YOUR CHOPS YOU GO . BOM. BOM.   BOM.   BOM.

. BOM. BOM.   THEN YOU START

FIFE & NICHOLS MUSIC COMPANY
1467 VINE STREET   HO 0534

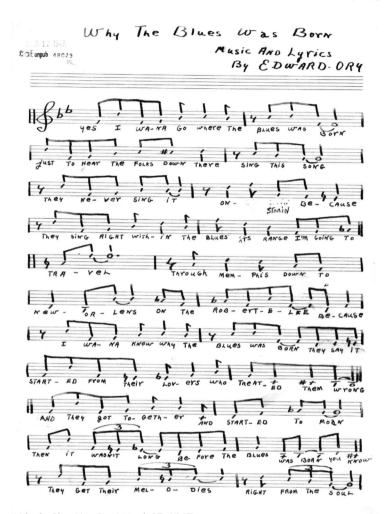

"Why the Blues Was Born" March 17, 1947

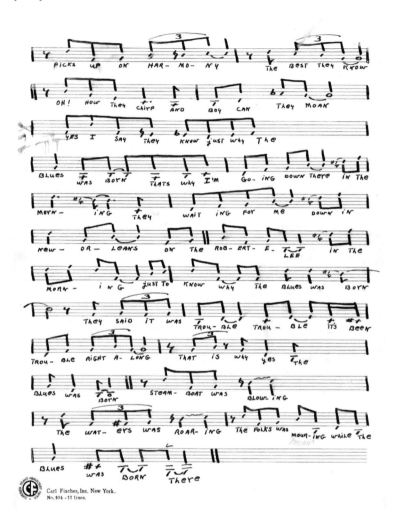

"Calling the Children Home" with Bud Scott, unknown date.

NOTES

CHAPTER 1

1. "the Woodland plantation"—St. John the Baptist Parish, "Mortgage Index" (St. John Parish Courthouse, Edgard, LA: 1898). Woodland Plantation sold to Ory Partnership by Emile Legendre—$65,000 for the house and 1,882 acres.

"the road"—Joy Lodrigues (granddaughter of John L. Ory) in interview with the author, September, 1999.

2. Claudia Montz Cambre and Etienne Cambre, *Getaway to Yesterday* (La-Place, LA: Cambre, 1983), 55.

3. U.S. Census, St. John the Baptist Parish, 1870: Population 6782—2718 white, 4044 black.

4. 1869 St. John the Baptist parish tax assessment rolls, Microfilm rolls: 1. 1863–65; 2. 1869–81. St. John the Baptist Parish Library, LaPlace, LA.

5. "birth of Ozeme"—Ozeme Ory Baptismal Certificate: St. John the Baptist Parish Church, baptism book page 280, act 47. Succession of Edmond Ory and Marie Irene Tregre. 4th JDC, St. John the Baptist Parish, microfilm page 537.

"for several generations"—Elida Millet Calliouet, *Lions on the River: A Potpourri* (Tuscon, AZ: 1989), 15, 16. The area was later known as Lions, named after postmaster Frank Lions.

6. "to Frederick County"—Glenn R. Conrad, "Some Maryland Germans who Settled in Louisiana", *Les Voyageurs*, vol. III, no. 4 (December 1982): 85–88.

"several more children"—Albert J. Robichaux Jr., *German Coast Families: European Origins and Settlement in Colonial Louisiana* (Rayne, LA: Hébert Publications, 1997), 780, 781. Ozeme Ory's paternal great-grandfather, Jean Mathias Ory (1749–1820), was a son of Nikolas's first marriage, while his maternal great-grandfather, Louis Ory (1763–1800), was a son of the second marriage.

7. Conrad, 85–88.

8. J. Hanno Deiler, *The Settlement of the German Coast of Louisiana and Creoles of German Descent* (Philadelphia: Americana Germanica Press, 1909), 74, 119, 124.

9. "in Terre Haute"—Succession of Edmond Ory and Irene Tregre. 4th JDC State Court, St. John Parish, page 537. Charles Nolan, ed., *Sacramental Register of the Roman Catholic Church of the Archdiocese of New Orleans*, vol. 10: 1810–12, 335; vol. 12: 1816–17, 376.

"They married . . . Marie Ory Tregre"—1850 Census, St. John the Baptist Parish, 8/13/1850, 270, vis. 373.

"when he was three"—Succession of Edmond Ory and Marie Irene Tregre Ory. 4th JDC, St. John Parish, 537.

10. "guardian of three-year-old Ozeme"—*Ibid*.

"about Ozeme's age"—1860 Census, St. John the Baptist Parish, slave schedule, 501.

"near LaPlace"—1870 census of St. John the Baptist Parish, Fourth Ward, page 21, line 36.

11. "(though his brother Edmond did)"—Andrew B. Booth, ed., *Records of Louisiana Confederate Soldiers and Louisiana Confederate Commands*, vol. III (Spartanburg, SC: Reprint Publications, 1984), 46. Edmond Ory was a private in Co. D 22nd Confederate Louisiana Infantry who enlisted 16 August 1864. Pardoned by Union authorities 13 May 1865 in Meridian, MS.

"Ory's daughter Marie"—St. John the Baptist Church baptismal book. *Les Voyageurs* (March 1996): 9.

"with the Triches"—St. John Parish Index of Oaths, Parish Court, Guardian Appointments, 2 June 1869. St. John the Baptist Parish Library, Microfilm roll GS 48-132.

12. "named Octavie Devezin"—St. Peter Church, Reserve, LA, Baptismal Book 2, FPC, 1864–1884.

"first child of Ozeme Ory"—1880 Census St. John Parish, 1 supp. Dist., ed. 63, sheet 18.

13. "ebony in the sunlight"—Ory autobiography.

"Listed as mulatto"—1880 St. John Parish, 1 supp., dist. 2, ed. 63, sheet 18, line 59. 1900 Census St. John, Fourth Ward, vis. 382. Octavie is listed in the sacramental register of St. Peter's Catholic Church as being 48 at the time of her death on September 5, 1900, meaning she was born in 1852. She is 30 in the 1880 census. The 1900 census lists her birth in December 1848.

"She worked as a washerwoman"—Joy Lodrigues, interview with author, 1999.

14. "child of Octave and Jacques Thomas"—Baptism of Charles Octave Thomas, November 4, 1869, St. Peter's Church, Reserve, LA, Baptism Book 2, Free People of Color (1864–84) 65–66, Act 64.

"there were slaves named 'Devezin'"—St. Peter's Church, Reserve, LA, Baptismal Book 1.

15. Thomas Brothers, *Louis Armstrong's New Orleans* (New York: W.W. Norton, 2006), 171.

16. "behest of the French"—Deiler, *The Settlement of the German Coast of Louisiana and Creoles of German Descent*. Deiler argues that Germans adopted the French language, eventually modifying their names to French-friendly pronunciations (e.g. "Tregel" to "Tregre"). This is a generally accepted argument among that group.

"called *plaçage*"—*Plaçage* was a practice going back to the founding of the Louisiana colony. Women of mixed French and African ancestry were often brought to balls where they were matched with white men who would support them as mistresses or *plaçees*.

17. Coleman Warner, "Le Monde Creole," *Times-Picayune*, April 6, 2003, 1.

18. The godparents listed on the respective Ory family baptismal certificates tended to be other Creoles of Color, for example, Charles Lapeyrolerie, who was Annie Ory's godfather. Annie Ory baptism, St. Peter's Church, Baptism Book 4 (1892–02), 38, act 49.

19. "November 1870"—Baptismal record Simon Leonce Ory, St. Peter's Catholic Church, Reserve, LA, November 19, 1870.

"not with Octavie"—1870 Census, St. John the Baptist Parish, Fourth Ward, page 21, line 36.

20. "also moved upriver"—1880 Census, St. John the Baptist Parish, Fourth Ward, ed. 162, page 41, line 13.

"Edward joined a family"—1880 Census, St. John Parish, 1 supp. Dist., ed. 63, sheet 18. Ory autobiography, ch. 1, page 2. Says brothers died before he was born.

"came in 1889"—Marie Lesida Ory baptism, St. Peter's Catholic Church, Reserve, LA, Baptism Book 3, (1880–91), page 221, act 6. January 12, 1890.

"followed in 1893"—Annie Ory baptism, St. Peter's Catholic Church, Reserve, LA, Baptism Book 4, page 38, act 49. April 1, 1893.

"family was very poor"—Ory autobiography, August 14, 1951, 2.

21. "native of Avoyelles Parish"—1880 Census Avoyelles Parish, LA, Second Ward, 17 June 1880, page 14 supp. dist. 2, ed. 1, line 8, 9.

"in central Louisiana"—Marriage certificate of Victor Bontemps and Louisa Ory, St. John the Baptist Parish, 21st Judicial District Court, 5 March 1895, St. John the Baptist Parish Library, LaPlace, LA.

"and owned property"—Succession of Louis Bontemps, Orleans Parish clerk of court.

"at the Woodland"—1900 Census St. John Parish, sup. Dist. 2, ed. 63, sheet 18, visitation 384. The Orys are on the same page a few lines away.

22. "Clay Haydel"—1880 Census St. John Parish, Second Ward, page 675, supp. Dist. 1, ed. 150.

"operated a store"—St. John Parish assessment rolls, roll 6, microfilm roll 52.147, St. John the Baptist Parish Library, LaPlace, LA. Haydel General Store, Third Ward, 1905, Clay Haydel and Co., 560 acres, 1906; Sybil Morial (Ory's great niece) interview with the author, 1999.

23. Ory autobiography, August 14, 1951, ch. 1, page 1.

24. "five consecutive months"—"Notice: Officer of the Super of PS, St. John Parish," *Le Meschacébé*, February 16, 1895.

"elementary school student"—The unedited examples of his writing are recipes he wrote down to share with others. Personal collection of Arthur GaNung, stepson of Kid Ory. Ory eschewed the printed word and few examples of his writing, apart from a few recipes, exist. After his tours of Europe in 1956 and 1959, he was inundated with reams of fan mail, none of which he ever answered.

25. Ory autobiography, August 14, 1951, ch. 1,pages 1–2.

26. *Le Meschacébé*, March 23, 1895, 2; *Lions on the River*, 67–72.

27. "joined the family holdings"—Alcee Fortier, ed., *Louisiana; Comprising Sketches of Parishes, Towns, Events, Institutions, and Persons, Arranged in Cyclopedia Form*, Vol. 3 (Century History Association: 1914), 690-692. *Lions on the River*, 68. Lodrigues, interview with author.

"younger than Dutt"—1900 Census, St. John Parish, Fourth Ward, vol. 38, ed. 63, sheet 17, line 63.

"experienced in birthing children"—Marcia G. Gaudet, *Tales from the Levee: The Folklore of St. John the Baptist Parish* (Lafayette: University of Southwest Louisiana Press, 1984), 58–60.

"Babies were born at home"—Harold Ory interview with the author, February 5, 2000, Compton, California.

28. Joy Lodrigues interview with author, 1999.

29. *Lions on the River*, 41–42. Harold Ory interview, February 5, 2000, Compton, CA.

30. *Les Voyageurs*, March 1996.

31. *Lions on the River*, 28.

32. Ory autobiography, August 14, 1951, ch. 1, 3.

33. *Ibid.*, 2–3.

34. Ory autobiography, pages titled "Rice Harvest," 1, 2.

35. "only liquor license for miles"— Bill Russell, *New Orleans Style* (New Orleans: Jazzology Press, 1994), 172.

"telephone was installed"—Advertisement for the Woodland Store, *Le Meschacébé*, March 23, 1895, 2.

"in the Woodland Plantation"—*Le Meschacébé*, March 23, 1895, 2; *Lions on the River*, 67–72.

36. Maria Ory Levet, interview with the author, 1999.

37. www.infoplease.com/us/supreme-court/cases/ar29.html#axzzowEQApMva.

38. Jean M Eyraud and Donald Miller, *A History of St. John the Baptist Parish* (Marrero, LA: Hope Haven Press, 1939), 20; *Times-Picayune*, April, 24, 1896, 9.

39. Contrasting the 1850 St. John census with that of 1900 shows the conversion of names like Jean to John, Edouard to Edward, and Noelie to Nellie.

CHAPTER 2

1. "Death of John Ozeme Ory," *Le Meschacébé*, August 3, 1901, 1. Ory said in his autobiography that he got the banjo within weeks of his father John's death on July 29, 1901.

2. "grew up with Ory"—Morris French, Hogan Jazz Archive, Tulane University (June 24, 1960), 1.

"Stonewall would get fired"—Joseph "Babe" Phillips, Hogan Jazz Archive, Tulane University (March 25, 1957), 5.

"Lewis, born 1887"—Louis C. Matthews World War I draft registration, Ancestry.com. Matthews's age is listed as 27. 1910 Census, New Orleans, sup. 1, ed. 29, sheet 2B, vis. 43. Census also lists Matthews's age as 23.

"not the musician Chif was"—Clarence "Little Dad" Vincent, Hogan Jazz Archive, Tulane University (December 11, 1959), 19.

3. "Edward 'Rabbit' Robertson"— 1910 Census, New Orleans, ed. 29, sheet 2B, vis. 43.

"Both of Duhe's sisters"— Austin Sonnier Jr., *Second Linin' Jazzmen of Southwest Louisiana 1900–1950* (Lafayette: Center for Louisiana Studies, University of Southern Louisiana, 1989), 1; 1900 Census, St. John the Baptist Parish, Fourth Ward, ed. 63, sheet 9.

4. Ferrand Clementin and Mathilda August Clementin, interview by Richard B. Allen, Hogan Jazz Archive, Tulane University (August 2, 1973), 22, 23.

5. Irene Therese Whitfield, *Louisiana French Folk Songs* (Baton Rouge: Louisiana State University Press, 1939), 122.

6. Sybil Kien, ed., *Creole: The History and Legacy of Free People of Color*, (Baton Rouge: Louisiana State University Press, 2000), 124.

7. Shirley Thompson, "'Ah Toucoutou, ye conin vous': History and Memory in Creole New Orleans," *American Quarterly* (University of Texas) 53, no. 2 (June 2001): 232.

8. "newspaper accounts of the time"—*L'Observateur*, May 24, 1913, 1, article advancing a concert at Woodman of the World hall in LaPlace featuring John Daniel Ory on flute, sister Ida on piano, and cousin George Lasseigne on cornet.

"organized music of any kind"—Joy Lodrigues, interview by John McCusker, LaPlace, LA (1999).

"Ory alludes to him"—Edward "Kid" Ory interview, April 20, 1957, 10.

9. "'The brass bands were used'"—Ferdinand "Pete" Valentine, Hogan Jazz Archive, Tulane University (June 24, 1960), reel 2, 4.

"thus a 'string band'"—Joseph "One-Eye Babe" Phillips, Hogan Jazz Archive, Tulane University (March 25, 1957), 7. Phillips recalled brass bands that had string band configurations, which played for dancing.

10. Edward "Kid" Ory interview, April 20, 1957, 3.

11. Lynn Abbott, "Mr. E. Belfield Spriggins: First Man of Jazzology," *78 Quarterly* 10 (November 1999): 46, 48.

12. "Humphrey was born"—1860 Sugar Census of Louisiana, St. John Parish, 16, 17. Plantation owner James Humphrey, Professor Humphrey's father, appears on the 1860 census in the First Ward of New Orleans and also shows up as James B. Humphrey on the St. John slave owners' census. James B. Humphrey death certificate, November 26, 1935, housed at the Louisiana State Archive, Baton Rouge, LA.

"with his wife Ella in 1878"— 1880 Census, New Orleans, vol. 11, ed. 85, line 19.

"maintained a home in Reserve"—Richard Knowles, *Fallen Heroes: A History of New Orleans Brass Bands* (New Orleans: Jazzology Press, 1996), 72.

13. "He was a leader"—*Ibid*.

"though others did not"—Joseph "One-Eye Babe" Phillips, Hogan Jazz Archive, Tulane University (March 25, 1957), 3.

"in a competition"—Edmond Hall, Hogan Jazz Archive, Tulane University (April 11, 1957), 1.

14. Knowles, 76; Sunny Henry, Hogan Jazz Archive, Tulane University (January 18, 1959), 5; Harrison Barnes, Hogan Jazz Archive, Tulane University (January 29, 1959), 1.

15. Earl Humphrey, Hogan Jazz Archive, Tulane University (November 30, 1968), 9.

16. Charles "Sunny" Henry interview (January 18, 1959), 5.

17. "Valentine led the Pickwick band"—Ferdinand "Pete" Valentine interview, June 24, 1960, reel 1, page 1. Valentine did not know his exact birthday but was likely born in the 1870s.

"When playing a gig"—Marshall Lawrence, interview by Richard Allen, Hogan Jazz Archive, Tulane University (June 28, 1960), 4.

18. Ferdinand "Pete" Valentine interview, June 24, 1960, 1.

19. Russell, 174.

20. "Kid" Thomas Valentine, Hogan Jazz Archive, Tulane University (May 22, 1957), 1.

21. Russell, 172.

22. "blues for dancing"—"Papa" John Joseph, Hogan Jazz Archive, Tulane University (November 26, 1958), 27.

"Charlie Galloway and Edward Clem"—Edward "Kid" Ory interview, April 20, 1957, 24.

23. "What Did Ory Say: The fabulous trombonist's own story in his own words," *Record Changer* (November 1947): 5.

24. Russell, 171.

25. "till his death in 1939"—Al Rose and Edmond Souchon, *New Orleans Jazz: A Family Album*, 3rd ed. (Baton Rouge: Louisiana State University Press, 1984), 109.

"Robichaux is said"—Daniel Hardie, *Exploring Early Jazz: The Origins and Evolution of the New Orleans Style* (iUniverse, 2002), 18, 75.

26. "St. Joseph Brass Band"—William J. Schafer and Richard B. Allen, *Brass Bands and New Orleans Jazz* (Baton Rouge: Louisiana State University Press, 1977), 99.

"Henry, Kaiser, and Nelson"—Papa John Joseph interview, November 26, 1958, 1.

27. "his home in Reserve"—"Kid" Thomas Valentine interview, May 22, 1957, 8.

"how to read their parts"—Manuel Paul, Hogan Jazz Archive, Tulane University (April 19, 1960), 10.

"played with the group"—Papa John Joseph interview, November 26, 1958, 12; Papa John Joseph interview, January 18, 1962, 1.

28. Clementin interview, August 21, 1973, 22.

29. Ory autobiography, chapter titled "Girls, Clothes, Mules and Horses," dated August 9, 1951, 1.

30. *Ibid.*, 3.

31. Notes by Barbara GaNung from an interview of Kid Ory. Babette Ory collection.

32. Ory autobiography, chapter titled "Girls, Clothes, Mules and Horses," dated August 9, 1951, 1.

33. *Ibid.*, 2.

34. "dramatic presentations"—"Concert at LaPlace," *L'Observateur*, March 24, 1913, 1; "Better Get Ready," *L'Observateur*, April 18, 1914, 1.

"until a late hour"—"St. John Euchre Club," *Le Meschacébé*, August 4, 1906, 4.

"The club was for whites"—*L'Observateur*, November 14, 1914, 1.

35. "was thoroughly woven"—Lynn Abbott, "Play That Barber Shop Chord: A Case for the African-American Origin of Barbershop Harmony," *American Music* 10, no. 3 (Fall 1992): 319; Lynn Abbott and Doug Sertoff, *Ragged but Right: Black Traveling Shows, "Coon Songs" and the Dark Pathway to Blues and Jazz* (Jackson: University Press of Mississippi, 2007), 358.

"early in their careers"—Abbott, "Play That Barber Shop Chord," 314.

36. *Oh, Didn't He Ramble: The Life Story of Lee Collins*, as told to Mary Collins, ed. Frank J. Gillis and John W Miner (Urbana: University of Illinois Press, 1974), 62. *Cowien* is the Creole word for turtle, but it can also refer to a function where it is served.

37. Russell, 171.

38. "Popular songs in the river parishes"—Marshall Lawrence interview, June 28, 1960, 4.

"it replaced 'Dixie'"—Abbott and Sertoff, 235. In 1903 the Acme Quartette said "Hiawatha" had taken the place of "Dixie" as a highly requested number.

39. Ory autobiography, handwritten page containing this paragraph.

40. *Ibid.*, two unnamed pages dated July 24, 1951.

41. Barbara GaNung, biographical notes for Ory autobiography, Babette Ory collection.

42. "Kid" Thomas Valentine interview, May 22, 1957, 7–8.

43. Florence Dymond memoirs, 1873–1962 ca. 1930, Howard Tilton Library, Tulane University.

44. Rose and Souchon, 69.

45. Ory autobiography, unnamed page dated March 9, 1950, 2.

CHAPTER 3

1. Ory autobiography, chapter titled "Description of Rice Harvesting," dated July 24, 1951, 2.

2. "over buckets of ice"—Marcia G. Gaudet, *Tales from the Levee: The Folklore of St. John the Baptist Parish* (Lafayette: Center for Louisiana Studies, University of Southern Louisiana, 1984), 22.

"about two feet high"—Joy Lodrigues (granddaughter of John L. Ory), interview with author, September 1999.

"prayers at graveside"—St. Peter's Catholic Church, Reserve, LA, Funerals Book, 1864–1901, 282, no. 44.

3. Ory autobiography, untitled chapter dated August 14, 1951, 2.

4. Ory autobiography, chapter titled "Description of Rice Harvesting," dated July 24, 1951, 2.

5. Ory autobiography, untitled chapter dated July 24, 1951.

6. Ory autobiography, chapter titled "Description of Rice Harvesting," dated July 24, 1951, 2.

7. "Ozeme 'John' Ory died"—St. Peter's Catholic Church sacramental register, Funeral Book vol. 12, 4.

"at the Woodland Plantation"—Ory mentions in his autobiography that the family broke up. Ory says that Johnny lived with the Haydels and that he lived with the Bontemps. Annie also lived with the Bontemps; it is unclear where Lizzie went to live.

8. Ory autobiography, untitled chapter, undated page.

9. The actual name of this area was Furatsville, but it came to be known as Cherokee Town after the Cherokee roses that grew there.

10. Ory autobiography, untitled chapter dated March 10, 1950.

11. St. John Parish tax records, Fourth Ward, LaPlace, LA, 1903. James Millet listed as owner of $160 house.

12. Ory autobiography, untitled chapter, loose page dated March 13, 1950.

13. "to build the house"—Ory autobiography, untitled chapter, dated March 10, 1950.

"paid off the lumber bill"—Ory autobiography, untitled chapter, loose page dated March 13, 1950.

14. *Ibid.*

15. Ory autobiography, untitled chapter, undated page.

16. Harold Ory, interview with author, Compton, CA, February 2002. Since Ory says "guitar" here and not "banjo," it must be assumed that event occurred some time after he got the banjo. He may have borrowed his brother Johnny's guitar. Johnny Ory's son, Harold, recalled that his father once played guitar.

17. Ory autobiography, untitled chapter, untitled pages, 4.

18. Henry Garon, *Donaldsonville, its businessmen and their commerce at the turn of the century* (Louisiana Lore Press, 1976), 108. The Picayune sawmill was a mile downriver from Donaldsonville. Ory may have been visiting a camp in the area.

19. Ory autobiography, untitled chapter, untitled pages. These pages are distinguished with III at the top of each page, presumably to represent chapter 3 of the autobiography.

20. Ory autobiography Unpublished biography, untitled chapter, undated page.

21. Ory autobiography, untitled chapter, undated page.

22. Ory autobiography, untitled chapter, loose page dated March 10, 1950.

23. *Ibid.*

24. *Ibid.*

CHAPTER 4

1. "It was a regular store"—Author interview with Sybil Morial, 1999.

"a card game going on"—Author interview, Harold Ory, Compton, CA, February 2002.

"trained to carry messages"—Author interview with Rudolph Dinvaut, 1999. Dinvaut's family bought the store when Ory sold it in 1937.

2. Louis C. Hennick and E. Harper Charlton, *The Streetcars of New Orleans* (New Orleans: Pelican, 1965); Ory autobiography, "Coffee Story." In his autobiographies, Ory recalls staying with his cousin "Coffee" in New Orleans while the

latter was installing the City Park streetcar line. That project was completed November 30, 1905. Since Ory says his trip to buy the trombone was his first to New Orleans, it might be assumed that the Bolden meeting happened before this date.

3. "Ory's sister Lena"—Succession of Warren Cotton, June 4, 1918, #124020, Civil District Court, Orleans Parish, Div. A, docket 1. In this document the marriage is acknowledged and considered legal but no date is given. There is no mention of Lena's daughter Maud, who was born in 1902. It must be assumed that she was the child of another man.

"corner of Jackson Avenue"—1906 Soards directory of New Orleans.

4. "often included the story"—Campbell Holmes, "Kid Ory: Another Pioneer of Swing," *Tempo* 1938, 19–20. In Ory's earliest known interview, he recalled the Bolden story, though it was paraphrased in the publication.

"the first jazz band leader"—Papa John Joseph oral history, Hogan Jazz Archive, Tulane University (November 26, 1958), 18.

5. Marquis, Donald M., *In Search of Buddy Bolden: First Man of Jazz* (Baton Rouge: Louisiana State University Press, 1978), 99.

6. Papa John Joseph, oral history, Hogan Jazz Archive, Tulane University (November 26, 1958), 18, 21.

7. Lawrence Duhe, oral history, Hogan Jazz Archive, Tulane University (June 9, 1957), 8; Duhe interview 1960, 2.

8. Nat Shapiro and Nat Hentoff, *Hear Me Talking to Ya: The Story of Jazz as Told by the Men Who Made It* New York: Dover, 1955), 35.

9. Abbott, *78 Quarterly*, 14.

10. Ory interview, Hogan Jazz Archive, Tulane University (April 20, 1957), 56.

11. *Ibid.*, 28–29.

12. "a baseball venue"—Johnson Park approved January 2, 1903, by city ordinance 1579/cal #2089; Lincoln Park May 30, 1902, New Orleans City Ordinance 1260. Mathilda August Clementin interview, Hogan Jazz Archive, Tulane University (August 2, 1973), 29. Clementin said New Orleans teams played country teams Sundays in Oleander Park, which was across the street from Lincoln and Johnson Parks.

"opened the Johnson Saloon"— Marquis, 62.

13. E Benfield Spriggins, "Excavating Local Jazz," *Louisiana Weekly*, April 22, 1933.

14. *Ibid.*

15. Mathilda August Clementin interview, Hogan Jazz Archive, Tulane University (August 2, 1973), 13.

16. Ory autobiography, "Lincoln Park," 1.

17. Kid Ory interview, Hogan Jazz Archive, Tulane University (April 20, 1957), 29–30.

18. Ory autobiography, "Funky Butt Hall," August 16, 1951, 1.

19. "Ory said Bolden"—Kid Ory interview, Hogan Jazz Archive, Tulane University (April 20, 1957), 24–25.

"goes back to that"— Bernard Klatzko, Liner notes to *Whole World in His Hands: 1927–36 [Sanctified, Volume 3]*. 1928 recordings by the Elder Richard Bryant on Victor feature a cornet, lending credibility to the notion of wind instruments being used in church. One song, "Everybody was There," is similar to the jazz tune "Bucket's Got a Hole in It," which is remembered as a Bolden tune.

20. Kid Ory interview, Hogan Jazz Archive, Tulane University (April 20, 1957), 35–36.

21. "Papa Mutt Carey, Gene Williams and Marili Stuart," *Jazz* (1943): 5.

22. Shapiro and Hentoff, [PAGE].

23. "a Baptist one"—Marquis, 28. The church was also known as the St. John Institutional Baptist Church. Originally on First Street near Bolden's home, the church is now a short distance away on Jackson Avenue, where a picture of the original church hangs in the foyer.

"others within walking distance"—Woods Directory 1912 (New Orleans: Woods Publishing, 1912).

24. R. Emmet Kennedy, *More Mellows* (New York: Dodd, Mead, 1931), 7.

25. Edward "Kid" Ory, interview by Richard Hadlock, *The Complete Kid Ory Verve Sessions* (Mosaic/Verve Records, 1960).

26. Marquis, 81.

27. Author interview with Floyd Levin and Ray Avery, February 2000.

28. John L. Ory's niece Joy Lodrigues said he hired Kid Ory's band to play the wedding reception.

29. Ory interview, Hogan Jazz Archive, Tulane University (April 20, 1957), 11.

30. *Ibid.*, 37.

31. Marquis, 116, 123, 131.

CHAPTER 5

1. "I had to go back home"—"What Did Ory Say," 5.

"changing the date of the event"—Alma Hubner, "Ory: That New Orleans Trombone," *Jazz Notes* (January 1946): 4; Alfred Scott, "Kid Ory," Carnegie Hall Program, April 30, 194[?]. In both of these sources, Ory gives his birth year as 1889 and says he brought the band to New Orleans in 1911. Edward "Kid" Ory, interview by Nesuhi Ertegun, Hogan Jazz Archive, Tulane University (April 20, 1957). In this interview he gives his correct birth year (1886), but changes the date of the move to New Orleans to 1907 or 1908. That the move occurred in 1910 and not 1907 is supported by the fact that members of the band show up in city directories and the census in 1910. Sometime between 1950 and 1957, Ory wrote to St. Peter's Church in Reserve, LA, and obtained a copy of his baptismal certificate to learn the year of his birth.

2. "What Did Ory Say," 5.

3. "for a Mr. Snow"—Lynn Abbott, "Mr. E. Belfield Spriggins: First Man of Jazzology," *78 Quarterly* 10 (November 1999): 41.

"down in Lake Pontchartrain"— 60–61.

4. Edward "Kid" Ory, unpublished autobiography, chapter titled "Lincoln Park," dated March 23, 1950, 1.

5. Marquis, 61.

6. Edward "Kid" Ory, interview, Hogan Jazz Archive, Tulane University (April 20, 1957); Kid Ory unpublished autobiography, chapter titled "New Orleans," dated March 23, 1950, 1–2; Ferrand Clementin and Mathilda August Clementin, interview by Richard B. Allen, Hogan Jazz Archive, Tulane University (August 2, 1973), 5. Lincoln Park regular Mathilde August Clementin also recalled the ping-pong as "a killer" to dance. The ping-pong featured a motion where the dancers swung from side to side. Clementin said they also danced the slow drag, turkey trot, bunny hug, and grizzly bear. These sexy new dances were then becoming popular, no doubt mirroring the evolution of dance music.

7. Kid Ory unpublished autobiography, chapter titled "New Orleans," dated March 23, 1950, 2.

8. "What Did Ory Say," 5.

9. "Ory himself misidentified him"—"What Did Ory Say," 5. Ory referred to his bass player as Alfred Lewis. Edward "Kid" Ory, interview by Nesuhi Ertegun. Ory says "Alfred," then corrects himself and says "Foster."

"Ory claims in an interview"—"What Did Ory Say," 5. Ory said his old bass player became a trombonist.

10. "just gotten married"—1910 Census, St. John the Baptist Parish, ed. 80, page 13, line 13. Louis is listed as 21 years old and having been married a year.

"band moved to New Orleans"—1910 Census, New Orleans, Louisiana.

11. "He could not remember"—"Papa" John Joseph, Hogan Jazz Archive, Tulane University (January 18, 1962), 2.

"kicker to Verrett's story"—Harrison Verrett interview, Hogan Jazz Archive, Tulane University (August 10, 1961), 14.

"Clarence 'Little Dad' Vincent"—Clarence "Little Dad" Vincent interview, Hogan Jazz Archive, Tulane University (November 17, 1959), 15.

12. "No musicians refer to"—The Hogan Jazz Archive at Tulane University maintains an index of band names that are mentioned in its vast collection of oral

history interviews. In these, the only reference to the Woodland Band is made by Ory himself. Others identify his groups as simply "Ory's Band," "Ory's Brown Skin Band," and later the Ory-Oliver band.

"probable culprit is GaNung"—The band is referred to as Ory's Brown Skin Band in an article by Cy Shain and Vivian Boarman, *Jazz Music* 3, no. 7 (1947). In 1950–51 fragments from his autobiography, co-written with Barbara GaNung, he refers to the plantation group as the Woodland Band.

13. Tom Stoddard, *The Autobiography of Pops Foster: New Orleans Jazzman* (Berkeley: University of California Press, 1971), 51.

14. Ory dates this "just before" his move to New Orleans in 1910. Moseman's saloon first shows up on St. John Parish conveyance records in 1905; Conveyances register, St. John Parish Book Q, page 217, St. John the Baptist Parish Library, La-Place, LA.

15. Ory unpublished autobiography, chapter titled "Instruments," dated March 10, 1950, 1. Louis Bontemps was actually his brother-in-law's brother.

16. Trevor Herbert, *The Trombone* (New Haven and London: Yale University Press, 2006), 267.

17. David Sager, "A Tale of the Slide Trombone in Early Jazz," *Jazz Archivist* 3, no. 1 (1988): 1, 2, 11.

18. "Ory mentions playing"—"What Did Ory Say," 6.

"confirmed Ory's membership"—Ferrand Clementin and Mathilda August Clementin, interview by Richard B. Allen, Hogan Jazz Archive, Tulane University (August 2, 1973), 20.

19. Spelling taken from draft registration. He is Robinson in other sources.

20. "What Did Ory Say," 6. The story suggests that Ory brought sheet music to Robertson to learn to play pieces by ear as Robertson played from the piece as written.

21. "Bill Matthews said"—Bill Matthews interview, Hogan Jazz Archive, Tulane University (March 10, 1959), 25.

"Ory said Delisle"— Ory interview, *Complete Kid Ory Verve Sessions*.

"though with less glissando"—For a head-to-head comparison, listen to Zue Robertson's recording with Morton of "Someday, Sweetheart" and Ory's recording of the same song with Morton's Red Hot Peppers in 1926.

22. Ory interview, *Complete Kid Ory Verve Sessions*.

23. Ory unpublished autobiography, chapter titled "Lincoln Park," dated March 23, 1950, 1–2. According to the *Indianapolis Freeman*, Lincoln Park was open in August, so it is possible that Ory got the year wrong or that Bartley was no longer manager.

24. Ernest "Kid Punch" Miller interview, Hogan Jazz Archive, Tulane University (May 25, 1958), 4.

25. "What Did Ory Say," 6.

26. "also presented there"—Milton Martin interview, Hogan Jazz Archive, Tulane University (December 21, 1964), 1.

"Gilbert 'Bab' Frank"— 1910 Census, New Orleans, Louisiana, ed. 185, page 8A, line 50. Birthday based on 1910 census where Frank is listed as 38 years old.

"Bass player Wellman Braud"—Wellman Braud interview, Hogan Jazz Archive, Tulane University (March 31, 1958), 6.

"He was one of the best"—"Papa" John Joseph interview, Hogan Jazz Archive, Tulane University (November 26, 1958), 68–69.

27. Ibid.

28. Ory unpublished autobiography, chapter titled "New Orleans," dated March 23, 1950, 2.

29. "Ory's band cut Frank"—Martin T. Williams, Jazz Masters of New Orleans (New York: Macmillan, 1967), 208.

"Ory solidified his gig"—Alex Bigard interview, Hogan Jazz Archive, Tulane University (April 30, 1960), 25.

30. Ory unpublished autobiography, chapter titled "When I first Met Freddie Keppard," dated July, 26, 1951, 3.

31. "Jones lived in"—Soards Directory, New Orleans, 1910, lists George Jones, musician, 520 Bertrand.

"He was also popular"—Eddie Richardson interview, Hogan Jazz Archive, Tulane University (October 29, 1960), 2.

"Johnny St. Cyr said"—Johnny St. Cyr interview, Hogan Jazz Archive, Tulane University (August 27, 1958), 32.

"He sawed through"—The G string is the thinnest one on the bass. Bows are traditionally made of horsehair.

32. Edward "Kid" Ory interview, Hogan Jazz Archive, Tulane University (1957).

33. "Edward Garland (1885–1980)"—Edward Garland, California Death Index, 1940–1997, January 22, 1980. search.ancestry.com/search/db.aspx?dbid=5180&cj=1&sid=dicadeath&o_xid=0000584978&o_lid=0000584978; Ed Garland interview, Hogan Jazz Archive, Tulane University (August 8, 1959).

"tipped Garland off"—Edward Garland interview, Hogan Jazz Archive, Tulane University (August 8, 1959), 3.

34. Ory unpublished autobiography, chapter titled "Tudi," undated page.

35. Edward Garland interview, Hogan Jazz Archive, Tulane University (August 8, 1959), 3.

36. Ory unpublished autobiography, unnamed chapter dated March 23, 1950.

CHAPTER 6

1. 1910 Census, New Orleans, Louisiana.

2. Henry A. Kmen, *Music in New Orleans: The Formative Years, 1791–1841* (Baton Rouge: Louisiana State University Press, 1966), 58, 149, 150.

3. *Ibid.*, 151.

4. *Ibid.*, 226.

5. *Ibid.*, 227.

6. *Ibid.*, 227, 228.

7. *Ibid.*, 229.

8. "horn and trumpet playing"—*Daily Picayune*, August 2, 1838, 2.

"musical funerals with brass bands"—*Daily Picayune*, August 21, 1853, 2.

"these societies that funded"—Though militia companies and fire companies also held parades into the twentieth century, it is the benevolent society procession that has endured within the same communities in New Orleans where they existed a century ago.

9. Kmen, 3.

10. For example, the Original Dixieland Jazz Band incorporated "That Teasin' Rag" into one strain of the "Original Dixieland One-Step."

11. "Ory had followed"—When asked to mention the other bands on the scene when he arrived in New Orleans, Ory mentions uptown bands like Jack Carey and Frankie Duson—not Creole dance bands.

"remembered bassist John Joseph"—"Papa" John Joseph interview, Hogan Jazz Archive, Tulane University (November 26, 1958), 28.

12. Wellman Braud interview, Hogan Jazz Archive, Tulane University (March 31, 1958), reel 1, page 6.

13. Earl Humphrey interview, Hogan Jazz Archive, Tulane University (November 30, 1968), reel 1,page 5. By "faking," Humphrey explained, he meant one who was not able to read music, who made up his own parts which he "used to his own distinction."

14. Stoddard, 51.

15. "his brother John's marriage"—John Ory marries Cecile Tregre of Reserve, LA. St. John marriage records, 1891–1916, part 2, February 18, 1909. Microfilm GS 48-17, St. John the Baptist Parish Library.

"John's daughter Pearl"—Pearl Ory baptismal notation, 1910, St. Peter's Catholic Church baptismal register, reprinted in *Les Voyageurs*, June 1997, 65.

16. "3201 Freret Street"—1910 Soards New Orleans City Directory. Soards places Ory at Freret Street. John Cotton, the brother of his sister Lena's husband Warren Cotton, is noted at that address in 1908. The 1910 census finds Ory at 2823 Second Street in June. The Ory autobiography says he lived at 2135 Jackson Avenue when

he first moved to New Orleans. Ory later shows up in the Soards directory at Jackson Avenue 1913–15. He likely lived at Freret Street with his extended family before moving in with Warren Cotton's family and sister Annie to 2823 Second Street by June 1910. From there he likely moved to Jackson Avenue. His occupancy at Jackson Avenue was a fluid one, as he also rented a house at 1906 Josephine in 1912.

"2823 Second Street"—1910 Census, New Orleans, Louisiana, Vol. 49, ed. 189, vis. 134. Annie Ory is listed living with the Cottons and Ory on Second Street.

"a few years earlier"—1900 Census, Baton Rouge, Louisiana, Sup. 6, Ed. 30, page 8, line 70.

17. 1910 Census, New Orleans, Louisiana; Sanborn Fire Insurance Map: New Orleans, 1910 (Vol. 2, Sheet 167). Both reference the 2100 block of Jackson Avenue.

18. 1910 Census, New Orleans, Louisiana, Ed. 189,page 6a, lines 51–73.

19. "from cousin Leana"—While genealogy of Ory's mother's family has proven elusive, it might be assumed that Leana Banks is a relative of Ory's on his mother's side of the family.

"Leana had married"—St. John the Baptist Parish marriage records 1846–1931, pt. 2, 1891–1916 GS 48-17, St. John the Baptist Parish Library.

"marble cutter and carpenter"—Ory unpublished autobiography, chapter titled "How I Started Promoting Dances," dated August 2, 1951, 2. The Judge Minor Wisdom Court of Appeal building on Camp Street in downtown New Orleans, once the city post office, was one of the buildings where Ory cut marble. Arthur Banks World War I draft registration, Ancestry.com. Banks is listed as a carpenter on his draft registration. Soards New Orleans directory lists Banks as a machinist in 1913 and a marble cutter in 1916.

20. Sanborn Fire Insurance Map: New Orleans, 1909 (Vol. 4, Sheet 401).

21. William Ivy Hair, *Carnival of Fury: Robert Charles and the New Orleans Race Riot of 1900* (Baton Rouge: Louisiana State University Press, 1976).

22. Ory unpublished autobiography, chapter titled "Chinches," dated September 5, 1951.

23. Ory unpublished autobiography, chapter titled "Storyville," dated July 29, 1951, 1–2.

24. Manuel Manetta and Edward "Kid" Ory interview, Hogan Jazz Archive, Tulane University (August 26, 1958), 1.

25. "businessman Peter Ciaccio"—Peter Ciaccio World War I draft registration, Ancestry.com. Address given as 1500 Iberville, the site of one of his two Storyville businesses.

"an ongoing business"—Johnny Lala interview, Hogan Jazz Archive, Tulane University (September 24, 1958), Reel 4, page 14.

26. Ory, Lewis Matthews, Edward Robertson, and Lawrence Duhe all appear on the 1910 census in New Orleans, which was taken in April.

27. Ory unpublished autobiography, chapter titled "Storyville-Spano's," dated August 7, 1951, 3.

28. *Ibid.*, 2.

29. Ory unpublished autobiography, loose page, dated March 23, 1950, 1.

30. Ory unpublished autobiography, loose page with two dates: July 26, 1950, and August 14, 1950.

31. *Ibid.*

32. *Ibid.*

33. "What Did Ory Say," 6.

34. *Ibid.*

35. *Ibid.*

36. Edward "Kid" Ory, interview by Nesuhi Ertegun, Hogan Jazz Archive, Tulane University (April 20, 1957), 88.

37. Louis Armstrong, *Satchmo: My Life in New Orleans* (New York: Da Capo, 1954), 141.

38. "Wooden Joe" Nicholas interview, Hogan Jazz Archive, Tulane University (November 12, 1956), Reel 2,page 11.

39. "Betsy Cole's maiden name"—New Orleans marriage index, May 30, 1887.

"purchased a lot of property"—New Orleans property records, October 25, 1909, 4th Municipal District, Sq. 393, Property bounded by Willow, Clara, Josephine, Jackson. #2 lot, 2732 Josephine Street.

"She was a spiritualist"—Lillian De Pass interview, Hogan Jazz Archive, Tulane University (June 20, 1960), 15.

40. Marili Ertegun, "Just Playing Music I Love, Says Kid Ory," *Down Beat*, August 10, 1951, 2.

41. "What Did Ory Say," 6. Ory thought he was 21. He probably did not meet Elizabeth when he was fifteen, as it has been established that Ory first visited New Orleans in 1905 when he was eighteen, but thought he was 15.

42. "John Wallace in 1907"—Tangiapahoa Parish State Court 25JDC, marriage record book 8, page 392. Los Angeles Superior Court divorce record, Ory vs. Ory, case D467592.

"they married and moved"—New Orleans Health Department, Register of Marriages, 1911, vol. 33,page 758. New Orleans Public Library.

"married Annie in January"—New Orleans Health Department, Register of Marriages, vol. 32,page 900. License filed Bk. 66, folio 52. New Orleans Public Library.

43. "to drift apart"—"What Did Ory Say," 5.

"Duhe and his new band"—Lawrence Duhe interview, Hogan Jazz Archive, Tulane University (June 9, 1957), 4.

"to pull the clarinet"— Stoddard, 53.

"twenty-year-old rice mill worker"—Ory unpublished autobiography, chapter titled "Dances," dated August 2, 1951. Ory says he sponsored his first dance in March 1912 and that Dodds was in the band.

44. Gene H. Anderson, "Johnny Dodds in New Orleans," *American Music* (Winter 1990): 417.

45. *Ibid.*

46. Edward Garland interview, Hogan Jazz Archive, Tulane University (April 20, 1971), 4. John Brown shows up as a furniture mover in the Soards New Orleans directory in 1910.

47. Anderson, "Johnny Dodds in New Orleans," 406, 413.

48. "Brown kept his job"—Stoddard, 53. Pops Foster confirms that Brown switched from clarinet to violin.

"the point of fisticuffs"—Edward Garland, Hogan Jazz Archive, Tulane University (August 7, 1951), 1, 3.

49. Stoddard, 52.

50. Ory unpublished autobiography, chapter titled "How I Started Promoting Dances," dated August 2, 1951, 3.

51. *Ibid.,* 4–5.

52. Fatima Shaik, "The Economy Society and Community Support for Jazz," *Jazz Archivist,* 2004, 2.

53. Ory unpublished autobiography, chapter titled "How I Started Promoting Dances," dated August 2, 1951, 4–5.

54. Shapiro and Hentoff, 48–49.

55. *Times-Democrat,* January 2, 1913.

56. *Ibid.*

57. Johnny St. Cyr interview, Hogan Jazz Archive, Tulane University (August 27, 1958), 23.

58. 1920 Census, Los Angeles, California, Vol. 56, Ed. 412, sheet 21, line 43. 1890 birthday based on census. According to the 1930 census, his birthday would be 1888. 1891 is the date given in Cy Shain article in *Jazz Music* (1946): 5–10. It is September 17, 1890, according to the online California Death Index, 1940–1997. His WWI draft registration says he was born in New Orleans on May 25, 1892.

59. Hentoff and Shapiro, 40.

60. "Carey's family"—Cy Shain, *Jazz Music* 3, no. 1, 5.

"604 Felicity Street"—Soards Directory of New Orleans, 1911, 211. Edward Garland interview, Hogan Jazz Archive, Tulane University (August 8, 1958), 14. Garland said Carey worked as a cotton inspector.

61. Hentoff and Shapiro, 40–41.

62. Joe Tullis, "Papa Mutt," *Jazz Tempo* (March 1944): 51.

63. Hentoff and Shapiro, 24.

64. "St. Cyr met Ory"—Johnny St. Cyr interview, Hogan Jazz Archive, Tulane University (August 27, 1958), Reel 6,page 23.

"at guitar/banjo"—St. Cyr played a six-string banjo tuned like a guitar. Sometimes called a guitjo or a banjitar, St. Cyr hand-made his from guitar and banjo parts.

65. Ory unpublished autobiography, chapter titled "Spano's," dated August 7, 1951; Bar permits, 1916, City of New Orleans. Spano's was located at 1235 Poydras in black Storyville.

66. Ory unpublished autobiography, chapter titled "New Orleans," dated March 23, 1950, 2.

67. "What Did Ory Say," 6.

68. Edward Garland interview, Hogan Jazz Archive, Tulane University (April 21, 1957), 2.

69. Johnny St. Cyr interview, Hogan Jazz Archive, Tulane University (August 27, 1958), 23.

70. "His legitimate job"—Lorenzo Staulz World War I draft registration, Sept. 12, 1918, Ancestry.com.

"a good banjo player"—Edward "Punch" Miller interview, Hogan Jazz Archive, Tulane University (May 25, 1958), 2.

71. 1920 Census, New Orleans, ed. 34, sheet 15b, line 95; Henry Martin, World War I draft registration, June 5, 1917, Ancestry.com.

72. "a great drummer"—Alfred Williams interview, Hogan Jazz Archive, Tulane University (February 3, 1961), 14.

"Martin would sometimes"—*Ibid.*, 1.

"dazzled by the playing"—Alex Bigard interview, Hogan Jazz Archive, Tulane University (April 30, 1960), 21.

73. Joe Watkins interview, Hogan Jazz Archive, Tulane University (March 16, 1960), 13.

74. Ory unpublished autobiography, loose page dated August 14, 1951.

75. Ory unpublished autobiography, chapter titled "Johnny Dodds and Frankie Dusen," August 21, 1951, 1.

76. "who lived next door"—Staulz and Duson show up next door to each other in the 1916 Soards directory. This story could have happened then or a little earlier.

"Staulz reported to Ory"—Ory unpublished autobiography, "Johnny Dodds and Frankie Dusen," August 21, 1951, 1–2.

77. *Ibid.*

CHAPTER 7

1. "Oliver was born"—Stella Oliver interview, Hogan Jazz Archive, Tulane University (April 22, 1959), 1.

"year is contradicted"—Joseph Oliver draft registration, serial number 1997, order number 646, September 12, 1918.

"on Dryades Street in 1885"—*Jazzmen*, ed. Frederic Ramsey Jr. and Charles Edward Smith (Harcourt Brace, 1939), 59.

"His father, Nathan Oliver"—Orleans Parish Recorder of Births, Marriages and Deaths, "Marriage License of Joseph Oliver and Stella Dominick," Vol. 33, 460; Stella Oliver interview, Hogan Jazz Archive, Tulane University (April 22, 1959), 2, 9.

"Nashville Avenue uptown"— 1900 Census, New Orleans, Ed. 130, sheet 1, line 22.

"Second and Magazine streets"—Ramsey Smith, *Jazzmen*, 60–61; Stella Oliver interview, Hogan Jazz Archive, Tulane University (April 22, 1959), 2; Manuel Manetta interview, Hogan Jazz Archive, Tulane University, 19.

2. "led by Walter Kenchen"—Walter C. Allen and Brian Rust, *King Joe Oliver* (London: Jazz Book Club, 1957), 1.

"'Monocles' and 'Bad Eye'"—*Ibid.*, 1, 2.

"He eventually took to playing"—*Ibid.*, 2; Laurie Wright, *"King" Oliver* (L. D. Wright/Storyville, 1987), 2; Richard Knowles, *Fallen Heroes: A History of New Orleans Brass Bands* (New Orleans: Jazzology, 1996), 66.

3. Ory unpublished autobiography, chapter titled "Naturals in the Jazz World," dated July 21, 1951.

4. Preston Jackson interview, Hogan Jazz Archive, Tulane University (June 2, 1958), 20.

5. *Ibid.*, 22.

6. Shapiro and Hentoff, 45–46.

7. Manuel Manetta interview, Hogan Jazz Archive, Tulane University (March 21, 1957), Reel 6,page 19.

8. Ory unpublished autobiography, chapter titled "Naturals in the Jazz World," dated July 21, 1951.

9. Shapiro and Hentoff, 42.

10. *Ibid.*, 41–42. (This story must have happened before the fall of 1917 when both Dodds and Garland left the band. The reference to "Eddie Polla" is curious. There was a New Orleans violinist named James Palao who toured in this period with the Original Creole Orchestra. Palao had an uncle named Edgar Palao who was a wind band musician.) John McCusker, "The Onward Brass Band and the Spanish American War," *Jazz Archivist* 1998, 27.

11. Thomas Brothers, *Louis Armstrong's New Orleans* (London: W.W. Norton, 2006), 245.

12. Manuel Manetta and Edward "Kid" Ory interview, Hogan Jazz Archive, Tulane University (August 26, 1958), 2. (The spelling of this name is based on the transcription of the oral history.)

13. Manuel Manetta interview, Hogan Jazz Archive, Tulane University (March 28, 1957), reel 2,page 6.

14. "News of the Players," *Indianapolis Freeman*, November 10, 1917, 5.

15. Edward "Kid" Ory interview, *Complete Kid Ory Verve Sessions*.

16. Shapiro and Hentoff, 42.

17. "Ory would sing songs"—Stella Oliver interview, Hogan Jazz Archive, Tulane University (April 22, 1959), 13.

"Ory had a pretty good ear"—Manuel Manetta interview, Hogan Jazz Archive, Tulane University (March 28, 1957), reel 6.

18. Ory unpublished autobiography, chapter titled "Do What Ory Say," dated August 16, 1951/August 21, 1951. (Johnny St. Cyr also claimed the song in his oral history, and it was published by Clarence Williams and Armond Piron with St. Cyr as a co-composer with Piron.) Johnny St. Cyr and Armand Piron, "Mama's Baby Boy," ed. John Robichaux Collection (Williams and Piron, 1917), Box 70, f6, 10818263, Hogan Jazz Archive, Tulane University.

19. Ory unpublished autobiography, chapter titled "Do What Ory Say," dated August 16, 1951/August 21, 1951, 1, 2.

20. *Ibid.*

21. Louis Armstrong, *Satchmo: My Life in New Orleans* (New York: Da Capo, 1954), 97–98.

22. "back with Dort"—Edward Ory draft registration, Ancestry.com. He is listed as married and a musician. Manuel Manetta said Ory had been running around on Dort, but ran back to her when he learned about the exemption.

"Ory, Manetta, and Dodds"—Oliver, Staulz, and Lyons would register at a later call-up in 1918. Draft registration cards of Joseph Oliver, Lorenzo Staulz, and Bob Lyons, Ancestry.com.

"got their deferments"—Manuel Manetta and Edward "Kid" Ory interview, Hogan Jazz Archive, Tulane University (August 26, 1958), 3–5.

23. *Indianapolis Freeman,* July 14, 1917, 5.

24. Gene H. Anderson, "Johnny Dodds in New Orleans," *American Music* (Winter 1990): 430.

25. *Ibid.*, 430–31; "News of the Players," *Indianapolis Freeman*, November 10, 1917, 5; *Chicago Defender,* September 28, 1918, 6.

26. *Indianapolis Freeman*, September 28, 1918.

27. "News of the Players," *Indianapolis Freeman*, November 10, 1917, 5.

28. "Macon and Chattanooga"—*Indianapolis Freeman*, December 8, 1917, 5, 6.

"Oliver had fallen in love"—Manuel Manetta interview, Hogan Jazz Archive, Tulane University (March 28, 1957), reel 2.

"She [Mary McBride]"—Manuel Manetta interview, Hogan Jazz Archive, Tulane University (March 28, 1957), reel 2.

"Billy Mack was arrested"—New Orleans Police Department arrest records, August 1, 1917, 1st Precinct.

29. *Times-Picayune*, March 2, 1919, 30.

30. Anderson, "Johnny Dodds in New Orleans," 429–32.

31. "Jimmie Noone (1894–1944)"—James Noone World War I draft registration card, Ancestry.com. 1894 given as year of birth.

"Noone was on tour"—Gene H. Anderson, "The Genesis of King Oliver's Creole Jazz Band," *American Music* (Fall 1994): 284; Lawrence Gushee, *Pioneers of Jazz: The Story of the Creole Band* (New York: Oxford University Press, 2005), 229; Lawrence Gushee, author interview, August 2010.

"His big break came"—Gushee, *Pioneers of Jazz*, 180.

32. Anderson, "Johnny Dodds in New Orleans," 419.

33. Ory unpublished autobiography, chapter titled "Naturals in the Jazz World," dated July 21, 1951, 5.

34. Wade Whaley World War I draft registration, Ancestry.com; Rose and Souchon, 126.

35. Anderson, "Johnny Dodds in New Orleans," 423. Foster's chronology connecting Dodds, Nicholas, and Whaley supports the notion that Whaley was with the band after Dodds left in 1917.

36. Gushee, *Pioneers of Jazz*, 217.

37. Rose and Souchon, 74.

38. Anderson, "Johnny Dodds in New Orleans," 423.

39. "Ory's old clarinetist"—*Indianapolis Freeman*, August 25, 1917, 5.

"Bob Lyons (1872–1949)"—Rose and Souchon, 78; Bob Lyons arrest card, New Orleans Police Department Arrest Cards 1914–47, roll 826 B, New Orleans Public Library.

40. "in King Oliver's band"—Rose and Souchon, 131.

"'Red Happy' Bolton (1885–1928)"—Anderson, "Johnny Dodds in New Orleans," 423.

41. Ory unpublished autobiography, undated page.

42. Arrest cards of Edward Ory and Joseph Oliver, New Orleans Police Department Arrest Cards, Oi–Paddio, 1914–47, roll 842B, New Orleans Public Library.

43. Shapiro and Hentoff, 49. An odd thing about this story is Dodds was the clarinetist on the job that got raided, but Ory refers to Jimmie Noone as his clarinetist.

44. "he hated the cold"—Anderson, "Johnny Dodds in New Orleans," 431.

"at the Dreamland Café"—Allen and Rust, 6.

45. "named him 'King'"—Ory unpublished autobiography, chapter titled "Naturals in the Jazz World," dated July 21, 1951.

"next time they met"—*Western Outlook*, March 25, 1922, 2.

46. Shapiro and Hentoff, 49.

47. Armstrong, *Satchmo*, 137.

48. *Ibid.*, 139.

49. Shapiro and Hentoff, 49.

50. Brothers, 28.

51. Armstrong, *Satchmo*, 145.

52. Brothers, 28.

53. Armstrong, *Satchmo*, 142.

54. "Shipyard workers had been exempt"—*Times-Picayune*, October 17, 1917.
"jumped atop a streetcar"—Manuel Manetta and Edward "Kid" Ory interview, Hogan Jazz Archive, Tulane University (August 26, 1958), 3.
"shut down for much of the summer"—City Counsel index of ordinances, card file, New Orleans Public Library, Louisiana Room. Also published in the *Times-Picayune*, July 7, 1918.

55. Manuel Manetta and Edward "Kid" Ory interview, Hogan Jazz Archive, Tulane University (August 26, 1958), 7.

56. Ernest "Kid Punch" Miller interview, Hogan Jazz Archive, Tulane University (April 9, 1957), reel 1.

57. Shapiro and Hentoff, 76.

58. *Ibid.*

59. "What Did Ory Say," 6.

60. Rose and Souchon, 86, 106.

61. The Volsted Act would not become law until 1920. A 1908 state liquor law, The Gay Shattuck Act, was enforced to close New Orleans establishments that served women and featured music. It also banned the serving of both blacks and whites at the same establishment.

62. *New Orleans Item*, October 24, 1919, 1.

63. Manuel Manetta and Edward "Kid" Ory interview, Hogan Jazz Archive, Tulane University (August 26, 1958), 7–8.

64. Ory unpublished autobiography, chapter titled "Promoting Dances," dated August 9, 1951.

65. "What Did Ory Say," 12.

66. "Sweet Lucy" can refer to either a bourbon-based liqueur or a wine.

67. Ory unpublished autobiography, undated page (Kid Ory said there was a railroad strike in Los Angeles when he arrived and that he worked as a cook preparing meals for replacement workers or "scabs."); *Los Angeles Times*, August 16, 1919, Sect. 1, page 1, and August 31, 1919, Sect. 2, page 1. Manetta said Ory left on a Friday. There are two Fridays in that window. It was likely August 22 that he left for Los Angles as the strike ended only three days after the second Friday. That leaves open the possibility of August 14, as the strike started the next day.

68. Ory unpublished autobiography, chapter titled "Promoting Dances," dated August 2, 1951, 1.

CHAPTER 8

1. "African Americans from the South"—Lawrence B. De Graaf, "The City of Black Angels: Emergence of the Los Angeles Ghetto, 1890–1930," *Pacific Historical Review* (August 1970).

"a very fast-stepping town"—Philip Pastras, *Dead Man Blues: Jelly Roll Morton Way Out West* (Berkeley: University of California Press, 2003), 75.

2. *Ibid.*, 76.

3. De Graaf, 332, 341, 342.

4. "older residents in [this] community"—De Graaf, 346.

"1001 E. 33 Street"—Los Angeles City Directory, 1922 and 1924 (Los Angeles Directory Company); 1920 Census, California, Vol. 54, Ed. 385, Sheet 6, Line 34.

5. Ory unpublished autobiography, "Arrival in Los Angeles," September 9, 1951, 1.

6. Alfred Williams interview, Hogan Jazz Archive, Tulane University (February 3, 1961), 3.

7. Ory, "Arrival in Los Angeles," 2.

8. Anderson, "Johnny Dodds in New Orleans," 432.

9. Manetta, Williams, and Carey all appear on the California census taken on January 2, 1920.

10. "an instant draw"—Manuel Manetta and Edward "Kid" Ory interview, Hogan Jazz Archive, Tulane University, (August 26, 1958) 10.

"We really did very well"—Ory unpublished autobiography, "Arrival in Los Angeles," September 9, 1951, 1–2.

"They [the Ory band] played"—Alfred Williams interview, Hogan Jazz Archive, Tulane University (February 3, 1961), 3.

"People could sit down"—Gene Williams and Marili Stewart, "Papa Mutt Carey," *Jazz* (March 1943): 6.

11. "busting open their doors"—Manuel Manetta and Edward "Kid" Ory interview, Hogan Jazz Archive, Tulane University (August 26, 1958), 3.

"We didn't get to Hollywood"—*Ibid.*, 3.

12. "shut down completely"—Alfred Williams interview, Hogan Jazz Archives, Tulane University (October 13, 1961), 10.

"in the fall of 1919"—1920 Census, California, Vol. 57, Ed. 430, Sheet 13, Line 44. Manetta was still in Los Angeles as late as January 1920, when he appears on the census there.

"mother was ailing"—Manuel Manetta and Edward "Kid" Ory interview, Hogan Jazz Archive, Tulane University (August 26, 1958), 4.

13. Pastras, 78.

14. "added "Jazz" to their name"—*Ibid.*, 80.

"The Black and Tan was"—Alfred Williams interview, Hogan Jazz Archives, Tulane University (April 30, 1960), 5.

15. Alfred Williams interview, Hogan Jazz Archive, Tulane University (February 3, 1961), 3.

16. Manuel Manetta and Edward "Kid" Ory interview, Hogan Jazz Archive, Tulane University (August 26, 1958), 10.

17. Floyd Levin, "Kid Ory's Legendary Nordskog Sunshine Recordings," *Jazz Journal International* (July 1993): 6.

18. Floyd Levin, "The Spikes Brothers: A Los Angeles Saga," *Jazz Journal* (December 1951): 12–14.

19. "wisely conceded the preeminence"—Pastras, 128.

"Ory first met the Spikes"—William Russell, *"Oh Mr. Jelly": A Jelly Roll Morton Scrapbook* (Copenhagen: JazzMedia, 1999), 552.

20. Alfred Williams interview, Hogan Jazz Archive, Tulane University (October 13, 1961), 10.

21. "Mutt Carey had gone"—Oakland City Directory: 1921 (Polk-Husted Directory Company).

"sent packing for New Orleans"—Alfred Williams interview, Hogan Jazz Archive, Tulane University (February 3, 1961), 4.

"California music promoter"—John Chilton, *Who's Who of Jazz: Storyville to Swing Street* (Philadelphia: Chilton Book Company, 1970), 235

"Creole Band member Dink Johnson"—Hal Smith, "Bennie Borders WWI Draft Registration Card (June 5, 1917)," February 2007. doctorjazz.co.uk/draft cards2.html.

22. "Reb Spikes said"—Tom Stoddard, *Jazz on the Barbary Coast* (Heyday, 1998), 113

"Charlie 'Duke' Turner recalled"—*Ibid.*, 138.

"club was crowded nightly"—*Western Appeal*, October 19, 1921, 3.

23. Polk's San Francisco City Directory 1922 (Crocker-Langley).

24. "event was advertised"—*Oakland Sunshine*, February 25, 1922, 1.

"Oliver was back"—Gene H. Anderson, "The Genesis of King Oliver's Creole Jazz Band," *American Music* (Fall 1994): 296.

25. Pastras, 116.

26. Russell, *Oh Mr. Jelly*, 551.

27. Pastras, 117.

28. Ibid., 118.

29. "Ragtime" Billy Tucker, "Coast Dope," *Chicago Defender*, May 20, 1922, 7.

30. *California Eagle*, July 1, 1922.

31. Levin, "Kid Ory's Legendary Nordskog Sunshine Recordings," 6.

32. "Ragtime" Billy Tucker, "Coast Dope," *Chicago Defender*, May 27, 1922, 8.

33. Arne Nordskog, *Down Beat*, August 10, 1951.

34. "What Did Ory Say," 12.

35. Levin, "Kid Ory's Legendary Nordskog Sunshine Recordings," 7

36. *Ibid.*

37. "each $20 richer"—"What Did Ory Say."

"just weeks away"—Levin, "Kid Ory's Legendary Nordskog Sunshine Recordings," 7.

38. "Ragtime" Billy Tucker, "Coast Dope," *Chicago Defender*, June 24, 1922, 8.

39. "live radio broadcasts"—"Negro Melody Features Air Program Today," *Los Angeles Examiner*, June 27, 1922.

"giving away radio sets"—advertisement, *Los Angeles Examiner*, July 1, 1922.

40. "Negro Melody Features Air Program Today," *Los Angeles Examiner*, June 27, 1922.

41. "What Did Ory Say," 12.

42. *Los Angeles Examiner*, July 6, 1922.

43. "Reb Spikes remembered"— Levin, "The Spikes Brothers: A Los Angeles Saga," 12–14.

"a 1925 Columbia recording"—Dan Mahony, *The Columbia 13/14000-D Series: A Numerical Listing* (Stanhope, NJ: Walter C. Allen, 1961), 28, 29.

44. Levin, "Kid Ory's Legendary Nordskog Sunshine Recordings," 8.

45. *Ibid.*, 7.

46. *Ibid.*, 8.

47. David Sager, "A Tale of the Slide Trombone in Early Jazz," *Jazz Archivist* 3, no. 1 (1988): 11.

48. "it crossed over to playing"—One telling notice in the California Eagle from December 12, 1924, notes that Ory will play at the Assembly Auditorium after playing for white folks the last year.

"One admirer of the Ory band"—Jane Kesner Morris Ardmore, *The Self-Enchanted: Mae Murray, Image of an Era* (New York: McGraw-Hill, 1959).

"the year was 1919"— Ory unpublished autobiography, "Mae Murray," September 9, 1951, 1.

"From 1921–22, Murray made"—Ardmore.

49. "Ragtime" Billy Tucker, "Coast Dope," *Chicago Defender*, June 10, 1922; *California Eagle*, July 19, 1922.

50. "Ragtime" Billy Tucker, "Coast Dope," *Chicago Defender*, July 22, 1922.

51. "correction later ran"—"Ragtime" Billy Tucker, "Coast Dope," *Chicago Defender*, August 5, 1922.

"photographed as a member"—Stoddard, *Jazz on the Barbary Coast*, 45. Though Stoddard dates the photo ca. 1915, the presence of Reb Spikes in the pictures means it was likely later.

52. "Ragtime" Billy Tucker, "Coast Dope," *Chicago Defender*, August 26, 1922.

53. "Ragtime" Billy Tucker, "Coast Dope," *Chicago Defender*, September 2, 1922.

54. "Ragtime" Billy Tucker, "Coast Dope," *Chicago Defender*, August 5, 1922.

55. "an attack of rheumatism"—Pastras, 118.

"It got so rough"—Russell, *"Oh Mr. Jelly,"* 551.

56. "Ory recalled playing"—"What Did Ory Say," 12.

"two to three times the salary"—Paul G. Cressey, *The Taxi-Dance Hall: A Sociological Study in Commercialized Recreation and City Life* (Chicago: University of Chicago Press, 1932), 3, 4.

CHAPTER 9

1. "The Hot Five Sessions, as told to Lester Koenig," *Record Changer* (July-August 1950): 17.

2. "actively recruited"—William Howland Kenney, *Chicago Jazz: A Cultural History, 1904–1930* (Oxford: Oxford University Press, 1993), 11.

"population of Chicago stood"—"Bronzeville." encyclopedia.chicagohistory. org/pages/171.html (accessed 2010).

3. Kenney, *Chicago Jazz*, 13.

4. *Ibid.*

5. *Ibid.*, 4, 14.

6. "The label was placed"—Charles Kouri, "Shining Through," *Chicago Tribune*, March 27, 1992.

"its own bustling downtown"—Excerpt from the National Register Nomination for Chicago's Black Metropolis. nps.gov/nr/twhp/wwwlps/lessons/53black /53factsr.htm (accessed 2010).

"new motorized buses"—"Public Transportation." encyclopedia.chicagohis tory.org/pages/1023.html (accessed 2010).

7. Gene H. Anderson, *The Original Hot Five Recordings of Louis Armstrong*, ed. Michael J. Budds (Hillsdale, NY: Pendragon, 2007), 75.

8. "The Hot Five Sessions," *Record Changer*, 17.

9. Anderson, *Original Hot Five Recordings of Louis Armstrong*, 15.

10. "The Hot Five Sessions," *Record Changer*, 17, 45.

11. *Ibid.*

12. Anderson, *The Original Hot Five Recordings*.

13. *Ibid.*, 74.

14. "Sidney Bechet suggested"—*Ibid.*, 74–75.

"his story about writing it"—Babette Ory still has the saxophone. Ory always referred to it as the horn on which he wrote "Muskrat Ramble."

15. Anderson, *Original Hot Five Recordings of Louis Armstrong*, 74.

16. "The Hot Five Sessions," *Record Changer*, 17.

17. Anderson, *Original Hot Five Recordings of Louis Armstrong*, 53.

18. *Ibid.*, 100.

19. *Ibid.*, 157.

20. *Ibid.*

21. Louis Armstrong, *Louis Armstrong, in His Own Words: Selected Writings*, ed. Thomas Brothers (Oxford: Oxford University Press, 2001), 136.

22. Anderson, *Original Hot Five Recordings of Louis Armstrong*, 181, 185

23. *Ibid.*, 189.

24. "The Hot Five Sessions," *Record Changer*, 17.

25. Anderson, *Original Hot Five Recordings of Louis Armstrong*, 192–93

26. "The Hot Five Sessions," *Record Changer*, 17.

27. *Ibid.*

28. "Dreamland was a black and tan club"—Anderson, *Original Hot Five Recordings of Louis Armstrong*, 11–12, 13.

"Louis had moved on"—*Chicago Defender*, December 12, 1925, 7.

29. "The Hot Five Sessions," *Record Changer*, 17.

30. Allen and Rust, 16–17.

31. Edward "Kid" Ory, interview by Nesuhi Ertegun, Hogan Jazz Archive, Tulane University (April 20, 1957).

32. Kenney, 22.

33. Allen and Rust, 20.

34. *Ibid.*, 19, 20.

35. "recalled as 'Schemmery'"—Ory unpublished autobiography, "Chicago 1925–26," 1, 2. In the Ory manuscript he refers to the teacher as "Schimmery." He almost certainly meant Cimera.

"One of his students remembered"—Kreig E. Garvin and Andre M. Smith, "Jaroslav Cimera, 1885–1972: Virtuoso Trombonist-Master Teacher," *International Trombone Association Journal* (Winter 1997): 34, 39.

36. *Ibid.*

37. Edward "Kid" Ory, interview by Nesuhi Ertegun, Hogan Jazz Archive, Tulane University (April 20, 1957), 81.

38. Allen and Rust, 21; Kenney, 22; "Bombs Damage Southside Cafe," *Chicago Daily Tribune*, July 10, 1926, 1.

39. "Bombs damage South Side café," *Chicago Daily Tribune*, April 10, 1926, 1.

40. "gunned down Weiss"—Jonathan Eig, *Get Capone: The Secret Plot That Captured America's Most Wanted Gangster* (New York: Simon and Schuster, 2010).

"Mystery Fire Causes Big Loss in Plantation Cafe"—*Chicago Daily Tribune*, March 31, 1927, 1.

41. *Ibid.*

42. Edward "Kid" Ory, interview by Nesuhi Ertegun, Hogan Jazz Archive, Tulane University (April 20, 1957), 84.

43. *Ibid.*, 86.

44. Allen and Rust, 21, 22.

45. *Ibid.*, 22.

46. Edward "Kid" Ory, interview by Nesuhi Ertegun, Hogan Jazz Archive, Tulane University (April 20, 1957), 90.

47. Allen and Rust, 23.

48. "2:19 Blues"—Jelly Roll Morton, interview by Alan Lomax (1938).

"at the Cadillac and Leak's Lake"—Pastras, 139–40.

49. Russell, *"Oh Mr. Jelly,"* 364.

50. Russell, *"Oh Mr. Jelly,"* 359, 360.

51. *Ibid.*, 364.

52. *Ibid.*, 125.

53. *Ibid.*, 125, 361.

54. Gunther Schuller, *Early Jazz: Its Roots and Musical Development* (Oxford: Oxford University Press, 1986), 155.

55. Kenney, 136.

56. Schuller, 155.

57. Schuller, 156.

58. *Ibid.*

59. "Thomas Brothers writes"—Brothers, *Louis Armstrong's New Orleans*, 242.

"William Howland Kenney offers"—Kenney, 137.

"Martin Williams notes"—Williams, *Jazz Masters of New Orleans*, 216.

60. David Sager, "A Tale of the Slide Trombone in Early Jazz," *Jazz Archivist* 3, no. 1 (1988): 12.

61. Chilton, 248.

62. *Chicago Defender*, June 15, 1929, 5.

63. Chilton, 248.

CHAPTER 10

1. "According to Johnny Ory's son Harold"—Author interview, Harold Ory, Compton, CA, 2002.

"died of a heart attack"—California death index online, 1930–39, vol. 6, file # 29601.

2. "magazine article on Ory"—*Tempo* (April 1938): 19–20.

"Other tunes penned by Ory"—Kid Ory papers in possession of Babette Ory.

Copywrite Office 284440 Are You Selling Songs Mister, copywrite office 287491 Mussoulini, Copywrite Office 280210Jaywal;k.

3. Russell, *"Oh Mister Jelly,"* 556.

4. *San Francisco Chronicle*, May 10, 1943, page 11, mentions Ory playing bass "in some dive."

5. Bigard, Barney, *With Louis and the Duke* (New York: Oxford University Press, 1986), 89–90.

6. Hubner.

7. "Dort's case fell apart"—Superior Court Records, Los Angeles County, Ory vs. Ory Case 467-592.

"she died in 1965"—California Death Index 1940–1997, Ancestry.com.

8. Arthur GaNung, author interview, Oceanside, CA, 2002.

9. Bigard, 90.

10. "died there of pneumonia"—Certificate of death, Hawaii Department of Health, research and statistics office, file 151, January 30, 1973.

"As the brass band descended"—Barry Martyn, author interview, New Orleans, 2010.

INDEX

Page numbers in bold refer to figures.